STP 1394

D1501474

Dimension Stone Cladding: Design, Construction, Evaluation, and Repair

Kurt R. Hoigard, editor

ASTM Stock Number: STP1394

ASTM
P.O. Box C700
100 Barr Harbor Drive
West Conshohocken, PA 19428-2959

Printed in the U.S.A.

Library of Congress Cataloging-in-Publication Data

Dimension stone cladding : design, construction, evaluation, and repair / Kurt R. Hoigard, editor.
      p. cm.—(STP ; 1394)
  "ASTM Stock Number : STP1394
  Includes bibliographical references and index.
  ISBN 0-8031-2875-4
  1. Curtain walls–Design and construction. 2. Stone veneers. I. Hoigard, Kurt, 1961.
  II. ASTM special technical publication ; 1394.

TH2238 .D47 2000
693'.1–dc21

00-046898

Photocopy Rights

Authorization to photocopy items for internal, personal, or educational classroom use, or the internal, personal, or educational classroom use of specific clients, is granted by the American Society for Testing and Materials (ASTM) provided that the appropriate fee is paid to the Copyright Clearance Center, 222 Rosewood Drive, Danvers, MA 01923; Tel: 508-750-8400; online: http://www.copyright.com/.

Peer Review Policy

Each paper published in this volume was evaluated by two peer reviewers and at least one editor. The authors addressed all of the reviewers' comments to the satisfaction of both the technical editor(s) and the ASTM Committee on Publications.

To make technical information available as quickly as possible, the peer-reviewed papers in this publication were prepared "camera-ready" as submitted by the authors.

The quality of the papers in this publication reflects not only the obvious efforts of the authors and the technical editor(s), but also the work of the peer reviewers. In keeping with long-standing publication practices, ASTM maintains the anonymity of the peer reviewers. The ASTM Committee on Publications acknowledges with appreciation their dedication and contribution of time and effort on behalf of ASTM.

Printed in Chelsea, MI
November 2000

Foreword

This publication, *Dimension Stone Cladding: Design, Construction, Evaluation, and Repair,* contains papers presented at the symposium of the same name held in New Orleans, Louisiana, on October 27, 1999. The symposium was sponsored by ASTM Committee C-18 on Dimension Stone. The symposium chairman was Kurt R. Hoigard of Raths, Raths & Johnson, Willowbrook, Illinois.

Contents

Overview

This book represents the efforts of a number of authors that presented papers at the *Symposium on Dimension Stone Cladding: Design, Evaluation, Construction, and Repair* held in New Orleans on October 27, 1999. The symposium was held in conjunction with a regularly scheduled meeting of the symposium sponsor, ASTM Committee C18 on Dimension Stone. Sincere thanks are offered to those involved with the development of the materials presented and to those that endured the pressure of the podium, as well as the patient staff in the ASTM Acquisitions and Review department.

The purpose of the symposium was to promote an exchange of information on the state of the art in stone cladding applications. In the twelve years since the 1987 Exterior Stone Symposium and the subsequent publication of *ASTM STP 996, New Stone Technology, Design, and Construction for Exterior Wall Systems*, a substantial amount of work has been done in the fields of new stone cladding and the rehabilitation of existing stone cladding installations. Sixteen presentations covering case histories, original research, and new concepts were grouped into four sessions: Stone Cladding Preconstruction Evaluation; Stone Weathering and Durability; Design of Stone Cladding Systems; and Investigation and Restoration of Existing Stone Cladding Installations. Written versions of thirteen of these presentations are assembled in this book.

Stone Cladding Preconstruction Evaluation

The three papers in this section are all based upon doctoral thesis research work performed at the University of Illinois. Authors Reis and Habboub present basic research regarding the use of impulse-generated stress waves as a nondestructive means of determining stone properties such as grain size and shape, texture, bedding anisotropy, porosity, permeability, Poisson's ratio, and modulus of elasticity.

Stone Weathering and Durability

The four papers in this section cover this diverse topic from a variety of directions. Authors Miglio, Richardson, Yates, and West present information pertaining to current methods of durability assessment in the United Kingdom used for evaluating limestones, and provide recommendations for their specification in new building construction. Erlin's paper discusses the relationships between crystalline structure, thermal hysteresis, and bowing of Carrara marble panels. Authors Scheffler and Lesak offer a case history assessing the root causes of weathering-induced damage to an 80-year-old granite facade, and evaluate a variety of restorative treatment methods explored. Authors Bortz and Wonneberger provide a summary of durability test methods currently in use and under development in the United States and the European Community.

Design of Stone Cladding Systems

Both of the papers in this section address granite design issues. Authors Gerns, Wonneberger, and Scheffler stray slightly from the cladding theme of the book by providing guidance on the selection of granites and supports for exterior stone paver systems. Authors West and Heinlein provide anchor strength recommendations based upon extensive ASTM C 1354 laboratory testing of granite specimens fitted with a variety of edge anchors.

Investigation and Restoration of Existing Stone Cladding Systems

The four papers in this section offer a variety of case studies, observations, and specific recommendations regarding investigative means and repair methods used to address distressed facades. Authors Hoigard and Mulholland provide practical repair methods for addressing common types of stone distress, including chips, spalls, cracks, missing pieces, and defective or deficient anchors. Chin provides an overview discussing some of the most commonly encountered types of stone distress and their causes. Solinski presents case studies involving the investigation and repair of two distressed stone facades. Authors Scavuzzo and Acri present a case history discussing in-place load testing procedures used to evaluate the performance of a stone cladding anchorage system

Summary

The papers assembled in this book demonstrate a continuing advancement in the understanding of stone cladding. Investigations of distressed stone installations, combined with preconstruction evaluations of new stone cladding materials, continue to improve the knowledge base from which designers of new buildings can draw. Likewise, the economic needs of building owners, combined with the creative abilities of rehabilitation specialists, continue to provide advances in the methods available for maintaining and prolonging the useful life of existing facades.

Kurt R. Hoigard
Symposium Chairman and STP Editor
Raths, Raths & Johnson, Inc.
835 Midway Drive
Willowbrook, IL 60521

Stone Cladding Preconstruction Evaluation

Henrique L.M. dos Reis and Amin K. Habboub[1]

Nondestructive Evaluation of Dimension Stone Using Impulse-Generated Stress Waves: Part 1 – Theoretical Aspects and Experimental Prospects

Reference: dos Reis, H. L. M., and Habboub, A. K., **"Nondestructive Evaluation of Dimension Stone Using Impulse-Generated Stress Waves: Part 1 – Theoretical Aspects and Experimental Prospects,"** *Dimension Stone Cladding: Design, Construction, Evaluation, and Repair, ASTM 1394,* K. R. Hoigard, Ed., American Society for Testing and Materials, West Conshohocken, PA, 2000.

Abstract: Energy-related processes in dimension stones are numerous and may collectively describe the mechanical and physical features of stone such as its viscoelastic and microstructural properties. Viscoelastic properties are concerned with evaluating the complex, stress-relaxation, and creep-compliance moduli. Microstructural properties include grain-size distribution, grain type, shape, texture, bedding anisotropy, and grain coating/surface-contact conditions. Other related energy-based intrinsic properties include noise-abatement and transport properties such as porosity, permeability, and tortuosity. Therefore, the study of the energy evolution processes within a given stone component/system by means of an impulse-generated stress-wave field may reveal the nature of the required stone features. Using principles of statistical energy analysis, SEA, diffuse-wave-fields, and analogies to solid media of architectural-acoustic theories on reverberant enclosures, the evolution of the wave field is studied and discussed, and the experimental means of performing spectral and energy analyses from a single impulse-echo test is presented.

Keywords: dimension stone, stone veneer, cladding, diffuse wave fields, attenuation, viscoelastic properties, impulse-echo, statistical mechanics, power-density, material characterization, energy partitioning

Energy loss processes of dimension stone components and systems include intrinsic (i.e., material) factors, as well as extrinsic (i.e., structural) factors [1-4]. Intrinsic factors include damage accumulation, inter-aggregate sliding friction, viscous dissipation, thermodynamic relaxation, squirt-flow, and several other material non-linearity factors such as higher-order mode generation [5,7]. Extrinsic factors include energy lost to adjacent media through couplings and connections [8,9] and aerodynamic damping, or into the transducer [10-12]. These extrinsic losses are characteristic of the stone structural system or the test equipment, respectively [2,5]. When evaluating a single stone component, extrinsic factors should either be eliminated, such as the case in the current tests, or quantified beforehand, but may not be neglected [8,10]. On the other hand, when system-coupling characteristics are desired, intrinsic dissipation must be pre-evaluated either from available material data or by other calibrated tests [2]. Accordingly, structurally-efficient stone material claddings may be designed and constructed (i.e.,

---

[1] Professor Henrique L.M. dos Reis and graduate student Amin K. Habboub are associated with the Department of Civil and Environmental Engineering at the University of Illinois at Urbana-Champaign, 104 South Mathews, Urbana, Illinois.

coupled together within a structural system) in such a way that the installed system provides enough (i.e., efficient) energy outlets when subjected to high input powers due to excessive transient loads acting on a particular loading mode. Such severe loading conditions may include high wind buffets, nearby explosions, earthquakes, or general dynamic loading. In this case, the rate of dissipated energy (i.e., power output) must be designed through efficient material selection and panel coupling details/structural configurations, to be higher than the input power. Otherwise, the excess energy may be violently relieved through the abrupt dissipation mechanisms of material breakage or system failure. The test method and equipment described in this paper provide the experimental means of verifying and evaluating such design criteria in the laboratory or in the field by inspecting the elastic storage capacity of the component and the readiness/efficiency of its particular modes to dissipate energy intrinsically or extrinsically. Stress-wave energy methods usually involve the construction of a scalar quantity from either the coherent or incoherent parts of the response signal, where an energy power balance condition needs to be satisfied at all times [13-15]. Typically, this quantity is described using power-density, i.e., energy-density decay rate. The evolution of the energy-density within the incoherent regime of the response signal may be described by a diffusion process, whose parameters are typically derived from the high frequency and late-time regime of an impulse response [16-20]. These two response zones guarantee that several-fold modal coupling and steady-state conditions are achieved, respectively. Several energy loss processes may be operating within the frequency band of the propagating stress wave. Each loss process mechanism can influence the diffuse state and may operate on preferential propagation modes [3,6,21].

In designing an energy-based stress wave test, the contributions of supports and transducer energy leakage should be quantified beforehand [22,23]. In this case, the volume-averaged intrinsic material properties of dimension stone material are the subject of inspection. However, if energy losses due to material-related processes (i.e., when the object is free of any structural attachments) have already been quantified by the same means or by another calibrated method, then the support couplings as well as the boundary conditions may become the subject of the testing. In Part 1 of this study, the theoretical foundations and the general test procedures of this approach are presented. In Part 2 and Part 3 of this study, the applications of the impulse generated stress-wave energy method in evaluating the viscoelastic properties and the microstructure characteristics, respectively, are presented and discussed.

Statistical Energy Analyses (SEA)

When the wave energy becomes statistically distributed amongst the various modes of excitation in the neighborhood of an excitation frequency, Statistical Energy Analysis, SEA, may be used in evaluating the energy characteristics such as energy partitioning of the wave field [16,24,25]. The SEA procedures allow the calculation of flow and storage of dynamical energy in an engineering system. Because SEA includes power balance information, it can be used to trace the flow of energy through the system from one subsystem to another and to help identify important transmission paths from energy source locations to other locations where the system response is observed [2]. The parameters of the SEA model are based on material and geometric properties of the system, and as the name implies, energy is the primary parameter of analysis. The general procedure of the SEA includes (1) defining subsystems containing groups of natural modes within each of the system subcomponents, (2) defining the physical coupling between the subsystems, and (3) defining the form of the external excitations to the subsystems [2].

In this study, each stone specimen was isolated from linkage/anchorage or coupling to any other subsystem, except for energy leaking into the transducer [11], and therefore may be considered as a single component with two subsystems, i.e., bulk and shear. The drop of a metallic ball on a hardened steel plate resting on the top surface of the test cylinder introduces the excitation. The stress pulse contains a broad band frequency range with sufficient low frequency components necessary to sample the thickness of the stone sample, and be able to reflect back and forth with suitable detectable, although attenuating, energies. This was produced by imparting the point source with 4-6 mm falling spheres from a 61 cm height along a guiding tube. The ball impacts the hardened steel plate resting on the top surface of the cylindrical test sample as shown in Figure 1. According to Hertz theory of elastic impact, which underestimates the actual contact time due to inelasticity, the contact time of the bearing ball impact on stone was calculated as 22-25 μ s, and, on a similar object made of steel, as 11-13 μ s. Because of the St. Venant's principle of localized deformation, which occurs in the steel plate, the last number may be adequate. However, in lieu of a rigor analysis, the contact time was estimated as $t_c = 15 \mu$ s, in which case the bearing ball exerts a maximum force of 87 N on the steel plate. A rigor analysis should consider the inelastic response for the impact on the steel plate resting on top of the stone specimen. Most energy is contained in frequencies less than $q = 1.0/t_c = 67$ kHz, however, some energy is contained in frequency components up to $1.5/ t_c = 100$ kHz, and additional energy is contained in loops extending over $1/t_c$ frequency ranges beyond the main loop [26]. The stress pulse transmitted into the medium, i.e., the impulse, is described by Equation (1), which includes the initial

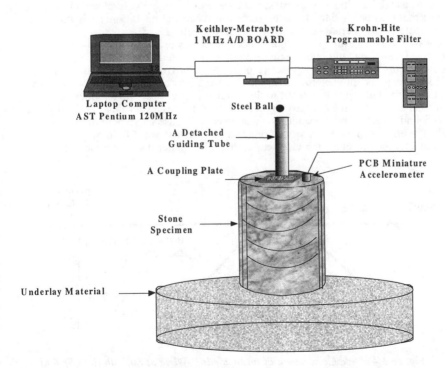

Figure 1 -- *The Testing Configuration of an Impulse-Generated Stress-Wave Procedure*

force amplitudes, F_{of}, at the various times. Equation (2) results from the Fourier Transform of the initial half-cycle sine force-time function described in Equation (1) [26].

$$F_0(t) = F_{max} \sin\pi \frac{t}{t_c} \tag{1}$$

$$F_{0f}(s) = \frac{t_c}{2} \left[\frac{\sin\pi(s-0.5)}{\pi(s-0.5)} + \frac{\sin\pi(s+0.5)}{\pi(s+0.5)} \right] \tag{2}$$

where $F_0(t)$ is the exerted force amplitude at time t and $s = f \cdot t_c$, where f is the frequency in Hz.

Energy Partitioning Due to Mode Conversion at the Specimen External Boundaries

In the case of a test object with reflecting surfaces that intercept the path of the propagating waves at non-perpendicular angles, mode conversions take place each time an incident wave is intercepted by the test object external boundaries. An incident wave may have been previously reflected from one boundary and became incident on another so that the reflected and transmitted waves contain both longitudinal and shear wave components, as shown in Figure 2. Therefore, the received signal by means of a transducer at a point on one surface of the test sample usually allows influx of both components, as well as, in some cases, surface waves. There are several sampling techniques that may be used to eliminate surface-wave sampling, before such waves either dissipate or degenerate into body wave components [27,28].

The wave evolves in time by the continuous processes of reflections, mode conversions/decoupling, and relative mode attenuation/modulation [6,21]. The various wave components travel at their respective phase velocities, therefore resulting in dispersion. The transient waveform that initially contains dominant bulk modes prolongs its duration as the bulk modes convert to the lower velocity shear wave modes [27]. However, shear waves typically have higher attenuation rates. After many reflections at external boundaries, and other conditions warranted, a diffuse wave field develops [18,19]. The effect of mode conversion on creating a diffuse wave field may be strengthened by the presence of a diffuse, i.e., irregular, rather than specular, external

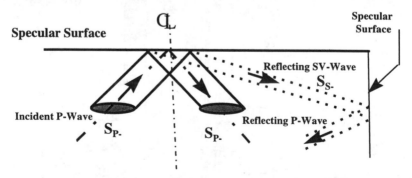

Figure 2 – *Mode Conversion of an Incident P-Wave at Smooth (i.e., Specular) External Boundaries of a Stone Panel or Component*

surfaces [10]. As a consequence, the wave field partitions its energy amongst the various wave modes according to the dynamic Poisson's ratio and irrespective of the original transient wave energy partitioning. This diffuse field is one which has evolved into a fully randomized state [11,29], preserving only minimal information contained in the frequency distribution of energy, but with no correlation in phase or amplitude between the extents of excitations of the different modes [16,20]. In the energy-partition scheme of Weaver for diffuse fields [19], each frequency is sought to describe a state of excitation, for which the normal modes in that frequency neighborhood, are each excited to equal energy. This implies that the amount of mechanical energy in a subspace is directly proportional to the number of the excited normal modes [17].

At a traction-free surface, the average energy transmission rates per unit area (i.e., acoustic intensity) for longitudinal and transverse waves, I_L, and I_T, from a p-wave impinging on this unit area of a smooth surface with an amplitude, A, as shown in Figure 2, may be expressed [27, 30,31] as follows

$$I_L = \frac{1}{2}(\lambda + 2\mu)\frac{\omega^2}{C_L}A^2 \tag{3}$$

$$I_T = \frac{1}{2}\mu\frac{\omega^2}{C_T}A^2 \tag{4}$$

where, ω is the circular frequency of the propagating wave (i.e., $\omega = 2\pi f$) and the Lame's constants, λ, and, μ are given in terms of the Young's modulus of elasticity, E , and the Poisson's ratio, v , [27,31] by

$$\lambda = \frac{vE}{(1+v)(1-2v)} \tag{5}$$

$$\mu = \frac{E}{2(1+v)} \tag{6}$$

The time average of the total energy, $\hat{E}_T$, may be computed as

$$\hat{E}_T = \frac{1}{2}\rho\omega^2 A^2 \tag{7}$$

For a beam of incident P-waves at an incident angle, θ_0 , the amplitude ratios of the reflected P-wave, A_1, and the reflected transverse wave, A_2, relative to that of the incident P-wave, A_0, (hence, the average energy partition transmitted over the reflected P-wave and the reflected SV-wave), can be determined using the following Equation (8)

$$\left(\frac{A_1}{A_0}\right)^2 + \left(\frac{A_2}{A_0}\right)^2 \frac{1}{\kappa\cos\theta_0}\left(1-\frac{\sin^2\theta_0}{\kappa^2}\right)^{1/2} = 1 \tag{8}$$

where

$$\kappa = \sqrt{\frac{2(1-\upsilon)}{1-2\upsilon}} \tag{9}$$

The losses at the interfaces might be superimposed to other losses. The amplitude due to interfacial transmission losses follows Equation (10)

$$A_f(n) = A_{f0}[1+\alpha_r]^n \tag{10}$$

where $A_f(n)$ is the amplitude of a given frequency upon the nth reflection. However, this attenuation mechanism was not considered in this study because little energy is lost to surrounding media in the test configuration used in this study. Figure 2 illustrates the occurrence of mode conversion of an incident P-wave at smooth external boundaries. Diffuse surfaces (i.e., rough surfaces) have an increasing effect on mode conversion rates.

Energy Partitioning Using Statistical Energy Analyses

The number of pseudo-longitudinal and pseudo-transverse normal modes ΔN_1 and ΔN_s may initially be considered to be uniformly distributed within a frequency interval Δf [19,20,29]. Accordingly, ΔN_1 and ΔN_s may be estimated for a test object of volume V, bounded by a surface area, A, within the frequency interval with a mean frequency, f, large compared with the inverse of the smallest linear dimension, l, [19,20], as follows

$$\Delta N_1 = 4\pi f^2 c_1^{-3} V \Delta f \tag{11}$$

$$\Delta N_s = 8\pi f^2 c_s^{-3} V \Delta f \tag{12}$$

Similarly, the number of incremental pseudo-surface wave normal modes on the surface, A, bounding the volume V, is given by

$$\Delta N_R = 2\pi f c_R^{-2} A \Delta f \tag{13}$$

In Equations (11) to (13), C_1, C_s, and C_R represent the longitudinal, transverse, and surface wave velocities, with typical measured values for dimension stone of 6800, 3700, and 2350 m/s, respectively. For a specimen of volume equal to 0.8 dm^3, and a frequency in the energetic spectrum of the propagating wave, say f = 50 kHz in the spectrum range of 8-200 kHz (i.e., Δf = 192 kHz) the number of pseudo-longitudinal and pseudo-shear normal modes, ΔN_1, ΔN_s are roughly estimated as 16 and 190 normal longitudinal and shear modes, respectively, which occur in the indicated spectral frequency range. By virtue of statistical energy analysis and Weaver's partitioning scheme, energy is regarded as uniformly distributed amongst the excited modes. Because the surface wave energy is either negligible or eliminated experimentally, energy partitioning between the body waves may be estimated. For the above case, the steady state diffuse wave field is mainly filled with shear wave energy relative to longitudinal wave energy by a proportion of 92.6 %. This value is consistent with the high rate of longitudinal to shear wave energy conversion of 92.9% predicted in the next section.

Energy Partitioning Using Modal Coupling Approach

The approximate shear wave energy proportion of 92.6 % was obtained by inspecting the role of modal coupling at external surfaces. Using sufficiently large stone specimens, with a characteristic dimension, l, that is large enough compared to the propagating wavelength (i.e., f >> $C_{1,t}/(2\pi l)$) in the frequency bandwidth of interest, the composite wave may be considered as a superposition of weakly coupled pseudo-modes. Each pseudo-mode is considered to be of a distinct wave type, and the energy partitioning factor, R, between the transverse and the longitudinal body waves [19,20,29] is given by

$$R = \frac{(dN_t/df)\Delta f}{(dN_d/df)\Delta f} = 2\left(\frac{C_l}{C_t}\right)^3 = 2\left(\frac{2-2\upsilon}{1-2\upsilon}\right)^{\frac{3}{2}} \tag{14}$$

For an average value of $\nu = 0.25$, which is typical of some stones, the partitioning factor, R, can be calculated according to the three relationships in Equation (14). It provides an approximate value of R at a high mode conversion factor of 13.1, i.e., leading to a relative high proportion of shear wave energy of 92.9 %.

As described by Egle [29], the partitioning factor, R, may also be given as

$$R = \frac{\gamma_{LT} C_l}{\gamma_{TL} C_t} \tag{15}$$

where γ_{LT} and γ_{TL} are the diffuse field mode conversion power ratios from longitudinal to transverse powers, and vise versa, respectively, resulting from solving the power balance equations [29], which solely depends on Poisson's ratio of the test object for elastic, homogeneous, and isotropic materials.

The diffuse-field solution for an impulsive source imparted at t = 0 is given by

$$\overline{\varepsilon_L}(t) = K_1 + K_2 e^{-\left(\frac{t}{t^*}\right)} \tag{16}$$

$$\overline{\varepsilon_T}(t) = RK_1 - K_2 e^{-\left(\frac{t}{t^*}\right)} \tag{17}$$

where ε's are the estimated average total mechanical energy densities at time t contained in the longitudinal and transverse wave components, and

$$K_1 = \frac{\left[\overline{\varepsilon_L}(0) + \overline{\varepsilon_T}(0)\right]}{(1+R)} \tag{18}$$

$$K_2 = \frac{\left[R\overline{\varepsilon_L}(0) + \overline{\varepsilon_T}(0)\right]}{(1+R)} \tag{19}$$

$$t^* = \frac{4V}{\left[S(\gamma_{LT}C_L + \gamma_{TL}C_T)\right]} \tag{20}$$

$$\overline{\varepsilon_L}(0) = \left(\frac{1}{V}\right) E_{L0} \tag{21}$$

$$\overline{\varepsilon_T}(0) = \left(\frac{1}{V}\right) E_{T0} \tag{22}$$

where E_{L0}, and E_{T0} are the longitudinal and transverse energies released by the source, which for this study are nearly, 0.0015 and 0.002 Joule, respectively, as S is the total external surface area. After a relatively short time, calculated as $t^* = 10$ μs, which is less than one transit time travels of 56 μs, the energy densities tend towards an equilibrium configuration that is predominantly in favor of the conversion towards transverse energy. A transducer placed on the surface will respond to longitudinal, transverse (only SV-), and surface waves that are incident on its surface. Therefore, the longitudinal power incident on the transducer [9] may be given by

$$P_{IL} = \frac{\gamma P_I}{(1+\gamma)} \tag{23}$$

$$P_{IT} = P_I(1+\gamma) \tag{24}$$

where

$$\gamma = \frac{C_L}{RC_T} \tag{25}$$

In Equations (23) and (24), the total, longitudinal, and transverse power that is incident on the transducer is denoted as P_I, P_{IL}, and P_{TL}, respectively.

As described earlier, the mode conversion rate generated at external surfaces of an elastic isotropic body is dictated by Poisson's ratio of the material [32,35]. Because shear waves propagate at slower velocities than bulk waves [14], and in the absence of scattering, the shear wave prolongs its residence in the test object, but rapidly decays due to several dissipation mechanisms that mostly affect shear waves [33,34]. Therefore, the late time regime, i.e., zone IV, as shown in Figure 3, will contain traces of shear waves, but is dominated by lingering bulk waves. Energy decay may be described by an exponential constant that is commonly termed the "diffuse energy density decay rate" or the "exponential decay parameter". Eventually, with most extrinsic attenuation mechanisms rendered inoperative at high frequencies at fairly late times [2], the whole test object becomes filled mostly with shear wave energy at intermediate times, i.e., zones II and III. Then the shear wave field depletes itself of energy and the lingering bulk wave modes dominate the wave field again. These lingering bulk-mode waves are the wave components which were immune to mode conversion or which have been converted in the opposite direction, i.e., from shear to bulk wave modes at the rate of 1/13.

Diffuse Field Approach

In the traditional impact-echo method [26], the stress pulse propagates in repetitive transit travels between two opposite parallel and reflective surfaces without undergoing significant mode conversions. Therefore, a p-wave injected to the system undergoes many reflections while substantially remaining in the same mode if the signal is sampled in the proximity of the impulse point. As a result, a resonance condition is staged at a frequency, $f=C'_p/2D$ for two pressure release surfaces; this frequency corresponds to the lowest normal mode of vibration, C'_p is the adjusted p-wave velocity in the material, and D is the distance between the two reflecting surfaces. C'_p is equal to C_p for infinitely extended surfaces — for other shapes, modal analyses is required. The amplitude of vibration of this mode is monitored with time, and an exponential decay parameter is derived. However, in the presence of many variously oriented reflective surfaces such as in the case of test cylindrical specimens, many normal modes are excited at any single excitation frequency and the signal can't be sampled with sufficient mode purity at any response mode. Furthermore, mode conversions also take place in the presence of external reflective surfaces intercepting the incident wave at non-perpendicular angles.

The diffuse wave field theory was originally developed within the context of architectural acoustics in order to study the collective (i.e., volume averaged) properties of reverberation chambers (i.e., acoustic enclosures). Although the theory has been around for several decades, only lately it has also been used to study oceanic and solid media [19,20,32].

The diffuse state had been described by Egle based on assumptions of isotropic random superposition of plane waves, with each having slowly varying amplitudes, and a random phase. Egle [29] applied power balance conditions to finite, isotropic, homogeneous, elastic media with traction-free boundaries to demonstrate that the wave field, after several reflections from the bounding surfaces, will partition its energy between transverse and longitudinal modes in fractions which are entirely attributed to Poisson's coupling at such surfaces, and independent of the initial energy partitioning of the source impulse. Later, however, by incorporating principles of statistical energy analyses, Weaver [16-20] modified this definition to suit anisotropic and inhomogeneous media, with consideration to normal modes rather than plane waves. The modified definition of Weaver regards the diffuse state at a particular frequency as one that excites each normal mode of the system with equal energy. This means that the excited subsystem acts as an energy "reservoir" with a capacity that is directly related to the number of normal modes occurring in the vicinity of the particular excitation frequency.

In diffuse field analysis, the test object is monitored for long times beyond impulse termination and after the elapse of several wave transit times. The monitoring time should be long enough such that edge reflections, and many other extrinsic loss mechanisms, cease to operate. Those extrinsic (i.e., structural) mechanisms include absorption mechanisms that are not related to internal energy dissipation. Examples of the extrinsic loss mechanisms include Rayleigh and phase (i.e., stochastic) scattering at external boundaries, transmission losses to other components (i.e., subsystems) aerodynamic radiation, as well as beam spreading within the test object.

Upon the elapse of several transit times, and all diffuse field conditions satisfied, the object is set into a steady state energy equilibrium condition with its surrounding, and therefore, will gracefully dissipate whatever energy it has accumulated [17,25,32]. This attenuation process is usually described by a simple first order differential equation whose solution has a constant decay parameter, which may be set to describe the energy processes taking place within the test object boundaries.

If the volume-averaged properties of a heterogeneous medium, such as dimension stone, are desired, the diffuse field should be established, and be governed by the external boundaries rather than internal grain boundaries [6,21] (i.e., the high frequency components should not be excessively high, because the wave fronts may become trapped within the grains – therefore, much higher frequency components are needed only if direct samplings of the grains are desired. If the transient impulse concurrently includes high frequency components that fall within the order of those microstructural lengths, the rate of mode conversion generated at the external boundaries by the relatively lower frequency components of the pulse, may be reversed, or strengthened, due to the modal energy partitioning of the high frequency components occurring at aggregate interfaces. This additional rate of mode conversion depends on the relative acoustic and geometric (i.e., shape, texture, roughness, etc.) properties of the interfaces.

At early times, the wave field is dominated by spherical wave fronts of bulk and shear waves in addition to Rayleigh wave. As the wave field evolves in time, modal energy conversion occurs at the external boundaries of the test specimens for lower frequencies as well as at the internal boundaries, i.e., aggregate/matrix interfaces, for higher frequencies (zones I and II shown in Figure 3). At the beginning of zone I, the shear and the bulk modes are fully coupled. Because of the estimated high net mode conversion rate in the stone specimens of 13/1 (for an average Poisson's ratio of $\upsilon = 0.25$) towards the shear wave mode, the wave field becomes dominated (nearly 93%) by shear wave components at later times (zone III). The wave field is then dominated by rapidly attenuating shear wave modes until it becomes again dominated by the lingering bulk wave modes which were immune to the external boundaries conversion rate (zone IV), and by bulk modes generated in the opposite direction (i.e., from shear to bulk waves at a conversion rate of 1/13). As the original wave field containing mainly bulk wave modes evolves towards a diffuse wave field, the mode conversion of dynamic strain energy from bulk wave modes to shear wave modes occurs mostly due to Poisson's coupling at the external surfaces of the test specimens. The resulting diffuse field is one which has evolved into a fully randomized state, preserving only minimal information contained in the frequency distribution of energy, but with no correlation in phase (i.e., coherence) or amplitude with those of the excitation source in the different modes. In the energy-partitioning scheme of Weaver for diffuse fields, each frequency is considered to describe a state of excitation, for which the normal modes within the neighborhood of that frequency, are each excited to equal energy.

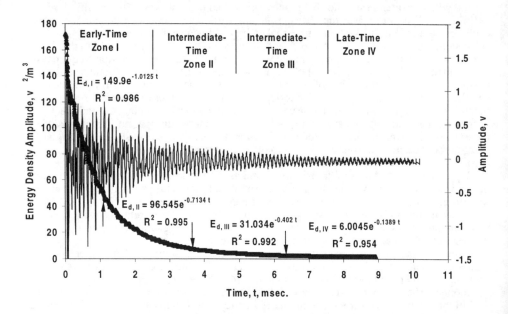

Figure 3 -- *Time Record Superimposed on the Corresponding Energy-Density Values in the Various Time Zones for the Granite Sample. Values are Fitted into Exponential Decay Functions*

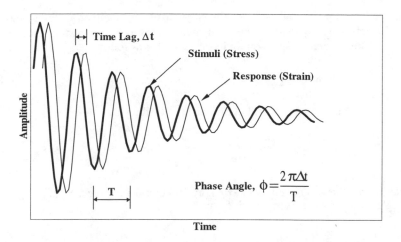

Figure 4 -- Propagation of Stress and the Delayed Strain Response

The Specific Damping Capacity (Damping Loss Factor)

The overall dynamic response level is inversely proportional to the damping level of test specimens. Assuming each test specimen, under the current testing configuration, to constitute a physical component that represents a total system composed of one single mode group (i.e., subsystem) [2,5,7] the power balance equation can be written as

$$\Pi_{in} - \Pi_{diss} = 2\pi f \eta E_{tot}$$ (26)

where Π_{in} is the input power, Π_{diss} is the dissipated power, E_{tot} is the total energy of the dynamical response in the subsystem at frequency f (in Hz), and ($2\pi\eta$) is the ratio of the energy dissipated per oscillation cycle to the total energy of the specimen. The inherent damping is related to the hysterisis loop in a load-deformation curve. Figure 4 shows how the stress stimulus is followed by a delayed strain response. The input energy to the subsystem is transformed into heat or other irrecoverable energy by internal friction or relaxation mechanisms, which results in power dissipation.

Assuming that all energy is being stored and dissipated by one subsystem, the strain lags the stress by a phase angle $\Phi = 2\pi\Delta T / T$, where T is the cycle duration, and ΔT is the lag time of the strain response. Expressing the strain as

$$\varepsilon = \varepsilon_{max} e^{j2\pi ft}$$

the Hook's law can be expressed as

$$\sigma = Re[(Q_r + jQ_i)\varepsilon]$$ (27)

where Q_r and Q_i are the real and imaginary parts of the complex dynamic modulus, respectively, and $Q_i/Q_r = \tan\Phi$. The dissipated energy per one loading cycle can be written as the area under the stress-strain hysteresis cycle as follows

$$E_{diss} = \pi \cdot Q_i \varepsilon_{max}^2 \qquad (28)$$

and the total dynamical energy stored in one cycle of loading as

$$E_{tot} = \int_0^{\varepsilon_{max}} \sigma d\varepsilon = \frac{1}{2} Q_r \varepsilon_{max}^2 \qquad (29)$$

By definition, the *specific damping capacity* (η) or the *damping loss factor* [2,7] due to the single mode of wave energy is given by

$$\eta = \frac{E_{diss}}{2\pi E_{tot}} = \frac{Q_i}{Q_r} \qquad (30)$$

where $\eta = \tan\Phi$, η is the *loss tangent*, and $Q_i = \eta Q_r$ is the *loss modulus* for that particular mode. Equation (30) demonstrates that, by measuring the storage modulus by customary elastodynamic analysis under linear response assumptions, the complex modulus can be calculated.

Experimental Procedure

In order to illustrate the principles of the proposed approach, a specimen typical of a triclinic crystal system extracted from an intact rock core and mainly containing the rhodonite mineral is used. This cylindrical specimen with dimensions of 100 mm in diameter and 180 mm in length is composed of a massive coarse aggregation resulting from the blocky prismatic habit of the rhodonite crystals. Rhodonite, which is pink-to-red in color, is usually associated with black manganese minerals and pyrite (i.e., (Manganese Iron Magnesium Calcium Silicate) or $(Mn, Fe, Mg, Ca)_5(SiO_3)_5$). Therefore, it belongs to the inosilicates subclass within the pyroxenoid group of minerals that usually exhibits a more erratic, twisted and almost helical chains of translucent/rarely-transparent crystals with hardness of 5.5 - 6.5 and a typical conchoidal fracture mode. Cleavage of rhodonite is perfect in two directions that form prisms with rectangular cross-section. The specific gravity is approximately 3.2 and the average grain size ranges from 4 to 9 mm. The dry bulk mass density was measured as 2870 kgm/m^3. The measured bulk and shear wave velocities were measured as 6840 m/s and 3630 m/s, respectively. The corresponding dynamic Poisson's ratio is calculated as 0.25. This material is similar to the Porkkala-Red (Finnish Koral) granite, which is large-grained and is quarried in large quantities and used for both exterior and interior purposes, mainly as a building stone for facades, floors and interior wall claddings. In the United States, similar geological compositions may be found in large quantities in New Jersey and in Pennsylvania.

Figure 1 shows the impact-echo data acquisition system used in this study. It includes a Laptop Computer, a Keithley Metrabyte Portable Data Acquisition System, a 1 MHz Keithley Metrabyte A/D converter, and a Krohn-Hite Eight-Pole Filter/Amplifier. The PCB Miniature Accelerometer (model 309-A) with a resonance frequency of 120 kHz was used as the receiving transducer; the use of this transducer allows the collection of the signal with a relatively flat transducer frequency response. A 6 mm diameter steel ball was used as the impactor and dropped on a heat-treated steel plate coupled to the test specimens using an ultrasonic couplant. In order to assure the repeatability of the impact, a 610 mm long metallic tube was used to control the height of the ball drop (impact energy). The PCB Miniature Accelerometer was placed just outside of the guiding tube and coupled to the surface of the test specimen.

All measurements were performed at room temperature of 17 °C without any static preload. For each test, including velocity measurements, the signal was captured starting at the first threshold triggering. Waveforms were obtained and digitized at a sampling rate of 400 kHz for a total monitoring time of 10.3 ms. Figure 3 shows the Impulse-Echo time domain waveform for each mixture and the resulting energy-density decay rate.

A fixed-size time window of 1288 μs was "slided," one digital point at a time, on the total domain record (i.e., 10.3 ms). At each window increment, the time signal contained in that fixed-size time window was processed by a Fast Fourier Transformation (FFT) algorithm, and the corresponding amplitude spectrum calculated. This process was performed for each window increment and the values of the energy density plotted against the gate time (i.e., initial time) as shown in Figure 3. An exponentially decaying function with respect to time was then fitted to these data points in each time zone.

Qualifying Diffuse Field Analyses for Dimension Stone

To qualify diffuse field analyses of the signals, Weaver's postulates [19,20], which may be regarded as essential requirements for statistical treatment of signals, need to be satisfied. Those requirements are based on the equipartitioning of energy amongst the different occurring modes, provided enough signal monitoring time and adequate bandwidth are available and in the presence of sufficiently weak absorption. With these requirements applied on the test specimens, and the frequency band used, the diffuse field analysis of the dimension stone specimens is justifiable.

To assure that the randomizing influences, due to the inevitable stochastic fluctuations, are rapid compared to the decay rate, a condition that sufficiently weak absorption exist should be satisfied, so that as the diffuse field decays, it remains in a state of energy equipartition, the following expression must be satisfied

$$\frac{l\alpha}{C_s} << 1.0 \tag{31}$$

where l is the average path length of an acoustic ray between randomizing reflections, α is the attenuation rate, and C_s is the shear velocity. The average path length, l, should not exceed the least dimension of the stone cylindrical specimens (0.075 m), and can be as short as a typical grain size (say 5 mm) if scattering from those internal interfaces is strong. If the volume averaged properties, rather than the microstructural ones, are desired, the length, l, should be taken as the one corresponding to external boundary reflections (i.e., not due to grain scattering) so that $l = 0.075$ m. At early times, the Rayleigh wave component may be neglected due to the sampling technique, and at late times it had already decayed or decomposed into body wave components. Therefore, in the current tests, modal energy exchange is considered to occur only between the longitudinal and shear wave components, mostly at external surfaces due to Poisson coupling. This consideration is assured by estimating the order of the mean free path length l, which must obey the following relation: $f << c_{l,t}/\alpha$, where $c_{l,t}$ is the frequency-range weighted average longitudinal, or shear wave velocity, and α is the attenuation parameter in Nepers/m. For the Porkkalla Red granite, α was measured as high as 1.0125 Nepers/ms at early times, and as low as 0.1389 Nepers/ms at very late times, see

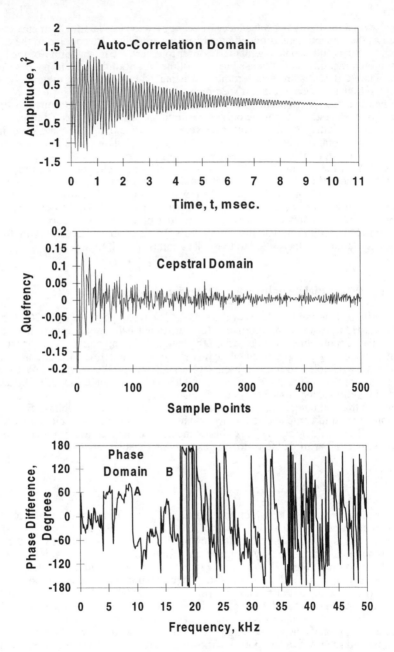

Figure 5 – *Auto-Correlation Domain, Cepstral Domain, and Phase Difference of the Impulse-Echo Signal for the Granite Sample*

Figure 2. Employing a typical wave velocity value of 5000 m/s for all stone specimens at all wave modes (i.e., regardless of the stress mode as it is being considered) l must be much smaller than 5 m corresponding to the early-time regime. Similarly, at very late times, l must be much smaller than 25 m for late time regime. All these bounding values constitute the practical range of l for which the propagating wavelengths should be selected.

The above calculations show that mode conversion is governed and is satisfied by the external surfaces, which have a minimum dimension of 0.075 m. Because of the special considerations mentioned above at low and high frequencies, the selection of an intermediate frequency band should be carefully evaluated to suit the size scales of the test object. The geometric limit set by Weaver which preserves a basic assumption of the diffuse field, that the wave amplitudes remain constant during measurement, is that the frequency, f , be such that the relation $f \gg c_{l,t}/(2\pi l)$ is satisfied. Because the wave field is mostly dominated by shear waves at late time for an intermediate impulse frequency band, $c_{l,t}$ should be taken as c_t. Using typical values of c_t and l for the stone specimens, external boundaries will control most of the diffuse state if f $\gg$ 10.6 kHz, which also must be above the lowest branch resonance frequency. Internal grain interfaces will start contributing to mode conversion when f $\gg$ 50 kHz. To allow external surfaces control of the diffuse state, a band pass filter of 10-50 kHz appears to be most appropriate for the stone specimens size and type ranges.

This last condition is equivalent to that of reverberant chambers in architectural acoustics concerning the diffuse field distance (i.e., the distance from an omnidirectional source for which the direct energy density is equal to the reverberant energy density) and is usually expressed in terms of a cross-over wavelength. Beyond this threshold wavelength (frequency), often called the "Schroeder frequency" [24], normal modes overlap instead of being initially distinctive (i.e., separable) and therefore, it marks the transition into the diffusive (i.e., statistical) range. A second constraint, which deals with the accuracy of the assessment of spectral amplitude density in a random process, [18,19] is expressed as follows

$$NT\Delta f \gg 1.0 \qquad (32)$$

where N is the number of independent receivers used in the amplitude averaging (only one receiver in this study). The signal monitoring time, T, is a sufficiently long time (in this study, T = 10.3 ms), and Δf is a sufficiently large frequency bandwidth over which, the averaged signal is being desired. Δf can be taken as the minimum observed frequency width between two normal modes such as the frequency spacing A-B, which is equal to 8330 Hz. For a typical test, Equation (32) is also satisfied.

In order to legitimize statistical analyses of the impact echo signal, a third constraint is also in place to assure that there are a large number of normal modes within the test bandwidth [18,19]. This constraint is expressed as follows

$$D(f)\Delta f \gg 1.0 \qquad (33)$$

where

$$D(f) \cong 8\pi f^2 \frac{V}{C_s}$$

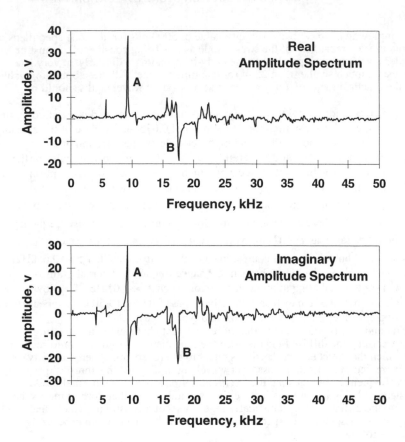

Figure 6 – *Real and Imaginary Amplitude Spectra of the Impulse-Echo Signal up to 50 kHz for the Granite Sample*

and, where V is the volume of a typical specimen (V=0.0008 m^3), c_t is taken as 3700 m/s, and f_{min} = 10.6 kHz, and Δf, is the frequency range over which the mean signal is desired, which should not be less than 3.5 kHz for $D(f)\Delta f$ =10 m^2/s^2 >>1, which is satisfied by the test bandwidth used in this study, and by the observed frequency spacing AB. Clearly, $D(f)\Delta f$ is much larger than unity.

In addition to these constraints, it is also necessary to allow the stress-wave pulse to undergo a couple of randomizing scattering trips such as two transit travels. This may be observed in the time record. The initial part of this domain is coherent and carries information about the source nature such as the contact time. To remove this unwanted coherent part of the signal, procedures usually include a lag on the start time of the signal, automatic truncation of the initially arriving waves with high energies and coherence, and magnifying the late times wave components relative to the early time ones.

Clearly, the stress wave field in this study decays rapidly (postulate 1) compared to

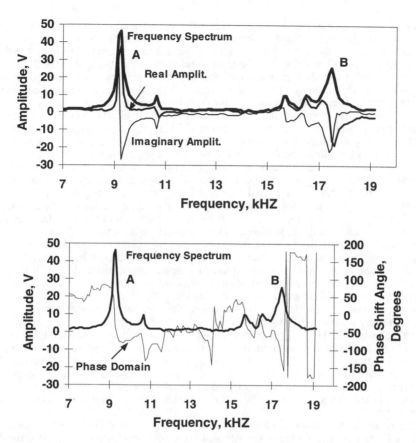

Figure 7 – *Amplitude Spectra of the Impulse-Echo Signal and its Phase Change for the Granite Sample*

other materials such as metals; however, for concrete and polycrystalline rock, the decay rate restriction is still satisfied. All other postulates are also satisfied, and the assumption that a maturely developed diffuse field satisfying the above constraints is verified. Furthermore, these results are also consistent with the solid media analog of Schroeder's statistical theory of reverberant enclosures [21]. For further study of Schroeder's theory adapted to solid media, the reader is referred to Reis et al [21]. Consequently, statistical energy analyses, based on diffuse field assumptions, is employed in this study.

Experimental Results

The impulse-generated time domain record and the corresponding energy-density decay curve are shown in Figure 3. The time record shown in Figure 3 is zoned into appropriate time zones that depend on the physical phenomenon being studied. The time domain waveform is divided into four main time zones where the time duration of each zone is decided upon inspecting the auto-correlation, cepstrum and phase functions of the waveforms to evaluate the corresponding signal state of coherence [35,36]. The first time regime (i.e., early time) where the impulse-echo signal maintain its coherence, consists of the beginning of the time record up to 1.2 ms, while during the third time regime where the impulse-echo signal had lost its coherence, is considered to be the time record after 3.5 ms. Figure 5 shows the auto-correlation, cepstrum, and phase domains of the impulse-echo signal. Figure 6 shows the real and imaginary amplitude spectra of the impulse-echo signal up to 50 kHz, and Figure 7 shows the changes of the frequency spectrum superimposed on the changes of the corresponding real and imaginary amplitudes, as well as the phase shift of the impulse-echo signal. In Figures 5 to 7, the resonance modes denoted by A, which occurs at 9225 Hz, and by B, which occurs at 17550 Hz, correspond to the shear-wave and dilatational wave transit resonance modes, respectively, which occur in the finite solid cylindrical test specimens. All shear-wave components of the impulse that have wavelengths larger than that corresponding to A, can transmit to surrounding media, and therefore, dissipate extrinsically. At frequencies above A, only the longer wavelength dilatational components can still transmit to surrounding media, and therefore, dissipate extrinsically, i.e., the shear wave components are confined within the test object. As the frequency increases and the boundaries appear increasingly reflective to the dilatational modes, less extrinsic dilatational-wave transmission, i.e., dissipation, occurs, as it is observed by the decreasing phase angle.

Because only shear wave components are reflected at A, and both body wave components become reflected at B, as depicted by the full angle phase shift at B, the relative phase difference between both shifts provide information about the shear-wave proportion in the wave field at the resonance frequency A, which is nearly 47% of the wave energy at point A (i.e., 9220 Hz). Therefore, the shear wave energy starts to dissipate entirely intrinsically above 9220 Hz, while the dilatational wave energy starts to do so only above 17550 Hz. This is an additional effect to mode conversion where the wave-field energy favors the accumulation of shear wave energy at point B (i.e., at the end of the bandwidth A-B). Therefore, if one is concerned about the time allocation of the occurrence of the frequency components (i.e., wavelet analysis) the high frequency regime (i.e., above B) will mainly correspond to the late-time regime. This provides experimental evidence that a diffuse field is extractable from the high-frequency late-time regime of the signal.

In the phase domain shown in Figures 5 and 7, above the dilatational mode transit resonance frequency (i.e., B) the stochastic scattering becomes immediately effective due to the role of the specimen-size/aggregate-size scales. Therefore, the phase shifts that occur above B, which produce incoherence of the signal, are mainly due to resonance scattering at grain boundaries, with higher frequencies being scattered by corresponding groups of smaller grains. As a consequence, the normalized frequency corresponding to each resonance (i.e., phase shift) provides the means to retrieve the relative proportion of grains of the same size. For example, it can be seen from Figure 5 that the grains are fairly densely packed with gaps in the intermediate size ranges, but with high fractions of smaller grains.

Phase shift analyses may be used in the calculation of the resulting phase differences and corresponding scattering and absorption cross-sections. Although the stochastic process that occurs above B is related to many factors (such as grain acoustic/elastic mismatch properties with those of the host media, grain crystallographic anisotropy, its volumetric extent, and grain separation distances), it strongly depends upon the grain size distribution, as this factor dominates the stochastic process of grain size-wavelength scale matching. Because of the high mode conversion rate towards shear waves and because of the higher extrinsic dissipation suffered by the dilatational waves, a relative pure shear wave field exists in this frequency domain (i.e., above B). Resonance of individual grains occurs when a wavelength becomes of a comparable size to a grain or a grain-size group. Accordingly, it may be adequate to consider that phase shifts that occur at individual frequencies correspond to shear-wave resonance scattering, for which scaling should be performed. Generally, phase shift increases with the grain size in the stochastic scattering regime (i.e., above B) up to the high frequency diffuse regime. A proper phase shift analysis is truly complex as it involves many parameters. For this reason, interpretations from the phase domain should be supported by concurrent interpretations of the response signal in several other domains. For a good review of phase shift analyses, the reader is referred to References [37-39].

Conclusions

The evolution in time of impulse-generated stress waves is described. The application of the presented methodology to dimension stones is expected to provide new and powerful capabilities for the evaluation and characterization of stone components and systems being treated as industrial end products. As will be demonstrated in Parts 2 and 3 of this study, this approach is used to retrieve the viscoelastic properties and some of the microstructural parameters of dimension stone. In addition to these two applications, other potential applications include the assessment of damage accumulation due to fatigue, creep, freeze-thaw, distributed damage or inclusions, low-temperature and durability cracking, as well as the intrusion of air pockets and water-filled voids. The approach can also be used in the estimation of sound absorption characteristics and transport properties of stone components.

Acknowledgements

This paper was prepared from a study conducted at the Center of Excellence for Airport Pavement Research. Funding for the Center of Excellence is provided in part by the Federal Aviation Administration under Research Grant Number 95-C-001. The Center of Excellence is maintained at the University of Illinois at Urbana-Champaign, which works in partnership with Northwestern University and the Federal Aviation Administration. Ms. Patricia Watts is the FAA Program Manager for the Air Transportation Centers of Excellence and Dr. Satish Agrawal is the FAA Technical Director for the Pavement Center. The authors are also very grateful to Professor Edward J. Cording, Director of the Rock Mechanics Laboratory at the University of Illinois at Urbana-Champaign, for providing access to the laboratory facilities.

Disclaimer

The contents of this paper reflect the views of the authors who are responsible for the facts and accuracy of the data presented within. The contents do not necessarily reflect the official views and policies of the Federal Aviation Administration. This paper does not constitute a standard, specification, or regulation.

References

[1] Kinra, V. K. and Yapura, C. L., "A Fundamental Connection Between Intrinsic Material Damping and Structural Damping," *M³D: Mechanics and Mechanisms of Material Damping, ASTM STP 1169*, Eds.: V. K. Kinra and A. Wolfenden, American Society for Testing and Materials, Philadelphia, 1992, pp. 396-420.
[2] Lyon, R., and DeJong, R., "Theory and Applications of Statistical Energy Analysis,"

Butterworth-Heinmann, second edition, 1995.

[3] Read, B., and Dean, G., "The Determination of Dynamic Properties of Polymers and Composites," *John Wiley Publ. - Halsted Press,* New York, 1978.

[4] Shatilo, A., Sondergeld, C., and Rai, C., "Ultrasonic Attenuation in Glenn Pool Rocks, Northern Oklahoma," *Geophysics,* Vol. 63, No. 2, 1998, pp. 465-478.

[5] Mavko, G., Mukerji, T., and Dvorkin, J., "The Rock Physics Handbook," *Cambridge University Press,* first ed., New York, 1998.

[6] Reis, H. L. M. dos, Habboub, A. K., and Carpenter, S. H., "Nondestructive Evaluation of Complex Moduli in Asphalt Concrete Using an Energy Approach," *To appear in the 1999 Transportation Research Record, TRR,* 1999.

[7] Zinoviev, P., and Ermakov, Y., "Energy Dissipation in Composite Materials," *Technomic Publ.,* Lancaster, PA, 1994.

[8] Clough, R., "The Energetics of Acoustic Emission Source Characterization," *Materials Evaluation,* Vol. 45, 1987, pp. 556-563.

[9] Clough, R., "A Scalar Approach to Acoustic Emission," *Am. Soc. of Mech. Eng.-NCA, Vibro-Acoustic Characterization of Materials and Structures,* Vol. 14, 1992, pp. 101-110.

[10] Dalenback, B., Kleiner, M. and Svensson, P., *"A Macroscopic View of Diffuse Reflection," J. Audio Eng. Soc.,* Vol. 42, No. 10, Oct. 1994, pp. 793-806.

[12] Dempsey, H. A. L., and Egle, D. M. "The Effects of Transducers on the Decay of a Diffuse Energy Field," *J. Acoustic Emission,* Vol. 4, 1985, pp. S46-49.

[12] Kautz, H. E., "Determination of Plate Wave Velocities and Diffuse Field Decay Rates with Broad-Band Acousto-Ultrasonic Signals," *National Aeronautics and Space Administration NASA, Lewis Research Center,* Report No. NASA TM-106158, Ohio, June 1993.

[13] Butkov, E., "Mathematical Physics," *First Ed., Addison-Wesley,* Menlo Park, California, 1968.

[14] Goebbels, K., "Materials Characterization for Process Control and Product Uniformity," *CRC Press,* First Ed., Boca Raton, Florida, 1994.

[15] Guo, C., Holler, P., and Goebbels, K., "Scattering of Ultrasonic Waves in Anisotropic Polycrystalline Metals," *Acoustica,* 59:112, pp. 112-120, 1985.

[16] Weaver, R. L., "Diffuse Waves for Materials NDE," *Proc. of a workshop on: Acousto-Ultrasonics, Theory and Applications,* Duke, J., Jr., Plenum Press, New York, 1988, pp.35-43.

[17] Weaver, R. L., "Diffusivity of Ultrasound in Polycrystals," *J. Mech. Phys. Solids,* Vol. 38, 1990, pp. 55-86.

[18] Weaver, R. L., "Indications of Material Character from the Behavior of Diffuse Ultrasonic Fields," *Nondestructive Characterization of Materials II,* Eds. J. F. Bussiere, J-P Monchalin, C. O. Ruud, and R. E. Green, Jr., Plenum Press, New York, 1987, pp. 689-695.

[19] Weaver, R. L., "On Diffuse Waves in Solid Media," *J. Acoustic. Soc. of America,* Vol. 71, 1982, pp. 1608-1609.

[20] Weaver, R. L., "On the Time and Geometry Independence of Elastodynamic Spectral Energy Density," *J. Acoustic. Soc. of America,* Vol. 80, No. (5), 1986, pp. 1539-1541.

[21] Reis, H. L. M. dos, Habboub, A. K. and Carpenter, S. H., "An Energy-Based Aggregate Geometric Packing Parameter for Asphalt Concrete," INSIGHT -- *Non-Destructive Testing and Condition Monitoring,* Vol. 41, No. 10, 1999, pp.650-656.

[22] Simpson, W., and McClung, R., "Quantitative Attenuation Technique for Materials Characterization," *Materials Evaluation,* Vol. 49, No. 11, 1991, pp. 1409-1413.

[23] Vary, A., "Ultrasonic Measurement of Mechanical Properties," *International Advances in Nondestructive Testing,* Vol. 13, (Ed. W. McGonnagle), Gordon and Breach Science Publ., New York, 1988, pp. 1-38.

[24] Schroeder, M. "The "Schroeder frequency" Revisited," *J. Acoustic Soc. of America*, Vol. 99, No. (5), 1996, pp. 3240-3241.

[25] Simpson, W., and McClung, R., "Quantitative Attenuation Technique for Materials Characterization," *Materials Evaluation*, Vol. 49, No. 11, 1991, pp. 1409-1413.

[26] Sansalone, M., and Carino, N., "Impact Echo: A Method for Flaw Detection in Concrete Using Transient Stress Waves," *Report No. NB SIR 86-3452, National Bureau of Standards*, Washington, D.C./PB 87-104444/AS, National Technical Information Service, Springfield, Virginia, Sept. 1986, pp. 222.

[27] Kuhn, G., "Symmetry of Energy-Transfer Ratios for Elastic Waves at a Boundary between Two Media," *J. Acoustic. Soc. of America*, Vol. 36(3), 1964, pp. 423-427.

[28] Pierce, A., "Acoustics: An Introduction to its Physical Principles and Applications," *First Ed., McGraw-Hill*, New York, 1981.

[29] Egle, D. M., "Diffuse Wave Fields in solid Media," *J. Acoustic. Soc. of America*, Vol. 70, No. (2), 1981, pp. 476-480.

[30] Achenbach, J. D., "Ultrasonics: Introduction," *International Centre for Mechanical Sciences: Courses and Lectures-330*, (ed., J. D. Achenbach), Springer-Verlag Pub., New York, 1993, pp. 1-9.

[31] Achenbach, J. D., "Wave Propagation in Elastic Solids," *Third Edition, North-Holland Pub.*, N. Y., 1980.

[32] Batchelder, L., "Reciprocal of the Mean Free Path," *J. Acoustic. Soc. of America*, 36(3), 1964, pp. 551-555.

[33] Grabovsky, Y., and Kohn, R., "Microstructures Minimizing the Energy of a Two-Phase Elastic Composite in Two Space Dimensions- II: The Vigdergauz Microstreucture," *J. Mech. Phys. Solids*, Vol. 43, No. 6, 1995, pp. 949-972.

[34] Gueguen, Y., and Palciauskas, V., "Introduction to the Physics of Rocks," *Princeton University Press*, Princeton, New Jersey, 1994.

[35] Gericke, O., "Cepstral Method for the Measurement of Ultrasonic Pulse Transmission Time Variations," *International Advances In Nondestructive Testing*, Mcgonnagle, W. J., Editor, Gordon and Breach Science Publishers, Vol. 15, New York, 1990, pp. 27-51.

[36] Malik, M., and Saniie, J., "Generalized Time-Frequency Representation of Ultrasonic Signals," *IEEE Trans. On Ultrasonics, Ferroelectrics and Frequency Control*, Symp. Proc. 2, 1993, pp. 691-695.

[37] Papadakis, E.P., "Revised Grain-Scattering Formulas and Tables," *J. Acoustic. Soc. of America*, 37(4), 1965, pp. 703-710.

[38] Papadakis, E.P., "Ultrasonic Diffraction Loss and Phase Change in Anisotropic Materials," *J. Acoustic. Soc. of America*, 40(4), 1966, pp. 863-876.

[39] Twersky, V., "Low-Frequency Scattering by Mixtures of Correlated Nonspherical Particles," *J. Acoustic. Soc. of America*, 84(1), 1988, pp. 409-415.

Henrique L.M. dos Reis and Amin K. Habboub[1]

Nondestructive Evaluation of Dimension Stone Using Impulse-Generated Stress Waves: Part 2 – Estimation of Complex Moduli

Reference: dos Reis, H. L. M., and Habboub, A. K., **"Nondestructive Evaluation of Dimension Stone Using Impulse-Generated Stress Waves: Part 2 – Estimation of Complex Moduli,"** *Dimension Stone Cladding: Design, Construction, Evaluation, and Repair, ASTM 1394*, K. R. Hoigard, Ed., American Society for Testing and Materials, West Conshohocken, PA, 2000.

Abstract: Using principles of Statistical Energy Analysis, a nondestructive evaluation methodology is presented to estimate the average Poisson's ratio and the average dynamic complex bulk, shear, extensional, and longitudinal moduli of dimension stone. The estimated moduli represent an average over the volume of the test specimen and over a frequency band up to 200 kHz. The proposed methodology is based upon the energy-density decay function of an impact-generated diffuse wave field using small dynamic strain amplitudes. Invoking the principles of linear viscoelasticity, various loss parameters are also extracted and discussed. The methodology allows the evaluation of the energy dissipation characteristics of different stone types, and their dependence upon the stone microstructure.

Keywords: dimension stone, material characterization, complex moduli, microstructure, stone veneer, vanities, cladding

The dependence of the long-term structural performance characteristics of dimensional stone upon its viscoelastic properties has been widely recognized [1-5]. However, these properties have not been typically included among the data provided by material suppliers, nor was it possible to evaluate them in the field. Therefore, the capability to perform viscoelastic measurements in the field, or when the stone components are in service, may provide new and effective industrial means of quality assurance/control of dimension stones.

When selecting a stone-type for a specific design, it may be advantageous to identify a stone that optimizes its stiffness and damping properties [6-8]. For example, load-bearing facades sustain considerable stresses that may also vary with height; therefore, their damping capacity should be limited in order to avoid excessive long-term wall deformations due to creep. On the other hand, the elastic-storage and damping capacities should be high enough in order to avoid easy fracture, and to accommodate arbitrary dynamic loading [9]. With thinner panel sections, these properties may become even more critical during manufacturing/handling or while the stone is in service. Stones that have high loss tangents, i.e., damping coefficients, but low stiffness, tend to be more compliant, which leads to larger permanent deformations [7,10-12]. Stones with low

[1] Professor Henrique L.M. dos Reis and graduate student Amin K. Habboub are associated with the Department of Civil and Environmental Engineering at the University of Illinois at Urbana-Champaign, 104 South Mathews, Urbana, Illinois.

damping will magnify the critical mode amplitude in a dynamic response, and therefore will experience reduced fracture toughness and fatigue resistance, which may result in reduced durability (i.e., accelerated weathering).

In each loading mode (i.e., shear, bulk, etc.) the viscoelastic properties may be adequately represented in terms of a complex modulus defined at a specific frequency, or as an average over a frequency bandwidth. The complex modulus is composed of two parts (i.e., the real and the imaginary parts), which correspond to the elastic and the inelastic, i.e., dissipation, parts, respectively. The first part represents the elastic-energy storage capacity of the component while the other represents its intrinsic damping capacity. Once the complex dynamic modulus is determined over several meaningful decades of time and frequency, the creep-compliance and the stress relaxation moduli may be derived [8,9,11-14]. Furthermore, the fracture toughness may also be evaluated empirically or analytically using principles of Statistical Energy Analysis (SEA).

Available mechanical test procedures on dimension stones include the elastic shear and compression moduli, density, moisture-absorption, thermal conductivity, short-term creep deflection, wear resistance by sliding friction, impact strength, as well as the compressive, shear and flexural strengths in the natural state, water-saturated, or after several freeze-thaw cycles [15-17]. Available physical tests include the specific and volumetric weights, degree of compactness, porosity, imbibition coefficients, and the coefficients of thermal expansion. In addition to impact strength tests, several ASTM test procedures are available to evaluate creep in hard and soft rocks such as the Standard Test Method for "Creep of Cylindrical Hard Rock Core Specimens in Uniaxial Compression"(ASTM D 4341-93), the Standard Test Method for "Creep of Cylindrical Soft Rock Core Specimens in Uniaxial Compression" (ASTM D 4405-93), and the Standard Test Method for "Creep of Cylindrical Rock Core Specimens in Triaxial Compression" (ASTM D 4406-93); however, the immediate evaluation of the viscoelastic properties of dimension stones in the field remains largely unavailable.

During excavation, by using hardness/elasticity correlations [18], the cutting energy consumption may be empirically developed. In the case of explosive blasting, the determination of the quantity of explosives that is needed to achieve a limited response at a specific location by "cube root" scaling and empirical correlations may require information about the intrinsic dissipation characteristics of the rock mass system [18]. As a general rule, the rate of the peak particle velocity attenuation decreases as the scaled range increases [18]. Furthermore, the increase of shear deformation of a stone element with time when the element is subjected to a constant deviatoric stress state (i.e., squeezing) is a common excavation problem which may require pre-knowledge of the viscoelastic properties [1,18]. Squeezing results in progressive ground movement into the excavation due to yielding and time dependent properties of the quarry [18]. This problem varies according to ground stress changes, stiffness and strength of the stone-ore, orientation and method of excavation, size and rate of excavation. Squeezing usually causes instability problems in excavations due to the short stand-up time and the development of large ground movements, which leads to an increase of load on the excavation supports with time. Therefore, pre-evaluation of such properties by geophysical [1,2] (i.e., large-scale) and by nondestructive (i.e., small-scale) means may be highly beneficial [3,5,19,20].

Within the quarrying industry, stress-wave based nondestructive testing and evaluation (NDE) methods had been traditionally used for rock mass characterization and for estimation of the in-situ rock moduli [18]. Lab measurements of bulk wave velocity for intact rock samples had been correlated to those in the field to estimate the Rock Quality Designation (RQD) [18]. The RQD is a measure of joints recurrence in the rock mass system due to foliation/bedding, or failure-induced jointing. The RQD is also a commonly used index to indicate continuity in a rock mass system, and it is also a measure of its structural integrity and quarrying feasibility [18]. Once the RQD is estimated, the 'effective' in-situ modulus of elasticity, which is frequently used in quarrying operations, can then be estimated [18]. Several in-situ stress-wave based NDE methods have been used at the macroscopic level to estimate certain parameters, such as thickness/velocity, joint depth/orientation, elastic moduli, density, and inspection of integrity of the dimensional stone block/component.

In this paper, by using a diffuse wave energy approach and principles of Statistical Energy Analyses (SAE) [7,21-25], an impact-echo methodology is presented that nondestructively estimates the viscoelastic properties of dimension stones. The proposed method is relatively fast, reliable, economical, and may be conveniently used in the laboratory or in the field [26,27].

The Dynamic Moduli

The complex modulus [7,9,14] in a particular constitutive mode (i.e., bulk, shear, etc.) is described as

$$M_m^* = M_{mr} + jM_{mi} = M_{mr}(1+j\eta_m) \tag{1}$$

where M_{mr} and $M_{mi} = \eta_m M_{mr}$ are the real and the imaginary (loss) parts of the particular mode m with loss tangent $\eta_m = \tan \phi_m$, and where ϕ_m is the strain phase lag angle relative to the applied stress. Several techniques can be used to evaluate the dynamic moduli of viscoelastic materials [7,11,13]. Here, these moduli are evaluated by measuring the velocity of propagation and attenuation of each wave mode in the test specimens [5,19,20]. Assuming the test specimens to be finite, homogeneous and isotropic, the bulk and shear storage moduli are determined from the corresponding modal velocities [5,19,20] by the following expressions

$$M_r = \rho(1+\upsilon)(1+2\upsilon)C_p^2/(1+\upsilon) \tag{2a}$$

$$M_r = \rho\,C_k^2 \tag{2b}$$

$$G_r = \rho\,C_s^2 \tag{2c}$$

where

$$\upsilon = (0.5(C_p/C_s)^2-1)/(\,(C_p/C_s)^2-1)$$

and where ρ is the mass density, M_r and G_r are the bulk and shear storage moduli, respectively, ρ is the Poisson's ratio and C_k, C_p, and C_s are the bulk, compressional, i.e., p-wave, and shear wave velocities, respectively. The extensional and longitudinal storage moduli [9,10,14] are obtained by the following expressions:

$$T_r = (9G_rM_r)/(3M_r+G_r) \tag{3}$$

$$L_r = M_r + (4/3)G_r \tag{4}$$

Using the correspondence principle of linear viscoelasticity, the dynamic (i.e., complex) extension, T^*, and longitudinal L^*, moduli can be obtained by replacing the elastic moduli in Equations (3) and (4) by the corresponding dynamic (i.e., complex) moduli [9-11,14].

The complex Poisson's ratio υ^* [14] is given by

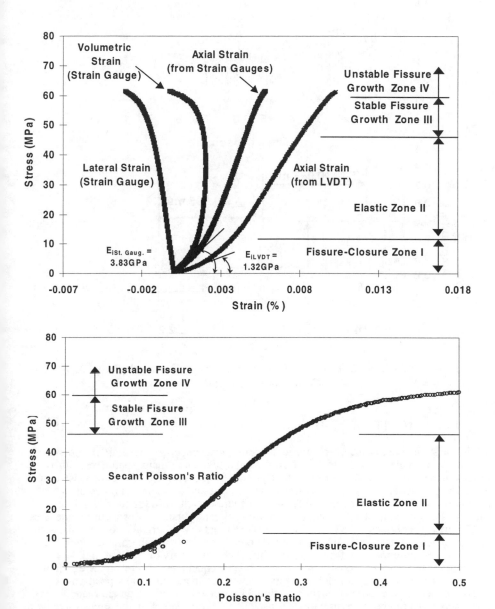

Figure 1 – Uniaxial Compression Response of Sandstone Test Sample

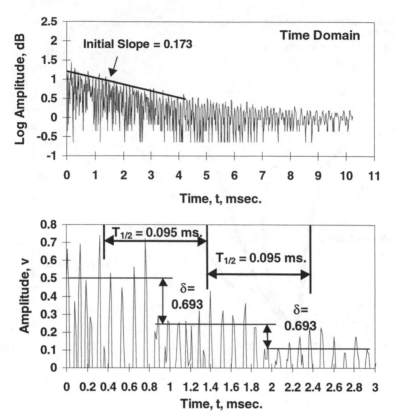

Figure 2 –*Time Domain Record of the Impact-Echo Signal Showing Different Methods of Calculating Decay Rates*

$$\upsilon^* = [T^*/(2G^*)] - 1 \tag{5}$$

In the statistical regime of the impact response, test specimens made of elastic and homogeneous materials are capable of exciting and sustaining many spatial resonance modes over time, which are n-fold coupled at high frequencies and at late response times. Therefore, the measured signal may not always correspond to the initial mode of excitation, as it may be expected when the procedure described in the Standard Test Method for "Fundamental Transverse, Longitudinal, and Torsional Resonant Frequencies of Concrete Specimens" (ASTM C 215-97) is extended to cylindrical or other finite-size test specimens. Because the excitation mode rapidly converts to other mode types, the detection of a pure mode in finite-size specimens becomes very difficult at high frequencies and computationally intensive at lower frequencies. Therefore, and in lieu of detecting the desired transit resonance mode directly as in a traditionally position-sensitive measurements, such as the traditional impact-echo method, an alternate approach to overcome such limitations is used by spatially averaging the stress wave field over all possible modes in a statistical manner, provided such treatment is warranted by diffuse wave energy analyses, and its statistical energy distribution requirements. This avoids the need to perform complex modal analyses of finite vibrating bodies. As

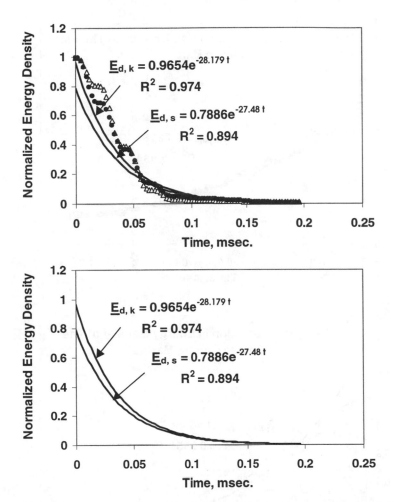

Figure 3 – *Convergence of the Normalized Energy Density Response Due to Bulk and Shear Impact Excitation for the Coarse Carrara Marble Test Specimen.*

discussed in Part 1 of this study, this can be assured by following Weaver's scheme of energy partitioning [23], or Schroeder's theory of reverberant enclosures modified to solid media [21], which were both verified for the current tests. This is the case when the volume-averaged properties, such as the various complex moduli, are desired over a frequency bandwidth of interest.

The loss factor $\eta_m = \tan \phi_m$ for each mode group (i.e., sub-system) is related to the corresponding specific damping ratio $\Delta W_m/W_m$, as follows

$$\eta_m = \Delta W_m/(2\pi W_m) \qquad (6)$$

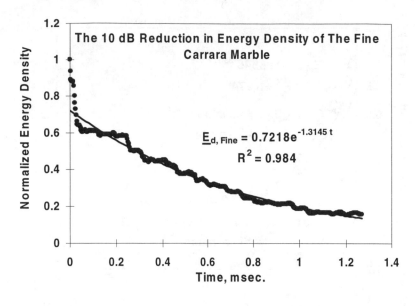

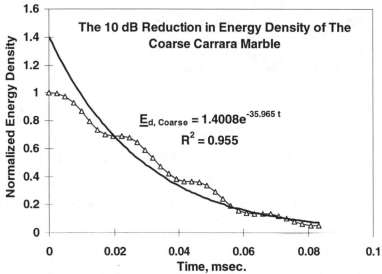

Figure 4 – *Normalized Energy Density Decay for the Fine and Coarse Carrara Marble Showing the Time Required for a 10 dB Reduction in Energy Density*

where ΔW_m represents the energy lost per cycle in a particular response mode and W_m represents the maximum elastic energy stored in that mode due to excitation. For small values of damping (i.e., $\tan \phi < 0.1$) and linear material response, which is achieved by introducing small dynamic strain amplitudes, the loss factor η may be related, or

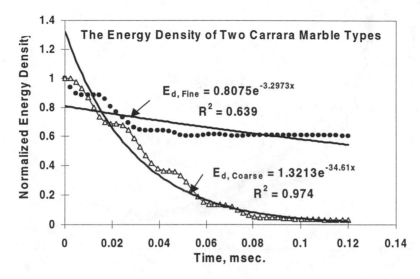

Figure 5 – *Normalized Energy Density Decay for Fine* (Ed Fine) *and Coarse*
(Ed Coarse) *Carrara Marble*

phenomenologically compared to other forms of damping measurements. The specific damping capacity values $\Delta W_m/W_m$ for the bulk and shear wave modes are retrieved from the energy-density decay curves at the early and late times of the impact-echo signal, respectively, and used to obtain the imaginary parts of the bulk and shear complex moduli, as described in Part 1 of this study.

Assuming linear viscoelasticity, the specific damping capacity [10,11,14] can be related to other measures of damping by the following equation

$$Q^{-1} = \frac{\Psi}{2\pi} = \eta = \frac{\delta}{\pi} = \tan\phi = \phi = \frac{M_{mi}}{M_{mr}} = 2\xi = \frac{\Delta W}{2\pi W} = \frac{\lambda a}{\pi} \qquad (7)$$

where

Q	= Quality Factor
Ψ	= Specific Damping Capacity, or, "Specific Loss"
η	= Loss Factor
δ	= Logarithmic Decrement of the Time Response Amplitude
ϕ	= Phase Angle by which strain lags the stress
M_{mi}	= Loss Modulus of a particular mode m
M_{mr}	= Storage Modulus of a particular mode m
ζ	= Damping Ratio or Damping Factor
ΔW	= Energy Loss per Cycle
W	= Maximum Elastic Stored Energy
λ	= Wavelength of the Elastic Wave Component = $c_{k,t}/f$
$c_{k,t}$	= Propagation Velocity of the Elastic Wave in the Dilatational or Shear stress-strain modes (m/s)
f	= The Cyclic Frequency of the Elastic Wave Component
α	= The Attenuation Coefficient given in Nepers/m

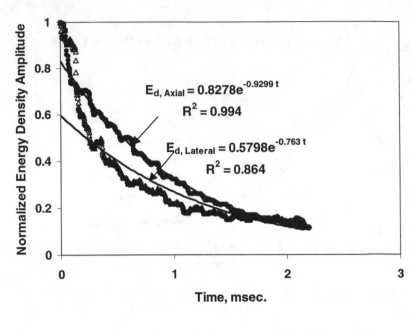

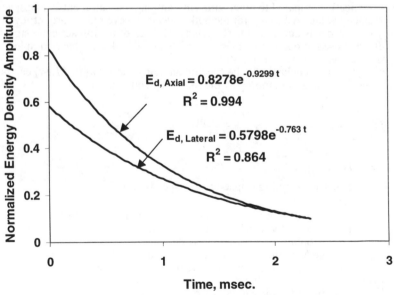

Figure 6 – *Energy-Density Decay of the Porkkala Red Test Cylindrical Specimen with Axial and Lateral Impact Excitations*

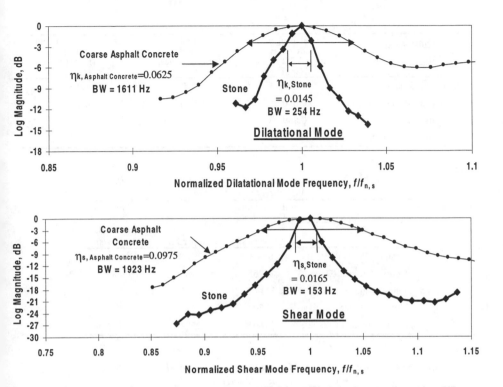

Figure 7 — *Modal Bandwidth, BW, Measurements for the Dilatational and Shear Modes*

Experimental Procedure

The data acquisition system and procedure is described in Part 1 of this study. Two excitation sources were employed; the first injects dilatational waves into the specimen by using a ball drop on the top surface of the test specimen, and the second impact injects shear waves by using a sliding friction pulse on the steel plate fixed on the top surface of the test specimen. Furthermore, to verify that, at late times, the wave field energy density becomes independent of the source-type, receiver location, and testing configuration, the test specimens were also excited by an impact in both the axial and the diametrical directions of the cylindrical test specimens. Because volume averaged properties were sought, a test frequency band up to 200 kHz was used in order assure that the propagating wavelengths were of a comparable size to the test specimens.

In addition to the granite test sample described in Part 1 of this study, test samples made of fine-grained and coarse-grained polycrystalline calcite (Carrara marble), Tirrasic Sandstone (Perea), and coarse asphalt concrete were also tested using this approach. The asphalt concrete sample is similar to dense coarse rock structures.

To retrieve the mechanical properties of dimension stones, structural tests were performed according to the recommended test method of the International Society for Rock Mechanics (ISRM) and the Standard Test Method for "Elastic Moduli of Intact Rock Core Specimens in Axial Compression" (ASTM D 3148-96). For the range of

Table 1 -- *Various Mechanical Parameters*

Specimen Material Type	Initial Tangent Modulus, E_i (LVDT) (Gpa)	Initial Tangent Modulus, E_i (Strain Gauge) (Gpa)	50% Stress Tangent Modulus, $E_{t50\%}$ (LVDT) (Gpa)
Granite (Porkkala Red)	62.5	62.5	62.5
Coarse-Grained Carrara	0.690	0.690	4.137
Fine-Grained Carrara	0.859	0.859	45.990
Tirrasic Perea Sandstone	1.32	3.830	18.823

Table 2 -- *Averaged Energy-Density Decay Rates in Various Time Regimes*

Specimen Material Type	Early Time Decay Rate (Nepers/s)	Late Time Decay Rate (Nepers/s)	Overall Time Decay Rate (Nepers/s)
Granite (Porkkala Red)	838.3	281.3	490.6
Coarse-Grained Carrara	35965	5.1	2748.0
Fine-Grained Carrara	1314.5	62.3	1205
Tirrasic Perea Sandstone	750	12	620.9
Coarse Asphalt Concrete	11661	2504	4772

Table 3 -- *Storage and Loss Moduli in the Bulk and Shear Modes Obtained Nondestructively*

Specimen Material Type	Bulk Storage Modulus (GPa)	Bulk Loss Modulus (GPa)	Dynamic Bulk Modulus (GPa)	Shear Storage Modulus (GPa)	Shear Loss Modulus (GPa)	Dynamic Shear Modulus (GPa)
Granite (Porkkala Red)	117.36	18.25	118.77	35.14	5.54	35.58
Coarse-Grained Carrara	35.09	2.66	35.19	17.14	1.00	17.17
Fine-Grained Carrara	63.48	9.88	64.24	18.01	2.74	18.21
Tirrasic Perea Sandstone	39.27	6.21	39.75	13.80	2.18	13.97
Coarse Asphalt Concrete	30.69	1.59	30.73	15.04	0.28	25.60

Table 4 -- *Extensional and Longitudinal Complex Moduli and Dynamic Poisson's Ratio Obtained Nondestructively*

Specimen Material Type	Extensional Storage Modulus (GPa)	Extensional Loss Modulus (GPa)	Dynamic Extensional Modulus (GPa)	Dynamic Longitudinal Modulus (GPa)	Dynamic Poisson's Ratio
Granite (Porkkala Red)	95.87	2.40	97.05	166.21	0.363
Coarse-Grained Carrara	44.21	0.43	44.30	58.08	0.290
Fine-Grained Carrara	49.35	1.20	49.92	88.53	0.370
Tirrasic Perea Sandstone	37.06	0.93	37.52	58.38	0.343
Coarse Asphalt Concrete	38.78	0.75	38.79	50.78	0.290

stone materials that were tested nondestructively, a summary of results that were obtained from the structural testing program is shown in Table 1. Results of a typical structural test on one specimen, with a length to diameter ratio of 2, are included in Figure 1. This test corresponds to a Tirrasic Perea sandstone specimen that was taken from the same core stretch with which the nondestructive test was performed. The results shown in Figure 1 demonstrate the procedure for calculating the initial tangent modulus that corresponds to low and slowly increasing stress levels. Also, at 50% of the failure load/stress, the tangent modulus may be calculated form the stress-strain curves that were independently monitored using strain gauges and Linear Variable Differential Transformers (LVDT) and from which the deflection due to the swivel may be calculated. The 50% stress level also corresponds to the design stress, and therefore, to the appropriate modulus for use in the working stress designs of dimension stones. The stress-strain relationships are consistent with other test results performed on the same material [18]. The relationships presented in Figure 1 reveal some of the nonlinear material properties of the stone that are attributed to the presence of fissures, cracks or distributed damage. For example, Figure 1 clearly shows four stress-strain regimes. These regimes correspond to the fissure-closure, elastic, stable and unstable-fissure-growth processes that, respectively, take place as the load increases [18].

The volumetric as well as the lateral stress-strain relationships are calculated from the readings obtained from the strain gauges and LVDT. From the volumetric stress-strain relationship, the bulk moduli may be derived at various stress levels. Furthermore, the tangent and secant Poisson's moduli may be calculated at each stress level. The results demonstrate the importance of the secant Poisson's ratio in monitoring damage accumulation in the stable and unstable fissure growth regimes at high stress levels. With increasing stresses, i.e., beyond the working stress levels, the axial, volumetric and lateral stress-strain shows variably less sensitivity to damage accumulation. This may constitute another important consideration when strength designs of dimension stones are considered.

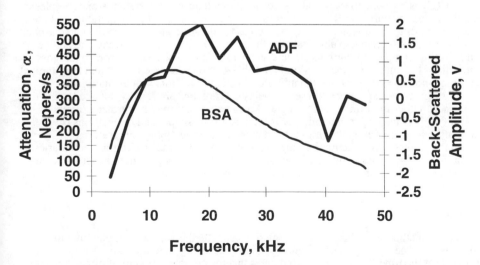

Figure 8 – *Attenuation Dependence on Frequency, ADF, and the Back-Scattered Amplitude, BSA, Spectrum*

Experimental Results

Figure 2 shows the time domain record of the impact echo signal illustrating different methods to calculate decay rates. In the first method, the decay rate is evaluated by calculating the initial slope of the logarithmic scale of the averaged amplitude; in the second method, the decay rate is evaluated by using a linear amplitude plot and a measure of the half-amplitude decay time ($T_{1/2}$) which is defined as the time required for the response amplitude to decay by one half, i.e., 6 dB. Figure 3 confirms that at late times the wave field partitions itself between body wave modes in a manner that is independent of the initial energy partitioning. It shows that for the two different excitation modes (i.e., initially bulk dominated and initially shear dominated) the energy density converges to the same rate of decay. Figure 4 shows the time required for 10 dB reduction of the normalized energy density for the fine and coarse Carrara marble. Figure 5 shows the normalized energy density versus time for the fine and coarse Carrara marble, illustrating the microstructure influence upon the intrinsic energy dissipation processes [16,28,29]. Figure 6 shows the normalized energy density decay response for Porkkala Red test cylindrical specimens for axial and lateral impact excitation. Results shown in Figures 3 and 6 show that, at late times, the wave field energy density becomes independent of the source-type, receiver location, and testing configuration, which provide significant testing advantages. Figure 7 shows the modal bandwidth measurement for the dilatational and the shear modes [5,7]. For comparison, Figure 7 also shows the modal bandwidth for the coarse asphalt concrete mixture, where the damping influence of the binder is clear. Figure 8 shows the attenuation dependence on frequency (ADF) and the back-scattered amplitude spectrum. While the first (i.e., the ADF curve) shows the time decay rate of each frequency component of the wave, which should be independent of the amplitude in linear-viscoelasticity, the back-scattered measurements show that amplitude. As Figure 8 shows, a significant portion of energy is contained within the lower frequency components, which correspond to the transit resonance modes where the waves are mainly reflected from the external boundaries of the specimen.

In Tables 2 to 4, experimental results are presented for the different stone samples made of granite (Porkkala Red), fine-grained and coarse-grained polycrystalline calcite (Carrara marble), Sandstone (Perea), as well as for the test sample made of coarse asphalt concrete for comparison. Table 2 shows the average energy-density decay rates in the various time regimes for various stone specimens. Table 3 shows the storage and loss moduli for the bulk and shear modes, and Table 4 shows the extensional and longitudinal complex moduli as well as the dynamic Poisson's ratio for the various materials.

For a given test specimen, these viscoelastic properties are readily obtained using this approach. Other important microstructural parameters that may be further examined using the NDE instrument include porosity, anisotropy, shape, and orientations of crystals, which are not dealt with in this paper. Another advantageous feature of estimating stress wave attenuation due to absorption and scattering at grain boundaries is the ability to estimate the intrinsic capability of the stone component to resist transient dynamic loads such as those due to wind-blow and earthquakes.

Conclusions

A fast methodology has been presented to estimate the various complex moduli in dimension stone. Analysis of the energy-density decaying function in the various time regimes of the time-domain record indicates that the complex moduli of dimension stones may be meaningfully characterized according to their energy dissipation characteristics. As it will be shown in Part 3 of this study, energy-density measurements may also be used to retrieve the grain scale parameters of stones. Based upon the complex moduli over a wide frequency band, the relaxation and the creep functions can also be estimated.

Acknowledgements

This paper was prepared from a study conducted at the Center of Excellence for Airport Pavement Research. Funding for the Center of Excellence is provided in part by the Federal Aviation Administration under Research Grant Number 95-C-001. The Center of Excellence is maintained at the University of Illinois at Urbana-Champaign, which works in partnership with Northwestern University and the Federal Aviation Administration. Ms. Patricia Watts is the FAA Program Manager for the Air Transportation Centers of Excellence and Dr. Satish Agrawal is the FAA Technical Director for the Pavement Center. The authors are also very grateful to Professor Edward J. Cording, Director of the Rock Mechanics Laboratory at the University of Illinois at Urbana-Champaign, for providing access to the laboratory facilities.

Disclaimer

The contents of this paper reflect the views of the authors who are responsible for the facts and accuracy of the data presented within. The contents do not necessarily reflect the official views and policies of the Federal Aviation Administration. This paper does not constitute a standard, specification, or regulation.

References

[1] Carcione, J. M., "Viscoelastic Effective Rheologies for Modeling Wave Propagation in Porous Media," *Geophysical Prospecting,* Vol. 48, 1998, pp. 249-270.

[2] Tutuncu, A. N., Podio, A. L., Gregory, A., and Sharma, M. M., "Nonlinear Viscoelastic Behavior of Sedimentary Rocks, Part I: Effect of Frequency and Strain Amplitude," *Geophysics,* Vol. 63, No. 1, 1998, pp. 184-194.

[3] Berryman, J. G., and Thigpen, L., "Extensions of Biot's Theory of Poroelasticity to Complex Porous Media," *In Am. Inst. of Physics- Conference Proc., Physics and Chemistry of Porous Media II*, Eds.: Banavar, J. R., Koplik, J., and Winkler, K. W., Ridgefield, CT, 1986, pp. 209-228.

[4] Gueguen, Y. and Palciauskas, V., "Introduction to the Physics of Rocks," *Princeton University Press,* Princeton, NJ, 1994.

[5] Sadri, A., Hassani, F., and Saleh, K., "Determination of Concrete Dynamic Elastic Constants Using a Miniature Seismic Reflection System," *Materials Evaluation,* July 1997, pp. 817-820.

[6] Grabovsky, Y., and Konh, R., "Microstructures Minimizing the Energy of a Two-Phase Elastic Composite in Two Space Dimensions. II: The Vigdergauz Microstructure," *J. Mech. Phys. Solids,* Vol. 43, No. 6, 1995, pp. 949-972.

[7] Lyon, R. H., and DeJong, R. G., *"Theory and Applications of Statistical Energy Analysis,"* Butterworth-Heinmann, second edition, Boston, MA, 1995.

[8] Zinoviev, P. A., and Ermakov, Y. E., *"Energy Dissipation in Composite Materials,"* Technomic Publ., Lancaster, PA, 1994.

[9] Nashif, A. D., Jones, D. P., and Henderson, J. P., *"Vibration Damping,"* John Wiley and Sons, 1985.

[10] Kinra, V. K. and Yapura, C. L., "A Fundamental Connection Between Intrinsic Material Damping and Structural Damping," M^3D: *Mechanics and Mechanisms of Material Damping, ASTM STP 1169*, V. K. Kinra and A. Wolfenden, Eds., American Society for Testing and Materials, Philadelphia, 1992, pp. 396-420.

[11] Christensen, R. M., *"Theory of Viscoelasticity - An Introduction,"* Academic Press, second edition, New York, 1982.

[12] McCrum, N. G., Buckley, C. P., and Bucknall, C. B., *"Principles of Polymer Engineering,"* Oxford University Press, second edition, New York, 1997.

[13] Kolsky, H., "The Measurement of the Material Damping of High Polymers Over Ten Decades of Frequency and Its Interpretation," *M^{3}D: Mechanics and Mechanisms of Material Damping, ASTM STP 1169,* V. K. Kinra and A. Wolfenden, Eds., American Society for Testing and Materials, Philadelphia, 1992, pp. 4-27.

[14] Read, B. E., and Dean, G. D., *"The Determination of Dynamic Properties of Polymers and Composites,"* John Wiley Publ. - Halsted Press, New York, 1978.

[15] Cadoret, T., Mavko, G., and Zinszner, B., "Fluid Distribution Effect on Sonic Attenuation in Partially Saturated Limestones," *Geophysics,* Vol. 63, No. 1, 1998, pp. 154-160.

[16] Cohen, J. M., and Monteiro, P. J. M., "Durability and Integrity of Marble Cladding: A-State-of-the-Art Review," *J. of Performance of Constructed Facilities,* Am. Soc. of Civ. Eng., Vol. 5, No. (2), 1991, pp. 113-124.

[17] Bell, F. G., "Durability of Carbonate Rock as Building Stone with Comments on Its Preservation," *J. of Environmental Geology,* Vol. 21, 1993, pp. 187-200.

[18] Cording, E.J., *Class Notes on Rock Mechanics, CEE 486 & 487,* Department of Civil and Environmental Engineering, University of Illinois at Urbana-Champaign, Urbana, Illinois, 1997.

[19] Sansalone, M., "Impact-Echo: The Complete Story,*" American Concrete Institute-Structural Journal,* V. 94, No. 6, November-December, 1997, pp.777-786.

[20] Rutter, E. H., "Use of Extension Testing to Investigate the Influence of Finite Strain on the Rheological Behavior of Marble," *J. Structural Geology,* Vol. 20, No. 2/3, 1998, pp. 243-254.

[21] Schroeder, M. R., "The "Schroeder frequency" Revisited," *J. Acoustical Soc. of America,* 99(5), 1996, pp. 3240-3241.

[22] Egle, D. M. "Diffuse Wave Fields In Solid Media," *J. Acoustic. Soc. of America,* 70(2), 1981, pp. 476-480.

[23] Weaver, R. L., *"*On Diffuse Waves in Solid Media,*" J. Acoustic. Soc. of America,* 71, 1982, pp. 1608-1609.

[24] Clough, R. B., "The Energetics of Acoustic Emission Source Characterization,*" Materials Evaluation,* V. 45, 1987, pp. 556-563.

[25] Clough, R. B., "A Scalar Approach to Acoustic Emission," *Am. Soc. of Mech. Eng.-* NCA- Vol. 14, Vibro-Acoustic Characterization of Materials and Structures, 1992, pp. 101-110.

[26] Reis, H. L. M. dos, Habboub, A. K. and Carpenter, S. H., "Nondestructive Evaluation of Complex Moduli in Asphalt Concrete Using an Energy Approach," *Transportation Research Record, Series 1681,* 1999, pp.170-178.

[27] Reis, H. L. M. dos, Habboub, A. K. and Carpenter, S. H., "An Energy-Based Aggregate Geometric Packing Parameter for Asphalt Concrete," INSIGHT -- *Non-Destructive Testing and Condition Monitoring,* Vol. 41, No. 10, 1999, pp. 650-656.

[28] Sidoroff, F., Cambou, B. and Mahboubi, A., "Contact Force Distribution in Granular Materials," *J. Mechanics of Materials,* Vol. 16, 1993, pp. 83-89.

[29] Shatilo, A., Sondergeld, C., and Rai, C., "Ultrasonic Attenuation in Glenn Pool Rocks, Northern Oklahoma," *Geophysics,* Vol. 63, No. 2, 1998, pp. 465-478.

Henrique L.M. dos Reis and Amin K. Habboub[1]

Nondestructive Evaluation of Dimension Stone Using Impulse Generated Stress Waves: Part 3 -- Microstructure Characterization

Reference: dos Reis, H. L. M. and Habboub, A. K., **"Nondestructive Evaluation of Dimensional Stone Using Impulse-Generated Stress Waves: Part 3 -- Microstructure Characterization,"** *Dimension Stone Cladding: Design, Construction, Evaluation, and Repair, ASTM 1394,* K. R. Hoigard, Ed., American Society for Testing and Materials, West Conshohocken, PA, 2000.

Abstract: A nondestructive testing and evaluation approach is presented to retrieve the microstructural characteristics and the grain size distribution of dimensional stone. The dimension stone test samples are typical of polycrystalline aggregations that represent quasi-monophasic rock structures with densely packed, elastic, and untextured grains. The grains of the test sample have a size distribution ranging approximately from 4 to 9 mm, and exhibit randomness in shape and in crystallographic axis orientation. Results indicate that this approach has the potential of being used for fast retrieval of microstructural features of dimension stone in the laboratory or in-situ.

Keywords: dimension stone, material characterization, complex moduli, microstructure, stone veneer, cladding

Limestone, sandstone, granite, and marble are popular building stones, which are typically used as structural and monumental components [1-3]. The role of microstructure in determining the physical and mechanical properties of dimension stone has been widely appreciated despite the fact that its parameters are not easily quantified and its effects are not fully understood. During the life-cycle design (i.e., production, design, evaluation, and repair) of dimensional stone components, knowledge of the microstructure-dependent physical and mechanical properties is often needed [4,5]. Although laboratory tests are available for this purpose, the in-situ characterization of microstructure remains a valued objective [1,4].

In addition to the effects on the structural qualities of the stone component, the long-term performance characteristics, including durability, are also governed by microstructure [6,7]. Unfortunately, convenient experimental means of retrieving microstructural characteristics in the laboratory or in-situ, are not yet readily available. As a result, current ASTM test methods, customary test procedures used by suppliers, and recent dimension stone design manuals, do not typically provide for direct microstructural evaluation. Instead, they provide testing procedures for several mechanical and physical properties that are variably and only phenomenologically influenced by microstructure [1,2,5,8]. Furthermore, none of the available test procedures provide directions on stone classification according to microstructure, nor do they quantify the corresponding intrinsic viscoelastic properties [1,5]. Intrinsic viscoelastic properties are needed to evaluate long-time creep and stress-relaxation processes, whose deformability effects may

[1] Professor Henrique L.M. dos Reis and graduate student Amin K. Habboub are associated with the Department of Civil and Environmental Engineering at the University of Illinois at Urbana-Champaign, 104 South Mathews, Urbana, Illinois.

be significant and may lead to a departure from the current design objectives of dimension stone.

Microstructural information is most beneficial when combined with experienced field observations and adequate in-situ experimental tests [4]. They are needed during stages of excavation, stone type selection, construction, and renovation [4]. When selecting a stone type, and during preservation designs of the dimension stone components, information may be sought about elastic and thermal anisotropy, degree of concentrated or distributed damage, and the remaining stiffness. Such information is directly affected by stone microstructure including grain and pore size distribution, texture, porosity, and permeability [1,3,9].

In addition to thermal fatigue [6,7] and bowing, i.e., curling, due to anisotropic thermal expansion [1,4,6,7], microstructure also affects stone durability [1,2], including susceptibility to freeze-thaw damage [2,10], and attack by atmospheric pollution (i.e., acid rain) [1,2]. Information about fractured grain interfaces (i.e., grain boundary microcracking) in the working stress range (i.e., below peak strength) and creep-induced porosity may also be of interest [1,4,6,7].

Clearly, an adequate means for field quantification of microstructural parameters is needed. A convenient and economic nondestructive test method for the microstructural characterization of dimensional stones is presented in this paper.

Distress Evaluation and Effect of Microstructure

When the stone is a structural (i.e., load bearing) component, grain size factors are pronounceable. For example, when samples, similar to those tested nondestructively, were structurally tested in an unconfined compression strength test [4], the coarse-grained stone test samples have exhibited, as expected, a relatively lower initial and tangent stiffness, higher Poisson's ratio, lower stiffness to strength ratio, lower creep deformation, less ductile post-peak behavior, and a higher strain level at failure associated with arbitrary planes of failure depending on crystal/grain size, orientations, load history, and elastic anisotropy [4]. Depending on the stone type and its grain size distribution, polycrystalline stone may be significantly strengthened, and also stiffened, by the presence of field confinement [4].

Load- and durability-related distresses include disaggregation, which results in loss of shape and boundaries, deformability, loss of flexural and compressive strength, curling, increased panel surface absorption, and grain/crack surface adsorption. Therefore, depending on the particular case, the evaluation of a potential rehabilitation effort may significantly benefit from any prior information about any of these aspects.

An important microstructural parameter, which is influenced by other morphometric and mineralogical factors, is elastic anisotropy [5,11,12,13]. Applied petrography research has consistently attempted at defining anisotropy and its relation to texture for various applications such as in stone classification and joint roughness characterization [3,4]. Stone components that are comprised of calcite crystals are extremely anisotropic such that different properties prevail in the crystallographic c-axis when compared to perpendicular directions [1,2,5,10]. When exposed to heat, the crystal expands along the c-axis, but contracts in a perpendicular one resulting in tensile stresses in the stone structure [5]. These stresses cause grain boundary microcracking or disaggregation. As a result, erosion, dusting, frost penetration, dissolution of the calcite binder and expansion of dissolved halite (i.e., salt) may all take place, resulting in accelerated weathering and chemomechanical weakening. Therefore, information about the anisotropic characteristics of polycrystalline calcite marble, such as Carrara types, may provide significant guidance about the preferred orientation in cutting panels from a quarried marble block for particular applications such as flooring, facades, or other vanities [5,10]. Another advantageous feature of estimating stress wave attenuation due to dissipation at grain boundaries is the estimation of the intrinsic capability of the stone component to resist transient dynamic loads such as wind and earthquakes loads.

The Grain Size Distribution (GSD) is statistically described by parameters, which include Average Size (D_o), Fineness Modulus (FM), Coefficient of Curvature (C_c), Coefficient of Uniformity (C_u), Maximum Aggregate Size (D_2), Minimum aggregate size (D_1), Size Range (D_2-D_1), and by a Gradation Curve. The gradation curve can be of discrete (i.e., stepwise) nature, or continuous such as that of a polynomial or a single-power relationship with exponent γ.

This research attempts at evaluating crystalline size parameters in addition to several other customary sonic-ultrasonic parameters such as moduli/density and velocity/thickness, by means of a single impact-echo test. The objective is to develop the necessary theoretical understanding and the practical experimental means to retrieve microstructure features such as the grain size distribution characteristic parameters from sonic-ultrasonic attenuation measurements on intact stone core components in the laboratory and in the field. Several test specimens of various types had been tested; however, because of space limitations, only results pertaining to one specimen are reported here to demonstrate the nondestructive testing methodology. Other important microstructural parameters that may be further examined using the current nondestructive test procedure include porosity, anisotropy, shape, and orientations of crystals.

Scattering Based Attenuation Measurements

Scatterers (i.e., grains, crystals, aggregates, or inclusions) that reside in the propagation path of the stress wave scatter, i.e., deflect, the sound beam from its original path, and therefore, attenuate it in that direction [11,14-18]. The attenuation dependence on frequency (ADF) relationships obtained from the high frequency impact-echo signal are phenomenologically affected by the scattering effects of the various grain sizes, and therefore, the ADF relationship is capable of sampling the grain size distribution [13,19]. The dominance in the Rayleigh scattering regime (i.e., isotropic scattering) may be more obvious for all wavelength components, which are shorter than twice the least significant dimension of the test sample, and longer than the maximum grain size by several orders of magnitude; therefore, this imposes a minimum size for the test object and a maximum detectable grain size for a test procedure which merely relies on a dominant Rayleigh regime [11,20]. On the other hand, a dominant diffusion, i.e., geometric, scattering regime may only be obtained in the ADF relationship if the pulse contains enough wavelength components shorter than the minimum grain size that needs to be sampled [20]. From the dominance/withdrawal characteristics of the various scattering regimes in a wide frequency range, information about several microstructural parameters of the grain size distribution may be retrieved [21-23]. To sample a wide grain size distribution, the stress wave also needs to contain widely ranged wavelength components [24-27]; it should also include wavelengths that are comparable to the expected grain sizes, therefore, requiring an adequately selected impact source [28]. Furthermore, the test object should be capable of propagating stress waves in that bandwidth, and the sensing and processing equipment should also be adequate for that same frequency range [29,30]. The scattering regimes include the Rayleigh (i.e., long wavelength compared to scatterer size), the stochastic (i.e., intermediate wavelength), and the diffuse (i.e., short wavelength) scattering regimes. However, when the microstructure exhibits a grain size distribution, the various scattering regimes may not be distinctively observed, as this phenomena also depends upon the geometric features, including the size of the test specimen, and the used frequency bandwidth.

Single Scatterer and a Single-Frequency Wave in an Infinite Elastic Medium

The simplest case of scattering consists of a single scatterer of a specific geometric shape such as a sphere, spheroid, or cylinder, in an otherwise elastic, homogeneous and infinite host medium, with a propagating mono-frequency stress wave [16,17,31]. In this case, the characteristics of scattering (i.e., intensity of sound deflected or reflected in the various azimuth directions) depend on various factors [16,32]. Those factors include the acoustic impedance mismatch at the grain boundaries, which will determine the relative compressibility and compliance, as well as grain shape, orientation, elastic anisotropy, roughness, interfacial conditions between scatterer and host medium, and the size scale of the scatterer compared to the wavelength. Accordingly, different scattering-based attenuation characteristics will be observed at early monitoring times (i.e., before the whole field is rendered diffuse upon the elapse of sufficient time) in the various sensing configurations, and the signal will attenuate in a manner depending on the interference produced by the scatterer in the direction of sensing and the propagating wave.

Single Scatterer and Wide-Band Frequency Wave Pulse in an Infinite Elastic Medium

In the case of a wide-band pulse propagating in the media with a single scatterer, each wavelength component will undergo different interfering scattering amplitudes by the same scatterer in the various directions [19,33]. Depending on the same factors described previously, three scattering regimes may be identified in the attenuation-dependence-on-frequency (ADF) domain if the wave bandwidth is wide enough. At low frequencies (i.e., wavelengths longer than a scale proportional to the scatterer size) the ADF relationship is dominated by Rayleigh scattering (i.e., the wave component notices the scatterer), but reaches beyond it in the same mode of wave propagation although at the expense of high intensity loss represented by a scattering cross-section [11,20]. At relatively high frequencies, i.e., at wavelengths shorter than a scale proportional to the grain size, the ADF relationship is reflected (specularly or diffusively) by the external boundaries of the inclusion, and therefore, the wave field becomes dominated by diffuse scattering. In between, the scatterer will resonate at a specific frequency with a substantial phase shift.

Uniform-Size Long-Spaced Scatterers and a Wide-Band Frequency in an Infinite Elastic Medium

The individual scattering effects of each scatterer may be superimposed at each frequency if the medium includes several individual (i.e., tenuous) concentrations of uniform size scatterers, which are separated by long distances (relative to the inverse of the wave number). When the media is propagated with the same wide-band stress wave (as above), the same superposition takes place at each individual frequency. These assumptions constitute the basis of single or independent scattering models. If each scatterer has its different characteristics (i.e., type, size, etc.) the individual scattering effects in the direction of interest can still be superimposed at each wavelength component provided the scatterer concentration remains tenuous (i.e., with negligible inter-scatterer interference).

Multiple Scatterers with a Size Distribution and a Wide-Band Frequency Wave in an Infinite Elastic Medium

In the presence of a wide scatterer size distribution with tenuous concentrations, the various scattering regimes, for a wide-band propagating wave, appear overlapping in the various zones of the attenuation-dependence-on-frequency (ADF) relationships. The ADF zones result from relative scattering-regime influences (i.e., dominance and/or withdrawal) of one or several overlapping scattering regimes corresponding to each grain size [24,25,34]. However, at very low frequencies (i.e., wavelengths much longer than the maximum grain size) the ADF relationship is dominated by Rayleigh (i.e., isotropic scattering) while at very high frequencies (i.e., wavelengths much shorter than the nominal-minimum grain size) the ADF relationship is dominated by diffuse (i.e., geometric) scattering if the bandwidth of the propagating wave is wider than the corresponding scales of all scatterers. In an intermediate range of frequencies, the wave field will resonate at individual frequencies, which correspond to discrete scatterer sizes, and this depends on how the individual scatterers present themselves to the propagating wave (i.e., dependence on size distribution). Since this process occurs stochastically, and is associated with successive phase shifts with frequency, this ADF zone is known as the stochastic, or, phase, zone. If the size range of scatterers is wider than the corresponding bandwidth of the propagating wave, no distinct regime absolutely prevails in any ADF zone, however, depending on the size distribution parameters, one regime may markedly dominate in narrower bands [20]. At high concentrations of scatterers, simple superposition is not warranted and multiple scattering effects between the scatterers themselves need be considered. This is the case of polycrystalline materials and many of the engineering materials whose grain volumetric concentration exceeds 50% [19].

Scattering in Finite Components

The preceding discussion is applicable for infinite media or large enough where no significant reflections exist from object boundaries. In that case, only the interference between the impinging wave and the scattered waves is considered. However, when the test object is finite with several reflective surfaces, this simple superposition may not hold, and the complex interference phenomenon between the reflected waves at many surfaces and the scattered waves need to be recognized. Therefore, although all of the basic scattering processes still hold, the interference with wave reflections from the object boundaries has to be inspected for each particular test object and testing configuration. In this case, the net ADF may substantially deviate from the phenomenological models and each test must be specifically designed with this phenomenon into consideration. As a consequence, energy partitioning and the onset of a diffuse field need to be taken into consideration. Therefore, when performing grain size analyses, the stochastic and diffuse scattering regimes are more adequate, rather than the Rayleigh scattering regime, whose conditions may not be satisfied for small-scale test objects with large grain sizes.

Elastic Wave Scattering in Inhomogeneous Materials – A Historical Review

The theoretical grounds describing stress wave propagation in random, or inhomogeneous, media had been around for several decades; however, much of the literature is fragmented and needs to be adapted to the elasticity models and to the frequency range corresponding to the geometric scales of the stone microstructure [25-27,35]. Available literature which present ultrasonic nondestructive testing theories and methods for microstructural characterization in solid media in the megahertz frequency range are intended for material types such as ceramics, metals, and powders [24,32,36,37]. In the characterization of engineering materials, investigations were performed considering single (i.e., tenuous) or various concentrations of multiple scatterers (i.e., grains). They were also performed using various testing configurations (i.e., monostatic such as backscattering and bistatic such as forward scattering). Only a few investigations address the relevance of the kilohertz frequency range bandwidth

[*38,39*], or consider the effects of the grain size distribution on attenuation measurements. Furthermore, in its current state, as described partly by Vary et al [*35*], much of the available literature is either ad hoc, over simplistic, too complicated, or deal with other wave types such as light or electromagnetic waves. Clearly, there is a need for validation and/or modification of existing theories for the time scales and constitution of stone components.

Wave propagation and scattering in random media had been investigated since, in 1894, Rayleigh developed an attenuation-dependence-on-frequency equation defining the Rayleigh, or isotropic, scattering regime for wavelengths (λ) much greater than the grain size (D) (i.e., $\lambda >> D$) as described by Equation (1). Many other experimental and theoretical investigations followed for the regions where the wavelengths are either of comparable size (i.e., $\lambda \cong D$) and therefore, are said to be in the stochastic or phase scattering regimes, which is described by Equation (2), or of much smaller scale than the grain size where the scattering amplitudes are independent of frequency and is called the geometric or diffuse scattering regime (i.e., $\lambda << D$) as described by Equation (3). Historically, the phenomena had attracted the attention of many researchers leading to several theories. For example, scattering in these regimes had been used to explain many important physical phenomena including the twinkling of the stars as they appear to fluctuate in brightness and position due to multiple scattering of light waves in the upper atmosphere, and the color of the sky as the higher frequency blue (i.e., shorter wavelength) scatters more than other wavelengths in the visible light spectrum.

Effects of Grain Size Distribution on Elastic Wave Scattering

Limits of the scattering regimes are defined with respect to the properties of the media as well as the propagating wave [*20,40,41*]. The attenuation in these regimes [*11,13,19,21,24-27,34*] is commonly defined in the literature as follows

1. In the Rayleigh scattering regime (i.e., $\lambda >> D$)

$$\alpha(\lambda, D) = C_r D^3 \lambda^{-4} \tag{1}$$

2. In the stochastic or phase scattering regime (i.e., $\lambda \cong D$)

$$\alpha(\lambda, D) = C_s D \ \lambda^{-2} \tag{2}$$

3. In the diffuse, or geometric, scattering regime (i.e., $\lambda << D$)

$$\alpha(\lambda, D) = C_d / D \tag{3}$$

where C_r, C_s, C_d are material constants [*11*]. In the case of quasi-isotropic materials, $(C_r V^4 = S)$, where S is the scattering parameter whose units is in $(mm/ms)^{-4}$, V is either the transverse or longitudinal propagation velocity. Similarly, $(C_s V^2 = T)$ and $(C_d = U)$ where T and U are scattering parameters. For spherical scatterers, D is the diameter. For irregular grains, fractal analysis is used to determine a representative diameter, but the largest dimension of the grain is usually taken. Pioneering investigations used an individual, or average, grain size, but later many considered the effects of grain size distribution and demonstrated the significance of considering the distribution even if the sample maintains the same average grain size [*13,14,18,21,22,42*].

Some other investigations considered the effects of shape, texture, orientation, location, and constitution such as anisotropy, compressibility, moduli, impedance mismatch, and grain-to-grain or grain-to-host medium interfacial conditions [*33,43,44,45*]. Much of this information is available and referred in the literature such as

Ishimaru [18], Goebbels [11], Serabian [46], Smith [31], Vary and Kautz [35], Nicoletti [14,24-27], Sanii and Bilgutay [23,47,48], Stanke and Kino [31], and Weaver [45].

Since Rayleigh's work in 1894, numerous other works followed. For example, in 1947 Lax and Feshbach [49] described a method of calculating the required phase shifts and corresponding scattering and absorption cross-sections by spherical and cylindrical scatterers near resonance based on boundary impedance. The work of Lax and Feshbach investigated resonance triggered when the reactive part of the impedance at the scatterer interface is capacitive; therefore, the treatment is applicable to the phase scattering regime. However, they provided approximate cross sections for very short and very long wavelengths.

The first meaningful attempt to retrieve the Grain Size Distribution (GSD) parameters from attenuation measurements is probably due to Papadakis [50], who considered the effects of grain size distribution on ultrasonic attenuation measurements and derived exponential area decay functions obtained from grain images, such as optical micrographs, to find volumetric distribution functions of grains [13,21,42,50]. He also develop corrected formulas for ultrasonic attenuation caused by Rayleigh scattering in metals by considering the effect of the grain size distribution on the averages of the third and the sixth power of the grain diameter where he indicated that the last sixth power has a better fit with experimental data. He investigated the attenuation-dependence-on-frequency in the three distinct regimes, computed the grain size distribution, and provided grain scattering formulas and tables to cover many grain-property combinations in the Rayleigh and stochastic regimes. He also demonstrated conformance of theory with experimental results, and indicated the importance of incorporating mode conversion effects because of their high attenuation effects on longitudinal waves in the Rayleigh regime.

Later in 1970, and based on experimentation with metallic specimens, Merkulova [18] showed that the scattering cross section, therefore, attenuation, must vary with frequency in the presence of a grain size distribution. He derived a relationship between distribution and ultrasonic attenuation and noted the significance of the transition between the Rayleigh regime and the stochastic scattering regime, also called the Rayleigh limit or the "corner frequency," in measuring the heterogeneosity of the coarser grains. However, his work is only valid in the Rayleigh regime, and considers size variations through one parameter which is the coefficient of variation of a log-normal distribution. In 1970, Grebennik [51] applied the resonance method in the stochastic scattering regime to estimate grain size in austenitic steel, and obtained amplitudes at the various grain sizes and frequencies. Kesler and Shraifel'd [52] considered in 1975 scatterer size distribution in the Rayleigh and stochastic regimes and found functional relationships for the relative contribution of each regime on total scattering as a function of frequency. They demonstrated that as the spread of the grain size increases, while maintaining the same average size, the total scattering cross section increased, and the relative contribution of stochastic scattering increased to approach that of Rayleigh scattering for high size variance.

In 1980, Serabian [46] investigated several metals for the limits and conditions necessary for Rayleigh and stochastic scattering as described by a scaled parameter of wavelength divided by average grain size ($\lambda/D_{avg.}$). In 1982, Smith [31] based his work on Papadakis' average of the sixth power of the grain size [50] to demonstrate that two specimens with the same mean grain size can have significantly different ultrasonic attenuation if their size distribution is different. This work showed that in the presence of a size distribution, no unique relationship of the overall ultrasonic attenuation-dependence-on-frequency (ADF) can exist in terms of average grain size.

In 1982, Crostack and Oppermann [20] described a theoretical model to determine an optimum center frequency for testing sound-scattering materials in the Rayleigh regime for various reflectors in order to maximize signal-to-noise ratio. The model was verified by experimental testing and indicated that the optimum testing frequencies occur in the stochastic regime, and that these optimum test frequencies are neither influenced by the depth position of the grains nor by variations in the sound attenuation coefficients.

Sanii and Bilgutay [23] introduced a technique relating the statistical characteristics of the measured signal to the mean ultrasonic wavelet and attenuation coefficient in various spatial regions of a test specimen and in all the scattering regimes. The wavelet technique works at removing randomness from the backscattered signal and meaningful parameters become, therefore, readily and clearly extractable. They used a homomorphic processing technique to estimate the mean ultrasonic wavelet and frequency-dependent attenuation, and incorporated absorption into the overall model as follows

$$\alpha(f) = \alpha_a(f) + \alpha_s(f) \tag{4}$$

where $\alpha_s(f)$ is the scattering coefficient and $\alpha_a(f)$ is the absorption coefficient. Equations (1-3) may, therefore, be rewritten as

1. In the Rayleigh scattering regime (i.e., $\lambda > 2\pi D_{avg}$),

$$\alpha(f) = a_1 f + a_2 D_{avg.}^3 f^4 \tag{5}$$

2. In the stochastic (or phase) scattering regime (i.e., $D_{avg.} < \lambda < 2\pi D_{avg.}$),

$$\alpha(f) = b_1 f + b_2 D_{avg.} f^2 \tag{6}$$

3. In the diffuse (or geometric optic) scattering regime (i.e., $\lambda < 2\pi D_{avg.}$),

$$\alpha(f) = c_1 f + c_2 / D_{avg.} \tag{7}$$

Saniie and Bilgutay [23] introduced a grain size evaluation approach based on examination of the spectrum of an ensemble of randomly distributed scatterers. However, their technique is limited to the Rayleigh regime and doesn't account for factors such as varying attenuation, anisotropy, multiple scattering, and correlation between grain size and echo amplitudes. The technique also loses sensitivity for increased standard deviation of grain size relative to the mean grain size. The spectral technique used in their investigation imposes the limitation that the grain sizes, whose values are to be experimentally estimated by the spectral technique must correspond to the frequencies within the flat response frequency band of the sending/receiving transducer. The technique is mainly concerned with estimating the average grain size but not the grain size distribution.

Goebbels [11] demonstrated that the average grain size of a specimen can be obtained from attenuation of the backscattered echoes with depth and showed that the scattered amplitudes of the ultrasonic waves in anisotropic polycrystalline metals decay with time according to an exponential decay. Non-exponential decay cannot be explained by conventional single scattering theory, which regards the scattered amplitude as a cumulative sum of the single reflections from grains. This was also discussed by Weaver [45], who attempted to explain the non-exponential decay of the energy density and suggested that diffusion measurements are not less important than scattering measurements.

A unified theory for elastic wave attenuation and dispersion in polycrystalline materials was developed in 1984 by Stanke and Kino [53] based on a perturbation method of the Keller approximation instead of the Born approximation used in preceding theories, therefore, making it unsuitable for the diffuse regime. However, their work is limited to small single crystal anisotropy, and did not account to texture. Furthermore, it disregards grain shape, or multiple scattering effects. The model, therefore, only takes a simplified account of mode conversions at grain surfaces, which are in fact responsible for a considerable portion of the scattering amplitude. In 1984, It was further observed by Stanke and Kino [53] that trends observed as a result of increasing the inhomogenuity mismatch between wave propagation parameters inside the grains and those of the host unperturbed medium, include a diminishing stochastic region, reduced overall attenuation in the diffusion regime, and less abrupt stochastic-diffusion transition. All these parameters can be observed from the ADF.

A transition matrix approach to evaluate scattering from an inclusion in an elastic medium was developed in 1984 by Hackman [54]. A major attempt to introduce a unified approach based on the transfer functions concept was also made in 1988 by Vary and Kautz [35], who described literature, which relates attenuation to specific microstructural factors over particular frequency ranges as either fragmented, ad hoc, over-simplistic or complicated. Their approach depends on treating the microstructure as elastomechanical "filters" characterized by a distinctively definable analytical transfer function, which is expressible in terms of the frequency-dependence-of ultrasonic-attenuation coefficient.

In 1991-1992, based on experiments with Nickel specimens, Nicoletti [14] obtained a simple relationship between the power law that describes the grain distribution in polycrystalline materials such as metals and the power-law dependence of attenuation on frequency. They also concluded that a relationship exists between grain size distribution obtained from micrographs and 3-D distribution. Later, Nicoletti [24,25,27] explored the ranges of applicability of such relationships, the range of frequency to be selected to generate the three types of scattering regimes, and introduced the "corner frequency" concept as an estimator of maximum aggregate size. In 1993, Ogilvy [55] described a numerical model for ultrasonic wave propagation in regions including random inclusions from which scattering field statistical parameters can be derived. For two-phase materials, Sayers [56] addressed the problem for highly porous media based on 1956 work of Ying and Truell [57].

Scattering of Elastic Waves in Rock-Like Materials

Only few relevant attempts at the microstructural characterization of concrete are known. In 1996, Marklein et al [39] developed a numerical model of ultrasonic wave propagation and scattering in concrete using an Elastodynamic Finite Integration Technique (EFIT) for isotropic homogeneous and isotropic inhomogeneous media in 3-D [39]. A normal pressure probe 5 cm in diameter with a center frequency of 80 kHz in the pulse-echo configuration was used. The numerical model allows image construction and visualization. The second effort introduced in 1997 by Haskins and Alexander [28] deals with a field device developed by the U.S. Army Waterways Experiment Station (WES) called the "Scanned Ultrasonic Pulse-Echo Results for Site Characterization of Concrete Using Artificial Neural Networks and Expert Reasoning (SUPERSCANNER)." Using this device, the grain size is compared to the pulse wavelength to characterize scattering.

Experimental Procedure

To verify that at later times, the wave field partitions itself between body wave modes in a manner that is independent of the initial energy partitioning (i.e., impact type) if a

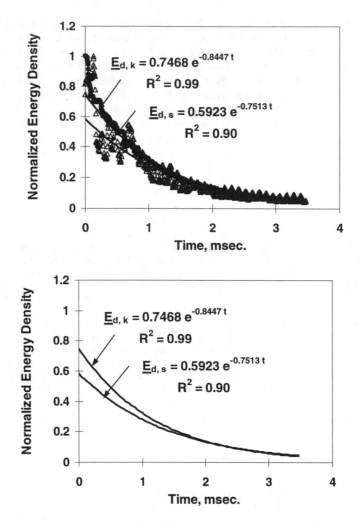

Figure 1 – *Normalized Energy Density Decay Rate for Bulk and Shear Modes of Excitation*

diffuse wave field condition is staged, two excitation impact types were used. The first impact is due to a source that mainly injects a dilatational wave into the test specimen (i.e., a ball drop on the top surface of the specimen) as described in Part 1 of this study. The second impact is due to a source that mainly injects shear waves into the specimen by imparting a sliding friction pulse on the steel plate that is fixed on the specimen surface. The Rhodonite test sample similar to Porkalla Red described in Part 1 of this study is also used in this paper to illustrate the microstructure characterization of dimension stone using this approach. However, in order to retrieve the microstructural characteristics, frequencies up to 200 kHz were used, which allows the observation of the diffuse scattering regime.

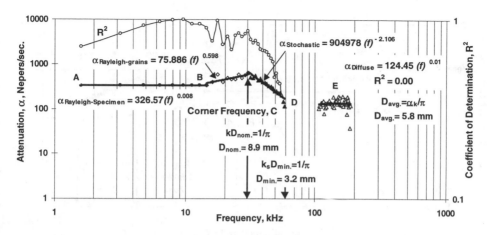

Figure 2 – *Attenuation Dependence on Frequency for Rhodonite Stone Test Sample*

Experimental Results

The energy density decay functions for both types of excitation are shown in Figure 1. Figure 1 shows that, irrespective of the nature of the source and its initial energy partitioning, the late time response is the same, indicating that in a diffuse field regime, the wave field evolves independent of the type of initial excitation. The emergence of the two decay curves therefore verifies the establishment of a diffuse field at the relatively late time of 2 msec. Furthermore, it also confirms that the wave field becomes mostly filled with shear wave energy, as the late time decay rate falls closer to the decay rate corresponding to the initial shear wave decay, as predicted in Part 1 of this study. Among many other dissipation mechanisms, shear waves generally dissipate energy according to the intrinsic dissipation mechanism of intergranular friction, which tends to produce a linear dissipation decay curve with time that influences the dissipation curve shown in Figure 1. However, because the shear excitation also produces dilatational waves and dilatational excitation also produces shear waves, a strictly linear dissipation curve due to shear excitation should not be expected, even if linear friction would be the only dissipation mechanism operating on the shear waves.

Qualitatively, attenuation increases with the grain size in the Rayleigh and stochastic regimes, but decreases with grain size in the diffuse regime. The various scattering regimes contribute to the Attenuation-Dependence-on-Frequency (ADF) relationships shown in Figure 2. Not only scattering effects contribute to the ADF, but also other mechanisms, such as the scale effects of the test specimen. As a consequence, the attenuation coefficient may not be entirely attributed to grain scattering, although such information is implicitly embedded in the measured attenuation parameter at each frequency component. Accordingly, in the measurement of the grain scale parameters, the experiment must be designed to maximize the scattering effects, that is the material and test parameters must be well characterized beforehand in order to isolate the scattering effects.

The microstructure grain scales are usually obtained by searching for the corner frequencies, which are a result of the changes in attenuation behavior attributed to the various scattering mechanisms, and therefore mark the limits of the various corresponding scattering regimes. These demarcations (i.e., corner frequencies) may

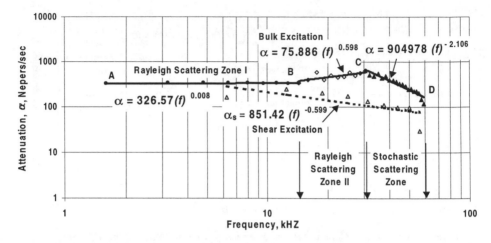

Figure 3 – *Comparison of the Attenuation Dependence on Frequency for the Initial Bulk and Shear Wave Excitation*

be best inspected using logarithmic scales, where the slope of the ADF also corresponds to the power of the grain size distribution in the stochastic scattering regime. To obtain a correspondence to grain size (i.e., diameter a) the frequency is normalized to the grain size by using the normalized frequency ka, where k is the wave number $= 2\pi cf / c_\varphi$ and where c_φ is the phase velocity at the particular frequency, which is usually obtained from dispersion analyses. Figure 2 shows four scattering regimes. The first regime (i.e., A to B) is the Rayleigh scattering regime, where the wave components isotropically scatter over the large-scale boundaries of the specimen. The second regime (i.e., B to C) corresponds to isotropic scattering over the grain microstructure scales. The corner frequency C indicates the start of the stochastic scattering regime that is prompted by the resonance of the largest (i.e., nominal maximum) grains. The openness of the angle subtended between the trend curves adjoining at C is an indication of the size range [18]; the broader the angle, the wider the size range. Resonance of individual grains continues in the stochastic resonance regime, where the wavelength becomes of a comparable size to the grain, until the scattering process substantially withdraws in favor of a diffuse scattering process that overlaps the stochastic regime depending on the grain size distribution. This occurs near point D. In the geometric (i.e., diffuse) scattering regime E, the ADF becomes independent of frequency as indicated in the slope of the relationship and its corresponding coefficient of determination. As shown in Figure 2, the grain distribution parameters were calculated and where found to correspond closely to the observed grain size parameters, that is a maximum size of 8.9 mm and a minimum size of 3.2 mm.

Figure 2 also shows that in the backscattering configuration of the test, the apparent reduction in attenuation in the stochastic scattering regime (i.e., between C and D) results from the interference of the reflected and propagating waves, which preserves the second-power dependence of the relationship as it is phenomenologically expected (i.e., Equation 2); as it is shown in Figure 2, this power dependence relationship was measured to be 2.1. Figure 3 shows a comparison of the attenuation dependence on frequency for both the initial dilatational and shear wave excitation, and demonstrates that the two wave fields are subjected to different attenuation mechanisms. Because the shear wavelengths are shorter than the dilatational ones, the shear wave components tend to remain within the test object boundaries; as a consequence, the abrupt changes in the ADF curve, as illustrated by point B in Figure 2, are not present in the ADF due to shear excitation as shown in Figure 3.

Conclusions

A methodology to characterize the microstructure of dimensional stone is presented. The methodology is based upon velocity, attenuation and backscattered amplitude measurements. The proposed methodology is relatively fast and can readily be used in the laboratory or in the field. Furthermore, it also provides a working model to reconstruct grain size distribution from a single nondestructive test.

Acknowledgements

This paper was prepared from a study conducted at the Center of Excellence for Airport Pavement Research. Funding for the Center of Excellence is provided in part by the Federal Aviation Administration under Research Grant Number 95-C-001. The Center of Excellence is maintained at the University of Illinois at Urbana-Champaign, which works in partnership with Northwestern University and the Federal Aviation Administration. Ms. Patricia Watts is the FAA Program Manager for the Air Transportation Centers of Excellence and Dr. Satish Agrawal is the FAA Technical Director for the Pavement Center. The authors are also very grateful to Professor Edward J. Cording, Director of the Rock Mechanics Laboratory at the University of Illinois at Urbana-Champaign, for providing access to the laboratory facilities.

Disclaimer

The contents of this paper reflect the views of the authors who are responsible for the facts and accuracy of the data presented within. The contents do not necessarily reflect the official views and policies of the Federal Aviation Administration. This paper does not constitute a standard, specification, or regulation.

References

[1] Bell, F. G., "Durability of Carbonate Rock as Building Stone with Comments on Its Preservation," *J. Environmental Geology,* Vol. 21, 1993, pp. 187-200.
[2] Cohen, J. M., and Monteiro, P. J. M., "Durability and Integrity of Marble Cladding: A-State-of-the-Art Review," *J. Performance of Constructed Facilities,* Am. Soc. of Civ. Eng., Vol. 5, No. (2), 1991, pp. 113-124.
[3] Mavko, G., Mukerji, T., and Dvorkin, J., "The Rock Physics Handbook," *Cambridge University Press,* first ed., New York, 1998.
[4] Cording, E. J., *Class Notes on Rock Mechanics, CEE 486, 487, and 498, University of Illinois-Urbana,* 1997.
[5] Widhalm, C., Tschegg, E., and Eppensteiner, W., "Anisotropic Thermal Expansion Causes Deformation of Marble Claddings," *J. Performance of Constructed Facilities,* Am. Soc. of Civ. Eng., February, 1996, pp. 5-10.
[6] Erskine, B. G., Heidelbach, F. and Wenk, H.-R., "Lattice Preferred Orientations and Microstructures of Deformed Cordilleran Marbels: Correlation of Shear Indicators

and Determination of Strain Path," *J. Structural Geology,* Vol. 15, No., 9/10, 1993, pp. 1189-1205.

[7] Rutter, E. H., "Use of Extension Testing to Investigate the Influence of Finite Strain on the Rheological Behavior of Marble," *J. Structural Geology,* Vol. 20, No. 2/3, 1998, pp. 243-254.

[8] Covey-Crump, S. J., "The High Temperature Static Recovery and Recrystallization Behaviour of Cold-Worked Carrara Marble," *J. Structural Geology,* Vol. 19, No. 2, 1997, pp. 225-241.

[9] Akabar, N., Dvorkin, J., and Nur, A., "Relating P-Wave Attenuation to Permeability," *Geophysics,* Vol. 58, No.1, 1993, pp. 20-29.

[10] Widhalm, C., Tschegg, E., and Eppensteiner, W., "Acoustic Emission and Anisotropic Expansion When Heating Marble," *J. Performance of Constructed Facilities,* Am. Soc. of Civ. Eng., February, 1997, pp. 35-40.

[11] Goebbels, K., "Materials Characterization for Process Control and Product Uniformity," *CRC Press,* First Ed., Boca Raton, Florida, 1994.

[12] Hirskorn, S., "The Scattering of Ultrasonic Waves in Polycrystalline Materials with Texture," *J. Acoustic. Soc. of America,* Vol. 77, No. (3), 1985, pp. 832-843.

[13] Papadakis, E. P., "Diffraction of Ultrasound Radiating into an Elastically Anisotropic Medium," *J. Acoustic. Soc. of America,* Vol. 35, No. (3), 1964, pp. 414-422.

[14] Nicoletti, D., "Scaling Properties of Ultrasonic and Grain Size in Metals," *PhD Thesis,* Drexel University, 1991.

[15] Bhatia, A. B., "Scattering of High-Frequency Sound Waves in Polycrystalline Materials," *J. Acoustic. Soc. of America,* Vol. 19, 1947, pp. 16-23.

[16] Huntington, H., "On Ultrasonic Scattering by Polycrystals," *J. Acoustic. Soc. of America,* Vol. 22, No. (3), 1950, pp. 362-364.

[17] Mason, W. and McSkimin, H., "Attenuation and Scattering of High Frequency Sound Waves in Metals and Glasses," *J. Acoustic. Soc. of America,* Vol. 19, No. (3), 1947, pp. 464-473.

[18] Merkulova, V., "Effect of Grain Size Distribution on Rayleigh Scattering of Ultrasonic Waves," *Sov. J. NDT,* 1970, pp. 223-25.

[19] Rose, J., "Ultrasonic Backscatter from Microstructure," *Rev. in Progress in Quantitative Nondestructive Evaluation,* Vol. 11, Eds.: D. O. Thompson, and D. E. Chimenti, Plenum Press, New York, 1992, pp. 1677-1984.

[20] Crostack, H. and Oppermann, W., "Determination of the Optimum Centre Frequency for Ultrasonic Testing of Sound-Scattering Materials," *Ultrasonics,* Vol. 20, 1982, pp. 19-26.

[21] Papadakis, E. P., "Ultrasonic Attenuation Caused by Scattering in Polycrystalline Metals," *J. Acoustic. Soc. of America,* Vol. 37, No., (4), 1965, pp. 711-717.

[22] Roney, R., "The Influence of Metal Grain Structure on the Attenuation of an Ultrasonic Acoustic Wave," *PhD Thesis,* California Institute of Technology, Pasadena, California, 1950.

[23] Saniie, J., and Bilgutay, N.M., "Quantitative Grain Size Evaluation Using Ultrasonic Backscattered Echoes," *J. Acoustic. Soc. of America,* Vol. 80, No. (6), 1986, pp. 1816-24.

[24] Nicoletti, D., and Anderson, A., "Numerical Modeling of the Ultrasonic Determination of Scatterer Size Distribution," *IEEE Trans. on Ultrasonics, Ferroelectrics and Frequency Control,* Symp. Proc. 2, 1993, pp. 701-704.

[25] Nicoletti, D., and Anderson, A., "Ultrasonic Discrimination of Samples with Differently-Distributed Grain Sizes and Equal Average Grain Size," *In Proc. Grain Size and Mechanical Properties: Fundamentals and Applications,* Mat. Research Society Symposium, Materials Research Society, Pittsburgh, PA, Vol. 362, 1995, pp. 123-128.

[26] Nicoletti, D., Bilgutay, N., and Onaral, B., "Power-Law Relationships Between the Dependence of Ultrasonic Attenuation on Wavelength and the Grain Size

Distribution," *J. Acoustic. Soc. of America,* Vol. 91, No. (6), 1992, pp. 3278-3284.

[27] Nicoletti, D., and Kasper, D., "Ultrasonic Attenuation Based on the Roney Generalized Theory and Multiple Power-Law Grain-Size Distribution," *IEEE Trans. on Ultrasonics, Ferroelectrics and Frequency Control,* Vol. 41, No. 1, 1994, pp. 144-149.

[28] Haskins, R., and Alexander, M., "Development of the Superscanner for Ultrasonic Pulse Echo Testing of Concrete," *Pre-Print Paper No. 97-0963: Trans. Res. Board,* Washington D.C., 1997.

[29] Sadri, A., Hassani, F., and Saleh, K., "Determination of Concrete Dynamic Elastic Constants Using a Miniature Seismic Reflection System," *Materials Evaluation,* July 1997, pp. 817-820.

[30] Sahay, S., Kline, R., and Mignogna, R., "Phase and Group Velocity Considerations for Dynamic Modulus Measurement in Anisotropic Media," *Ultrasonics,* Vol. 30, No. (6), 1992, pp.373-382.

[31] Smith, L., "The Effect of Grain Size Distribution on the Frequency Dependence of the Ultrasonic Attenuation in Polycrystalline Materials," *Ultrasonics,* Vol. 21, No. (9), 1983, pp. 211-214.

[32] Thorne, P., Hayhurst, L., and Humphrey, V., "Scattering by Non-Metallic Spheres," *Ultrasonics,* Vol. 30, No. (1), 1992, pp. 15-20.

[33] Stanke, F. and Kino, G., "A Unified Theory for Elastic Wave Propagation in Polycrystalline Materials," *J. Acoustic. Soc. of America,* Vol. 75, No. (3), 1984, pp. 665-681.

[34] Roney, R., "The Influence of Metal Grain Structure on the Attenuation of an Ultrasonic Acoustic Wave," *PhD Thesis,* California Institute of Technology, Pasadena, CA, 1950.

[35] Vary, A. and Kautz, H., "Transfer Function Concept for Ultrasonic Characterization of Material Microstructures," *International Advances in Nondestructive Testing,* Vol. 13, Editor: W. McGonnagle, Gordon and Breach Science Publ., New York, 1988, pp. 193-249.

[36] Healey, A., Leeman, S., Betts, M., and Ferrari, L., "A Novel Pulse-Echo Attenuation Estimation Technique," *IEEE Trans. On Ultrasonics, Ferroelectrics and Frequency Control,* Symp. Proc. 2, 1993, pp. 715-718.

[37] Mignogna, R., Delsanto, P., Rath, B., Vold, C., and Clark, A., Jr., "Ultrasonic Measurement on Textured Materials," *Nondestructive Characterization of Materials II,* Eds.: J. F. Bussiere, J-P Monchalin, C. O. Ruud, and R. E. Green, Jr., Plenum Press, New York, 1987, pp. 545-553.

[38] Haskins, R. and Alexander, M., "Development of the Superscanner for Ultrasonic Pulse Echo Testing of Concrete," *Pre-Print Paper No. 97-0963: Trans. Res. Board,* Washington DC, 1997.

[39] Marklein, R., Langenberg, K. J., Barmann, R., Brandfab, "Ultrasonic and Eletromagnetic Wave Propagation and Inverse Scattering Applied to Concrete," *Review of Progress in Quantitative Nondestructive Evaluation,* Vol. 15, Eds.: D. O. Thompson and D. E. Chimenti, Plenum Press, New York, 1996, pp.1839-1846.

[40] Howard, P. and Gilmore, R., "Ultrasonic Noise and the Volume of the Ultrasonic Pulse," *Review of Progress in Quantitative Nondestructive Evaluation,* Vol. 15, Eds.: D. O. Thompson and D. E. Chimenti, Plenum Press, New York, 1996, pp.1495-1502.

[41] Howard, P., Burkel, R., and Gilmore, R., "The Statistical Distribution of Grain Noise in Ultrasonic Images," *Review of Progress in Quantitative Nondestructive Evaluation,* Vol. 15, Eds.: D. O. Thompson and D. E. Chimenti, Plenum Press, New York, 1996, pp.1517-1524.

[42] Papadakis, E. P., "Revised Grain-Scattering Formulas and Tables," *J. Acoustic. Soc. of America,* Vol. 37, No., (4), 1965, pp. 703-710.

[43] Thompson, R., "A Generalized Model of the Effects of Microstructure on Ultrasonic Backscattering and Flaw Detection," *Review of Progress in Quantitative Nondestructive Evaluation,* Vol. 15, Eds: D. O. Thompson and D. E. Chimenti, Plenum Press, New York, 1996, pp.1471-8.

[44] Thompson, R., Han, K., Yalda-Mooshabad, I., Rose, J., and Margetan, F., "Influence of Texture on Backscattered Ultrasonic Noise," *Materials Science Forum,* Vol. 157, No. 6, 1994, pp. 221-226.

[45] Weaver, R., "Diffusivity of Ultrasound in Polycrystals," *J. Mech. Phys. Solids,* Vol. 38, 1990, pp. 55-86.

[46] Serabian, S., "Frequency and Grain Size Dependency of Ultrasonic Attenuation in Polycrystalline Materials," *British J. of NDT,* 1980, pp. 69-77.

[47] Saniie, J., Bilgutay, N.M., and Nagle, D., "Evaluation of Signal Processing Schemes in Ultrasonic Grain Size Estimation," *Review of Progress in Quantitative Nondestructive Evaluation,* Vol. 5A, Eds: D. O. Thompson and D. E. Chimenti, Plenum Press, New York, 1986, pp.747-753.

[48] Saniie, J., Wang, T., and Bilgutay, N.M., "Statistical Evaluation of Backscattered Ultrasonic Grain Signals," *J. Acoustic. Soc. of America,* Vol. 84, No. (1), 1988, pp. 400-408.

[49] Lax M., and Feshbach, H., "Absorption and Scattering for Impedance Boundary Conditions on Spheres and Circular Cylinders," *J. Acoustic. Soc. of America,* Vol. 20, No. (2), 1948, pp. 108-124.

[50] Papadakis, E. P., "Grain-Size Distribution in Metals and Its Influence on Ultrasonic Attenaution Measurements," *J. Acoustic. Soc. of America,* Vol. 33, No. (11), 1961, pp. 1616-1621.

[51] Grebennik, V. S., "Experimental Investigation into Ultrasonic Methods of Testing Grain Size of the Metal in Stainless Steel Kh18N9T Boiler Pipes," *Sov. J. NDT,* 1970, pp. 529-535.

[52] Kesler, H. A., and Shraifel'd, L.I., "Dispersion of Ultrasonic Waves in Polycrystalline Metals with Statistically Distributed Grain Size," *Sov. J. NDT,* 1975, pp. 76-80.

[53] Stanke, F. and Kino, G., "A Unified Theory for Elastic Wave Propagation in Polycrystalline Materials," *J. Acoustic. Soc. of America,* Vol. 75, No. (3), 1984, pp. 665-681.

[54] Hackman, R. H., "The Transition Matrix for Acoustic and Elastic Wave Scattering in Prolate Spheroidal Coordinates," *J. Acoustic. Soc. of America,* Vol. 75, No. (1), 1984, pp. 35-45.

[55] Ogilvy, J. A., "A Model for the Effects of Inclusions on Ultrasonic Inspection," *Ultrasonics,* Vol. 31, No. 4, 1993, pp. 219-228

[56] Sayers, C., "Ultrasound in Solids with Porosity, Microcracking and Polycrystalline Structuring," *International Centre for Mechanical Sciences: Courses and Lectures-330,* Ed.: J.D. Achenbach, Springer-Verlag Publ., New York, 1993, pp. 249-300.

[57] Ying, P. C. and Truell, R., "Scattering of a Plane Longitudinal Wave by a Spherical Obstacle in an Isotropically Elastic Solid," *J. Applied Physics*, Vol. 27, 1956, pp. 1086-1097.

Stone Weathering and Durability

Bruno F. Miglio, [1] David M. Richardson, [2] Tim S. Yates, [2] David West [3]

Assessment of the Durability of Porous Limestones: Specification and Interpretation of Test Data in UK Practice

Reference: Miglio, B. F., Richardson, D. M., Yates, T. S., and West, D., **"Assessment of the Durability of Porous Limestones: Specification and Interpretation of Test Data in UK Practice,"** *Dimension Stone Cladding: Design, Construction, Evaluation, and Repair, ASTM STP 1394,* K. R. Hoigard, Ed., American Society for Testing and Materials, West Conshohocken, PA, 2000.

Abstract: This paper discusses the methods currently used in the UK to evaluate the durability of limestones when used as stone cladding. This review is combined with an analysis of the data obtained in a study of all commercially available UK building limestones and provides advice concerning the use of various test properties as a guide to durability. Within this review, recommendations demonstrating how these tests may be specified in UK practice are also given.

Keywords: durability, frost damage, limestone, petrography, porosity, salt crystallization, stone cladding, specification, testing,.

Introduction

Traditionally, limestones have been widely used materials for external walling of major buildings in the UK. Perhaps the best known example is that of Portland stone which found favour with Sir Christopher Wren in the extensive rebuilding of London following the Great Fire of 1666. One of the greatest monuments to this period is argueably St. Paul's Cathedral. However, Portland stone is not alone and there are many other limestones with a successful track record of use in the UK.

However, in older construction, prior to the early 1900's, limestone was typically used in thicknesses in the order of 100 mm for smaller applications, such as ashlar, and in much greater thicknesses for load bearing blocks.

While the modern trend is to use stone as a non-structural cladding, the current edition of the relevant British Standard [BS8298:1994] still calls for limestone cladding to be a minimum thickness of 75 mm thick. In the US the Indiana Limestone

[1] Associate, Arup Façade Engineering, 13 Fitzroy Street, London W1P 6BQ, UK
[2] Senior Geologist and Principal Scientist respectively, BRE, Garston, WD2 7JR, UK
[3] Associate, Arup Façade Engineering, PO Box QVP, Sydney, Australia

Institute strongly recommends that Indiana Limestone not be milled to dimensions less than two inches (51 mm). In contrast, the trend in Continental Europe has been to use considerably thinner limestone, usually between 30mm and 40mm. Consequently, there is pressure in the UK to move to thinner stone sizes. This was recognised in a recent BRE Information Paper [1] that provided outline guidance on the use of thin stone cladding. However, this paper dealt largely with issues of strength rather than durability.

For limestones considerable caution is required if thicknesses are to be reduced. Unlike many other commonly used cladding stones such as granite, limestones may suffer considerable weathering during the design life of the building. Given that limestones usually exhibit significantly lower compressive and flexural strengths than stones such as granite, on thin panels this weathering and consequent loss of strength may lead may lead to rapid failure in service as the stone becomes unable to sustain imposed structural or wind loads. The problem facing stone designers is, therefore, how to reliably assess the potential weathering performance of limestone in service. This paper describes some of the approaches currently being used in the UK to determine the durability of porous limestones.

Durability Considerations

The durability of a stone may be defined as the ability to resist weathering and retain its physical and mechanical characteristics, appearance and shape over time. It is important to note that once worked any stone will be liable to undergo some change in appearance, and possible decay, as an inevitable consequence of weathering. However, in addition to the properties of the stone itself some specific factors, given below, will be particularly important.

Environment - While no stone will resist the action of the environment indefinitely the durability and the influence of any particular agent may vary depending on location (e.g. coastal, inland, urban, rural, cold or temperate).
Usage - The degree of weathering that is acceptable is an important consideration as the loss of several millimetres in thickness from a 100 mm thick granite wall may be acceptable but in a 30mm thick curtain-walling panel this may prove disastrous. Some limestones may perform perfectly well on sheltered plain walling but weather very badly if they are used in more exposed positions such as copings.
Design Life - What is the required durability of the stone? The design life for a supermarket may be 25 years; the New Parliamentary Building in London is 200 years.
Maintenance - What is the likely maintenance regime for the building to ensure contaminants from exposed surfaces are removed? What remedial action will be taken if defects, such as water penetration, are discovered?

Mechanisms of Weathering

Acid Dissolution

By definition limestones are predominantly composed of calcium carbonate which renders them liable to attack by acids. While this was once an important mechanism in highly polluted atmospheres it is less important today. Although stones are still liable to attack from carbonic acid formed by the dissolution of atmospheric carbon dioxide in rainwater this is usually a relatively slow process.

Frost Action

Frost damage to stone may be due to several mechanisms, given below.
Volumetric Expansion - Unlike many other liquids, upon freezing water expands by almost ten percent. Ross [2] showed that given the low tensile strength of many limestones the pressures caused by even modest freezing could be potentially damaging and could affect other porous stones such as sandstones and dolomites.
Ice Lens Formation - Ross [2] also suggested that damage may be due to a more complex crystallization process in which water flows to a growing ice crystal from elsewhere in the stone and therefore this crystal continues to expand causing damage. As the freezing point of water is known to be depressed in fine pores, ice will tend to grow in the larger pores. Once the ice has filled an individual pore either the crystal can continue to grow into surrounding pores or it will begin to exert pressure on the pore boundaries as it tries to grow in a confined space. If the former occurs then no damage will ensue. If the growing crystal exerts pressure on the pore boundaries then damage will be caused, unless the stone is strong enough to resist the crystallization pressures. An important requirement for lens formation is that, for the ice crystals to grow, the water in the stone must be in a continuous phase to allow it to flow.
Hydrostatic Pressure - There has also been some suggestion [3], that as the water is expelled from a pore by the growing ice crystal the hydrostatic pressure in the water will increase causing damage.

Salt Crystallization

Salt damage may be an important form of weathering in polluted environments, coastal locations and where salts are used for de-icing. Again, several mechanisms are likely.
When salts crystallize out of a saturated solution the process is often accompanied by an increase in volume. If this occurs within the individual pores of a stone, pressure upon the pore boundaries may be exerted resulting in damage. Problems may also

occur if a salt occurs naturally within the stone in several hydration states (such as sodium sulfate) as damage may result from a volume change in moving from one hydration state to another.

Physical Characteristics of Limestones

Porosity

In the early twentieth century, with his work on the Hard and Soft Headington limestones, Schaffer [4] demonstrated that physical characteristics such as pore structure, rather than chemical characteristics were responsible for differences in durability.

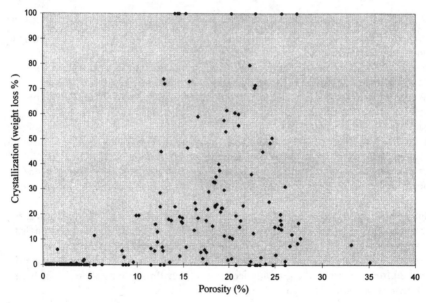

Figure 1. Graph of Salt Crystallization Results versus Porosity

Stones which exhibit low porosity values are generally found to be relatively more durable. This is to be expected as water is one of the main agents of weathering – either by entering the stone and freezing and thawing or by the transportation, deposition and hydration of salts. Water will be less able to penetrate low porosity stone types, and therefore less able to promote damage.
As part of a research programme at the BRE, physical testing has been carried out on all of the UK's commercially available limestone dimension stones. Figure 1 demonstrates that for the stones tested those which perform best in the salt crystallization test, and by implication have a better durability, are those with a

porosity of either less than 5% or greater than 30%. Below 5% porosity it is likely that improved durability results from only a limited amount of water entering the structure of the stone and the fact that this water is unlikely to be in a continuous phase. Above 30% it is likely that the structure of the stone is so open that the available pore space can accommodate any expansion generated during freezing or salt growth. Between 5% and 30% it appears that durability is affected by the size and distribution of the pores present. For example, it is likely that a stone with a large number of interconnected, small diameter pores will have a lower durability than a stone with a smaller number of unconnected large pores.

Microporosity - Micro-pores are defined as those with a diameter of 5 microns or less. As micro-pores will influence the lowering of the freezing point of water and act as constraints to the free passage of water (thereby setting up pressure gradients) they may influence durability. Figure 2 represents graphically the relationship between salt crystallization and microporosity for the major UK limestones that are commercially available. In general terms, the BRE data shows that the greater the microporosity the

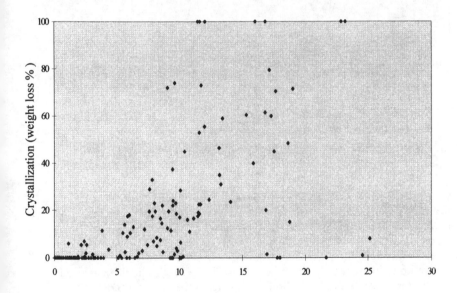

Figure 2. Graph of Salt Crystallization Results versus Microporosity

lower the durability. This can be broadly demonstrated using the salt crystallization test as a performance measure for durability.

Macroporosity - By definition these are pores that are greater than five microns in diameter. The BRE data broadly shows that durability increases with increasing macroporosity. Figure 3 shows the graphical relationship between salt crystallization and macroporosity, again using the salt crystallization test as a performance measure for durability.

While the relationship is not as clear as that for microporosity, it appears that above a critical value, the greater the macroporosity the lower the salt crystallization loss.

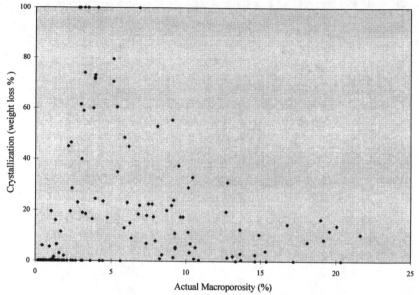

Figure 3. Graph of Salt Crystallization Results versus Macroporosity

Capillarity

As water usually enters a stone by capillary action the amount of water that a stone absorbs by capillarity will therefore have a profound effect on its durability. This was recognised many years ago by Hirschwald [5] and led to the development of the saturation coefficient. This is defined as the ratio of the volume of water absorbed by a sample immersed in cold water for 24 hours to the volume of pores in the sample. Experimental work by Hirschwald demonstrated that stones tended to be susceptible to frost damage if the saturation coefficient was greater that 0.80.

Again, this can be demonstrated using the BRE data. Figure 4 shows the relationship between saturation coefficient and salt crystallization loss for UK limestones. The higher the saturation coefficient the greater the salt crystallization loss.

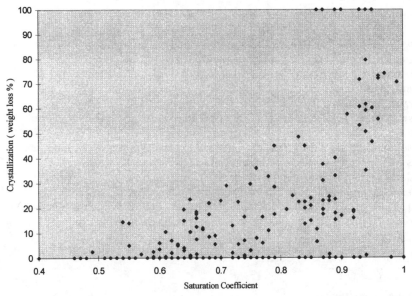

*Figure
4. Graph of Salt Crystallization versus Saturation Coefficient*

Tests for Durability

Index Property Tests

Porosity and Microporosity - In the UK, porosity is measured using the method given in BRE Report 141 [6] which will be superceded by a European Standard EN1936. Using the UK test the porosity is determined by saturating the sample in water for 24 hours and measuring the weight of the water absorbed. In the European Standard two porosities are recognised, open and total porosity. The open porosity is equivalent to the porosity determined under vacuum in the saturation coefficient test (given below). The total porosity includes closed pores and is determined after crushing the sample. There is no standard method for determination of microporosity. The most commonly used approach is the water plate method. In this test, small specimens are vacuum impregnated with water and then subjected to a known and predetermined suction. A clear relationship has been established between suction and the removal of water from pores of different diameters. In addition, the percentage of pores less than a certain size can be determined.

Saturation Coefficient - This is measured using the method given in BRE Report 141[6]. Cube specimens are first dried, allowed to cool and then placed in a vessel attached to a vacuum pump. The cubes are subjected to a vacuum for at least 2 hours and water is then allowed to enter the vessel until the cubes are covered in water. Air is then allowed into the vessel to restore atmospheric pressure. The samples are soaked in this way for at least 16 hours and then weighed. Following drying, the porosity is determined by soaking in water for 24 hours. The saturation coefficient is then calculated from the various weights determined.

Interpretation of Index Property Tests - These are considered basic properties of a stone and, unlike direct frost and salt crystallization tests that make take several weeks, these are simple tests which can be carried out quickly. Therefore, they are not only useful in any initial appraisal of a stone but in subsequent production control testing.

The results for the individual tests may be useful in their own right as demonstrated in Figures 1 to 3. However, a significant amount of testing on UK limestones, particularly Portland, has indicted that the results may be more useful in when considered in combination.

The A112 value (named after the original BRE report [7] in which it was first used) is based on saturation coefficient and microporosity and is calculated as follows;

$$100*S + 0.5*M \qquad (1)$$

where
S = Saturation coefficient
M = Microporosity expressed as a percentage of total porosity.

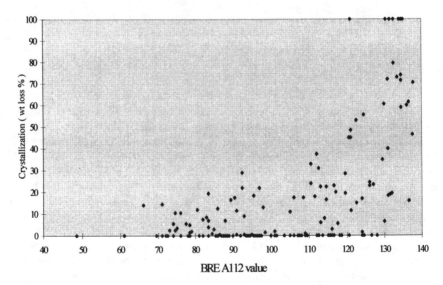

Figure 5. Graph of Salt Crystallization Results versus BRE A112 Value

Again, using the BRE UK limestone data the relationship between the A112 value and the salt crystallization test is shown in Figure 5.

As expected, given the relationship between both saturation coefficient and microporosity to salt crystallization, a clear trend emerges relating A112 value to salt crystallization loss. This relationship has been used by the BRE to develop the classification of limestones, particularly Portland, shown in Table 1 that is becoming increasingly used in the UK.

Class	Expected Performance	A112 value
A	Exceptionally good service in large towns and coastal districts	Must not exceed 79
B	Good service in large towns and coastal districts	Must not exceed 95
C	Good service in large inland towns but not very satisfactory in coastal districts	Must not exceed 115
D	Poor service everywhere except possibly in rural districts inland	Exceeds 115

Table 1 Classification of expected limestone performance in relation to A112 Value

Direct Tests

Salt Crystallization - This test involves the soaking of samples in a solution of sodium sulfate followed by oven drying and cooling to room temperature. This cycle is repeated 15 times and the percentage mass change is then measured.
Until very recently this test was carried out using the BRE method given in report 141[6]. However, the test was found to give variable results which was observed in the use of various control samples in the test. Such variability was caused by many factors and it has been recognized that the drying of the samples may be critical.
This variability has been addressed by the new European Standard EN12370 which is similar to the BRE method except that the test conditions are more rigorously specified. In the European test the mass change is recorded without any classification being applied. In the BRE test, limestones are classified according to their weight loss and assigned to one of the following classes.

A   weight loss less than 1%
B   weight loss less than 5%
C   weight loss less than 15%
D   weight loss less than 35%
E   weight loss greater than 35%
F   disintegrated before the end of 15 cycles

Frost Test - The UK has no standard direct frost test for stone. However, the most commonly used method is the German method described in DIN 52 104. There are no pass/fail criteria specified but the condition of the stone is visually assessed throughout the test and any defects noted. The test involves cycling the stone between −20 and +20 degrees C. There are a variety of conditions of freezing and thawing allowed but in practice freezing the samples in air followed by thawing in water has been found to produce consistent results.

The stones are assessed for visual damage at the end of the test. If there are any doubts as to whether any damage has been caused, the samples are subjected to compressive strength testing.

Specification and Use of the Test Methods.

Initial Appraisal

For a stone without a strong track record of use in the environment for which it is proposed, a comprehensive suite of tests including freeze thaw and salt crystallization may be required, although this may not always be the case. While not set out in any standard, the following approach is suggested by the authors.

- Obtain a petrographic description of the stone. With respect to limestones it will be important to determine the nature of the porosity, particularly the presence of micropores, the nature of the inter-granular cement, the presence of any lenses of clay or sand, the presence of stylolites and any filling they may contain.
- Consider the fundamental index properties of the stone. Assuming that the petrography has shown no problems then it may not always be necessary to carry out frost or salt crystallization tests to confirm durability. This is likely to be the case if the porosity is below 5%, the saturation coefficient is below 0.6 and most of the pores are greater than 5 microns in diameter. This situation is recognized by the European Standard for salt crystallization that states that the purpose of the test is to "assess the relative resistance of natural stones with an open porosity of greater than 5% when measured in accordance with EN1936". It states that the test "is not necessary for low porosity stones".
- If the stone falls outside the parameters listed above then further testing will be required. However, these would only normally be necessary at initial or design stage testing and it is likely that the production control testing for the stone can be carried out using the index property tests such as microporosity and saturation coefficient.

Accelerated Tests

If the index property tests indicate that further testing is necessary, then one or all of the following tests may be necessary depending on the proposed environment.

Frost Testing - There is much evidence that limestones, along with other rock types, may suffer a significant loss of strength through freeze-thaw cycling. Usually this is complete by about 25 cycles and commonly does not involve any visual manifestation such as cracking or spalling. In the context of façade design it is important to determine such changes and is increasingly common to combine freeze thaw cycling with flexural strength testing. Based on experience the authors suggest the following approach.

- For each block to be tested take 50 specimens of the dimensions given in ASTM C880 (Determination of Flexural strength of Dimension Stone) or EN1237.
- Before freeze-thaw commences (0 cycles), test five specimens for flexural strength in both the wet and dry condition.
- Commence freeze-thaw cycling in accordance with DIN 52104 with the samples frozen in air and thawed in water. Remove ten specimens from the test for flexural strength determination (both wet and dry, as above) after 5 cycles, 10 cycles, 25 cycles and finally after 50 cycles.
- Flexural strength should then be plotted against number of cycles. The shape of the curve is of importance, if the strength loss appears to have stabilized by 25 cycles then this is the flexural strength to be used as the basis for design calculations. If, however, there is no evidence that the strength has stabilized, the stone should either be rejected, as potentially frost susceptible, or further testing be carried out to determine the ultimate strength loss.

Salt Crystallization Testing - This should be carried out as specified in the new European Standard with particular care being paid to the drying regime. For the UK the results have traditionally been interpreted using the data reproduced in Tables 2 and 3[6]. In this interpretation (based on a BRE review of UK Meteorological Office data) London is considered "a low pollution, no frost area" and even class E or F stones would be suitable for plain walling provided they exhibited acceptable strength properties. However, for the more exposed locations of a building in London, a greater degree of salt crystallization resistance would be required. In reality it would be unusual to use Class F stones on a building without considerable supporting evidence indicating the durability of the stone, for example frost tests, in service record etc..

Limestone durability class	Crystallization loss (%)	Inland				Exposed Coastal			
		Low pollution		High pollution		Low pollution		High pollution	
		No frost	Frost	No frost	Frost	No frost	Frost	No frost	Frost
		Zones #	Zones	Zones	Zones	Zones	Zones	Zones	Zones
A	<1	1 - 4	1 - 4	1 - 4	1 - 4	1 - 4	1 - 4	1 - 4	1 - 4
B	1 to 5	2 - 4	2 - 4	2 - 4	2 - 4	2 - 4	2 - 4	2* - 4	2* - 4
C	>5 to 15	2 - 4	2 - 4	3 - 4	3 - 4	3* - 4	4	-	-
D	>15 to 35	3 - 4	4	3 - 4	4	-	-	-	-
E	>35	4	4	4*	-	-	-	-	-
F	Shatters early in test	4	4	-	-	-	-	-	-

* Probably limited to 50 years life
# Exposure zones are detailed in Table 3

Table 2   Durability classes for limestones, based on weight loss in the crystallization test, and the suitability of the stones for use in particular exposure zones of a building under different environmental conditions

Exposure Zone (see Table 2)	Typical location on building
1	Paving, steps
2	Copings*, chimneys*,cornices*, open parapets, finials, plinths*
3	Strings, plinths*, quoins, tracery hood moulds, solid parapets (excluding coping stones*), cornices*, mullions, sills
4	Plain walling

* A stone normally suitable for Zone 3 could be used for copings and cornices in Zone 2 if it were protected by lead. Similarly, a plinth in Zone 2 could be considered as Zone 3 if there were protection against rising damp.

Table 3   Exposure zones in buildings

Applicability of Durability Tests in Different Countries.

This paper provides a review of UK practice in the determination of durability of porous limestones for national use. It should be noted that the interpretations applied to some of the tests such as the salt crystallization test and A112 value should only be regarded as valid for the particular climatic regime of the UK.

The approach outlined is also biased towards the historical development of certain tests in the UK, which have evolved with specific regard to the types of limestone typically found and used in the UK. Our geographically close and geologically similar European neighbours have developed quite different tests and methods of interpretation. One of the last European Standard stone tests to appear will be the frost test, not least because of the difficulty of the European member states in agreeing to the number of cycles of freezing and thawing.

One area where French and Belgian experience is to become more widespread is that of capillarity testing. In the UK only the fairly crude saturation coefficient test is used but both France and Belgium have more sophisticated tests to determine various capillarity coefficients, all of which are used in the assessment of durability. A variant of one of these tests has been issued as the new European standard for capillarity testing. However, at present there is very little UK experience of this test.

Summary and Conclusions

The concept of a single test and a single number by which the durability of a limestone could be judged will be almost impossible to realize given the different factors that may affect durability. These factors include the various mechanisms of weathering that may affect the stone, the different environments (climate, pollution) in which the stone might be used and the design of the building. Any assessment of durability will therefore be based on a subjective assessment of these factors combined with the results of the various tests described above.

While a single number or test to define durability is unlikely, it seems clear that the fundamental key to the durability of limestones lies in their pore structure, particularly the pore size distribution. It is in this area that more research is required to gain a deeper understanding of limestone durability.

For the present, this review has outlined the significance of microporosity and how, in combination with saturation coefficient, it may be a useful durability indicator for some UK limestones.

Given the advent of harmonized European Standards it is hoped that considerably more data will be generated on a wider range of stones than those currently included in this study. In addition, some of the newer European tests, such as capillarity measurements, will be applied to UK stones again increasing our knowledge of the properties of these rocks.

However, it is still possible to make significant progress in the durability assessment of a limestone if a reasoned and coordinated program of testing is followed.

References

[1]. Yates, T. J. S., Matthews, S. L., and Chakrabati, B., "External Cladding: How to Determine the Thickness of Natural Stone Panels", Building Research Establishment (BRE) Information Paper BRE IP 7/98, 1998.

[2]. Ross, K. D., "The Assessment of the Durability of Limestone and Other Porous Materials: A Review," Building Research Establishment (BRE), 1984.

[3]. Powers, T. C., "A Working Hypothesis for Further Studies of Frost Resistance in Concrete," *Journal of the American Concrete Institute*, Volume 16, No. 4, pp245-272, 1945.

[4]. Schaffer, R. J., "The Weathering of Natural Building Stones," Building Research Special Report No. 18. HMSO, 1932, Reprinted by BRE 1991.

[5]. Hirschwald, J., "Hanbuch der bautechnischen gesteinsprufung," Borntraeger, Berlin, 1912.

[6]. Ross, K. D., and Butlin, R. N., "Durability Tests for Building Stone," Building Research Establishment Report (BRE) 141, 1989.

[7]. Building Research establishment (BRE). "The Selection of Portland Stone for Various Conditions of Severity of Exposure,". BRE Report A112, 1963.

1

Bernard Erlin[1]

Contribution to a Better Understanding of the Mechanism Causing Dishing Failures of the Carrara Marble When Used for Outside Building Facades

---

Reference: Erlin, Bernard, **"Contribution to a Better Understanding of the Mechanism Causing Dishing Failures of the Carrara Marble When Used for Outside on Building Facades,"** *Dimension Stone Cladding: Design, Construction, Evaluation, and Repair, ASTM STP 1394*, K. R. Hoigard, Ed., American Society for Testing and Materials, West Conshohocken, PA, 2000.

Abstract: The famed Carrara marble has been used as outside-exposed, thin, facade panels that have failed because of out-of-plane distortions; a phenomenon referred to as dishing, cupping, and bowing. Theories have been advanced to explain that phenomena. This paper expands the explanations, and is based upon the relationships of thermal hysteresis the stone is known to possess and stone dimensions.

The marble consists of a mosaic of fine, essentially equi-axial calcite crystals devoid of defined crystal boundaries. Calcite has a known anisotropic thermal response wherein the crystal expands (as would be expected) in the direction of the 'c' crystallographic axis, but contracts (as would not be expected) in the direction of the three 'a' crystallographic axes, which are oriented normal to the 'c' axis. Very slight repositioning of the crystals result because of dislocations along crystal boundaries, which interfere with the return of the crystals to their original locations. The resulting slight increase in volume of the marble is accumulative with continued thermal cycling.

When the front of panels undergo more thermal cycles and/or reach higher temperatures than the back of panels, the result is a differential volume increase front to back with the front expanding more than the back. Based upon laboratory experimental work, when the ratio of lateral dimensions of the panels to their thickness is appropriate, out-of-plane distortions reconfigure the panels in the form of a permanent slight dish.

The physical effects of the thermal hysteresis on the marble causes; dishing, increased volume, increased porosity, decreased strengths because of stress along crystal boundaries and, ultimately, disintegration of the marble into sugar-like granules.

Marbles having coarser grain sizes and mosaic textures do not undergo similar thermal hysteresis effects as the Carrara marble because there are fewer crystals to interact.

Keywords: marble, Carrara, thermal hysteresis, dishing, bowing, facades

[1] President – Petrographer, The Erlin Company, Latrobe, PA 15650

Introduction

The eons old Carrara marble has been used for centuries as statuary and building stone – and has served well, subject to the wear and tear of long exposure in the hands of man and to the elements. It was, by choice, the stone of Michelangelo where its pure, white, fine-grained and massive-textural properties created an aura of purity and handsomeness. Near the mountain from which it is quarried is the Italian Riviera extension of the French Riviera; the walled fortress town of Piatrasantra, which the Allies and Axis powers had an unwritten agreement to not shell during World War II – so it has been reported; and where Michelangelo came to escape the torrid summer heat of Rome, and perhaps to select the next chunk of marble for his new sculpture – and that may have been after a visit to the tavern he frequented, which still exists and is now named after him. And somewhat nearby is the villa and lake where famous Lord Shelley and his wife Mary came, and where she, during a weekend there, wrote historic Frankenstein – or so the story goes. And it is from here, from the nearby towns of Forte de Marme and Carrara, the famous marble was, and is still, dispatched by boats to destinations throughout the world. It was also, by choice of building owners and architects, the marble of numerous building facades where it has performed poorly during very short periods of service.

So, the Carrara marble, which has captured fame as the fine-grained, pure, white stone used by Michelangelo, has also captured infamy as a building stone when used outside as thin facade units. Why the fame of the past, and why the current infamy? For the former, ask those who look at its sculptured beauty; for the latter, ask the owners of buildings, short and tall, and consultants, contractors, architects, engineers, stone fabricators, attorneys, and insurance companies.

There have been some unfortunate facade failures of the marble, in terms of dollar replacement values – and also in terms of litigation, where the reason for the failures becomes of great interest, let alone scientific curiosity, and where there is a great need to identify the mechanism(s) that deploy to ravage the stone and slowly render it structurally unsuitable. Its initial engineering design safety factor of 5, after outside exposure, can drop to 1 or less – a level where it becomes a potential life-safety problem.

From a several story bank building in Austin, to a colossal, tall, white, giant high-rise building overlooking Lake Michigan and the City of Chicago, to a medium sized building in Rochester whose curved fins were once clad in the luxuriant white Carrara marble, and to numerous others, the stone cladding became an engineering nightmare.

Should we have known about its problems and not have overextended its use? We know that it should be used cautiously outside, where exposure to atmospheric pollutants, such as acid rain, attack the stone polish by eating away the surface and creating gypsum as a by-product – but it can be used without a polished face because we recognize that with time the surface will dull. That polish loss is due primarily to the very slow and almost self-limiting chemical failure, which is not as great a consequence as a physical failure. The latter was not a problem years ago when the stone was used as thick ashlar units. But, recently, it has been used as thin panels having thicknesses of $^7/_8$ to $1^1/_2$ inches (22 to 38 mm), and large lateral sizes up to 4 x 5 feet (1.2 to 1.5 m).

The Carrara marble is volume unstable when exposed to cyclic heating – it has an uncontrollable "thermal hysteresis" that is dramatically invoked when the stone is used outdoors as thin, broad units. The result, out-of-plane building facade panels that are dished, cupped, or less appropriately referred to as bowed. The former two describe the distortion best because corners of the panels distort inwards more than the edges. The edge of a dished panel is shown in Figure 1.

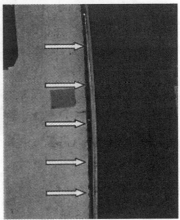

Figure 1 – Distorted edge of a marble panel on a facade.

The thermal hysteresis is interpreted to be a result of the non-linear (anisotropic) expansion and contraction of the millions of very fine calcite crystals that constitute the marble, and the internal interference to the expansion and contraction movements because, in part, of the excellent cleavages of the calcite crystals. Based upon experimental laboratory work that is partially the basis for this paper, it is the relationship of thickness to lateral dimensions that is an instrumental contributory factor to the recent failures. There certainly should be more research completed to establish if any other parameters may be contributory.

This paper is intended to assist and provide direction to others for future research. Reported reverse dishing (concave in contrast to the convex dishing) is not addressed in this paper because the experimental work that is described herein was not directed toward evaluating and explaining that phenomenon.

This paper describes a probable mechanism causing the thermal hysteresis, and how the accumulative expansion affects building facades where the marble is used. The primary distortive effect is due to higher temperatures and differential thermal cycles from front to back of the panels, which results in different magnitudes of expansions and changes to the physical properties of the stone. The latter includes significant degradation of strength.

The Marble

The Carrara marble of interest, with respect to this paper, is the relatively pure, white and clean appearing marble to the variable off-white to very light grey, and sometimes irregularly streaked, marble. The stone is massive-textured, dense, and consists of relatively pure calcitic marble that is nominally uniformly fine-grained, and contains anhedral calcite crystals having nominal sizes of 0.004 inches (0.10 mm) (Figure 2). The crystals are interspersed as randomly oriented units having a mosaic texture.

Figure 2 – General physical data for the Carrara marble.

- Very uniformly fine-grained, dense, vug-free, massive-textured
- Relatively pure calcitic marble (95-98%)
- White to variegated light grey

The marble has excellent physical properties (Figure 3) that should, from esthetical and strength points of view, make it quite suitable for use on building facades. It conforms to the requirements for marble as given in ASTM C503, "Marble Dimension Stone (Exterior)".

But, the marble when used outdoors, and particularly in urban environments where acid rain prevails: (1) is vulnerable to chemical alteration, such as conversion to gypsum ($CaSO_4 \cdot 2H_2O$); (2) has a low numerical hardness as measured on Moh's scale (3 on a log scale of 10), which makes its surface vulnerable to abrasion by atmospheric particulates; and (3) is volume unstable because of its thermal hysteresis, which adversely affects its strength and other physical properties, and can cause dishing.

Figure 3 – Carrara marble, nominal physical properties.

- Absorption -- 0.37 %
- Specific gravity -- 2.69
- Unit weight -- 169 pcf
- Compressive strength: ≈ 16,000 psi
- Modulus of rupture : ≈ 1,400 psi
- Flexural strength: ≈ 1,200 psi
- Nominal grain size: ≈ 0.10 mm

A number of factors have been proposed as possible contributors to the dishing, such as: (1) relief of naturally inherent internal stress in the marble after it has been quarried and fabricated; (2) loading, such as from vertical dead loads and building shortening; (3) stress corrosion and attendant cracking due to exposure in chemically aggressive environments; (4) restraint to thermal expansion, such as from anchors that hold panels rigorously in place; (5) some internal accommodation of imposed stress (creep); (6) differential thermal cycling and attendant differential expansion between front and back of panels; and (7) differential moisture cycling and attendant differential expansion between front and back of panels.

If (1) were the case, thin, unused panels stored in a static environment (e.g. attic samples) should distort, unless something else is needed to unleash the built-in stress – panels so stored do not exhibit any distortion. If (2) were the case, there should be no permanent distortion unless the strain caused cracks and/or disloca-tion of crystals, and panels would bow (rather than dish) normal to the direction of the restraining force. If (3) were the case, there should be evidence of chemical changes (e.g. gypsum) – there is none. If (4) were the case, the anchorage would have to rigidly hold the panels at each corner – the designs and field investigations do not indicate that is the case. If (5) were the case, there would be no distortion.

If (6) were the case, thermal hys-teresis would eventually cause dish-ing of panels without the need of an-chorage re-straint – which has indeed hap-pened. If (7) were the case, dishing could indeed occur.

The thermal hys-teresis phe-

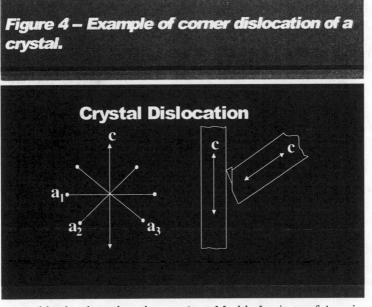

Figure 4 – Example of corner dislocation of a crystal.

Crystal Dislocation

nomenon of some marbles has been long known (e.g. Marble Institute of America, Inc.). There have been hypotheses about mechanism(s) causing that hysteresis, such as the anisotropic thermal expansion of calcite ($+24 \times 10^{-6}/°C/in.$ in the di-rection of the 'c' crystallographic axis, and $- 5 \times 10^{-6}/°C/in.$ in the direction of the three 'a' crystallographic axes); however, details of the specific internal mechanism causing the hysteresis have not been given.

All other things being equal, relaxation of the calcite crystals to their origi-nal position after heating should not cause any length change unless there is something that denied their complete return. That denial can be a result of solid material lodging in spaces between crystals, which are created when the calcite crystals expand and contract during heating and cooling.

Calcite has three excellent cleavages. Mechanical slippage along cleavage planes can be induced simply by using a knife blade to impose a force along an appropriate edge that is near a corner of a calcite crystal. The corner will glide and slide along the cleavage plane and, when the load is released, it will be tightly affixed and offset from its original location. That effect is shown in Figure 4 for two adjacent and differently oriented crystals. That mechanical dislocation, plus breakage along grain boundaries, will produce particles that interfere with the return of crystals to their exact original locations.

Experimental Studies

As a means of evaluating the effects of thermal cycling on volume instability of the marble, panels were exposed to cyclic heating on their front and, after heating, to cooling on their backsides. Panels of the fine-grained Carrara marble and two coarser-grained marbles were tested. Comparative grain sizes of the marbles are shown in Figure 5.

Fabricated for the studies were panels having lateral dimensions of 8 x 12 inches (20 x 31 cm) scaled to the 4 x 5 x 1¼ in. (1.2 x 1.5 x 0.03 m) size of panels on a building where dishing occurred except for thicknesses of $^1/_4$, $^3/_8$, $^5/_8$, and $^3/_4$ inch (6.4, 9.5, 15.9, 19.1 mm). Whitemore gage points for measuring length changes were installed along diagonals on the front and back faces of the panels. Front faces of the panels were heated for 1 hour using a battery of infrared lamps to a temperature of 140F (60C), and the panels were cooled to a temperature of 70F (21C) by spraying water on their back faces for 1 hour immediately after the heating period. One cycle thus is 2 hours.

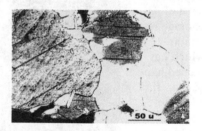

After 550 cycles, there were no measurable changes in length for the two coarser grained marbles. The out-of-plane distortions along the diagonals of the Carrara marble were calculated using the following formula:

Figure 5 – Thin sections of the three marbles.

$$D = S_c \times L^2 / 8T$$

D = out-of-plane distortion along panel diagonal.
S_c = strain differential (length difference between front and back of panel).
L = diagonal length.
T = thickness (in.).

The calculated out-of-plane distortions for different panel thicknesses are shown in Figure 6. As can be noted, for these panels the optimum thickness for obtaining the maximum out-of-plane distortion is $^3/_8$ inch (9.4 mm). This is explainable as follows: (1) the front of panels undergo more thermal cycles and/or attain higher temperatures, because of direct exposure to outdoor ambient temperatures than the back of the panels (Figure 7); (2) when panels are thinner than optimum, front and back undergo similar increases in volume so significant out-of-plane distortions do not occur (panels get uniformly larger); (3) when the ratio of lateral dimensions to thickness is appropriate, the accumulated incremental expansion (due to thermal hysteresis effects) of the front is greater than the back; (4) out-of-plane distortions progressively increase; and (5) for thicknesses greater than optimum, there is sufficient back restraint to partially, or completely, offset the expansive force at the front of the panels.

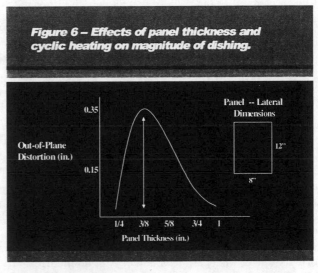

Figure 6 – Effects of panel thickness and cyclic heating on magnitude of dishing.

Figure 7 -- Factors contributing to the dishing.

- Greater number of thermal cycles to front face of panel
- Greater linear increase across front versus back of panel
- Greater linear increase along diagonal of panel

Discussion

Based upon the experimental work and field observations coupled with theoretical considerations, the following is offered as a mechanism causing the out-of-plane distortions that result in dishing of the Carrara marble panels and the ultimate fate of the panels.

The front of panels undergo expansion due to hysteresis from thermal cycling in contrast to the back of panels, which either reach lower temperatures and undergo fewer cycles, or both, at an appropriate panel thickness.

The thermal hysteresis is a result of anisotropic response of the mosaic of fine, randomly oriented calcite crystals to cyclic temperatures. When the calcite crystals relax to their original locations during temperature drop, dislocations along crystal edges keep crystals from returning to their original positions, resulting in a slight volume increase and slight increase in porosity due to dislocations along crystal boundaries. The changes are accumulative. The hysteresis causes progressive and permanent volumetric and linear increase to the marble (Figure 8) accompanied by increased porosity, progressive loss of strength (because of stress along crystal boundaries), and ultimately breakup of the stone into fine sugar-like granules (Figure 9) sometimes accomplished using a slight rapping force, as has been observed and reported.

Figure 8 -- Mechanism causing thermal hysteresis.

- NON RECOVERABLE INCREASED VOLUME FROM THERMAL EFFECTS ON CRYSTALS :
  - Crystals expand along c axis into spaces created by contraction along a axes
  - Crystal dislocation from stress to cleavage planes
  - New fixation of crystals -- permanent increased volume after each cycle
  - Progressive increase in volume

If the ratio of lateral dimensions to thickness is appropriate, and the back is shielded from direct heat that contacts the front of the panel, and/or there is a cooling environment behind the panels (such as cool airflow), the front of the panels are heated to higher temperatures and undergo a greater number of thermal cycles and attendant expansion than the back of the panels. The dishing occurs because of the greater hysteresis effect to the front of the panels, and greater linear expansions along diagonals of the panels than along their width or height.

Figure 9 -- Effects of thermal hysteresis on the marble.

- Increased volume
- Increased porosity
- Decreased strength
- Ultimately, granulation into very fine sugar-like particles

The above provides an explanation for concave dishing of the marble panels on building facades. It may also assist in explaining convex dishing if consideration is given to different environmental and ambient conditions to which panels are exposed.

Michael J. Scheffler[1] and John D. Lesak[2]

Natural Weathering of Granite: A Case Study

Reference: Scheffler, M. J. and Lesak, J. D. **"Natural Weathering of Granite: A Case Study,"** *Dimension Stone Cladding: Design, Construction, Evaluation, and Repair*, *ASTM STP 1394*, K. R. Hoigard, Ed., American Society for Testing and Materials, West Conshohocken, PA, 2000.

Abstract: Over the past few decades, natural stone granite claddings have become very widely used. The long-term weathering behavior of granite has been less studied than that of other natural stones, such as marble, that were more extensively used in the past and have experienced notable weathering related problems when used as an exterior veneer cladding in certain climates.

A white domestic granite, in place for more than 80 years and exposed to a northern midwestern climate, was studied to determine the cause of weather-related surface deterioration. The exterior walls of this monumental building, constructed of granite blocks mostly more than 200 mm (8 inches) thick experienced weathering distress including surface sugaring (saccarification), exfoliation, spalling, and discoloration. A loss of as much as 3 mm (1/8 inch) of granite from the bush-hammer surface of units was documented. The surface deterioration has had no apparent structural effect on the 200 mm thick units. However, similar deterioration, if it were to occur on 20 to 30 mm-thick veneer cladding, made of this material, would have a significant structural, as well as aesthetic impact. The major impact on the stone in this study was aesthetic. The weathering deterioration caused the stone surface color to alter and become irregular. The stone surface, which was originally uniformly light gray to white, became blotchy, ranging in color from white to dark gray.

Studies of the deteriorated granite included documentation of the extent and various types of distress present, as well as laboratory studies of removed distressed and intact samples. The effects that weathering exposure have on the degree of deterioration and overall aesthetic impact were explored. Scanning electron microscope studies, petrographic analysis, and x-ray diffraction analysis were also performed.

This paper presents the results of the studies performed to determine the chemical cause of the deterioration observed and provides a basis for understanding the fundamental causes of natural weathering of this granite. Also presented are the results of various treatment methods that were evaluated to determine if there is an effective means of restoring or providing a more uniform granite finish.

Keywords: granite, weathering, stone, deterioration, cleaning

[1]Consultant, Wiss, Janney, Elstner Associates, Inc., 330 Pfingsten Road., Northbrook, IL 60062.

[2] Senior Architect/Engineer, Wiss, Janney, Elstner Associates, Inc., 330 Pfingsten Road, Northbrook, IL 60062.

Introduction

Natural stone granite claddings are widely used in architectural applications. However, because granite tends to be more durable and exhibit less distress than other stones such as sandstone and marble, it has received less attention than those stones in terms of evaluation and repair. In particular, long term weathering of granite has been studied and documented less than that of other natural stones such as marble, which have experienced notable weathering-related problems when used as an exterior veneer cladding in certain climates. Often consideration of the long term effect of weathering is not considered when selecting granite for construction, as weathering effects on granite occur slowly relative to the human time frame.

A light gray domestic granite, in place for more than 80 years, was studied to determine the cause of weathering related surface deterioration. The granite, a medium grained light gray granite, consisting primarily of quartz, feldspar, and mica minerals, exhibited visible surface deterioration and a highly variable appearance. The study included detailed documentation of the overall deterioration and variability in granite appearance, field and laboratory petrographic examination, as well as X-ray diffraction and scanning electron microscope (SEM) studies to determine the cause of deterioration. Studies were also performed to evaluate cleaning and redressing treatments for the granite, in terms of both aesthetic effectiveness in restoring the appearance of the granite, and acceptability according to preservation standards. Field samples of cleaning and redressing treatments were performed, followed by field petrographic examination to evaluate the effects of the treatments on the stone.

Information obtained on the weathering effects, and successful treatments, of this common 80 year old granite may provide us with insights on what can be expected in the future for other similar granites, as their service lives reach and exceed 40 years. This information will be particularly useful in addressing weathering effects on other historic granite facades; as well as thin stone granite veneers, in which even a minimal loss of panel thickness can have a significant effect on the structural capacity of the granite panel.

Background

The light gray granite that was the subject of this study makes up more than 23 200 square meters (250 000 square feet) of the exterior facade of a monumental historic building in the northern midwest United States. The exterior facade is constructed primarily of large granite blocks, some of which are highly detailed and decorative. The stone units vary in thickness, but are typically more than 200 mm (8 inches) thick. The exposed surfaces of the granite facade were primarily finished with a "bush-chiseled" finish, which created a subtle lined surface texture. The bush-chiseled finish consists of approximately three to five grooves per cm (eight to twelve grooves per inch), approximately 1.6 mm (1/16 inch) deep, in the surface of the stone. This surface treatment enhanced the whiteness of the stone as compared to its unfinished light gray appearance.

Archival documents indicate that the building's exterior granite were cleaned with an acidic cleaner in 1964. It was reported that the cleaning solution used was mixed at the site and was a combination of hydrofluoric acid and hydrochloric acid. The long term effect of this type of cleaning process on granite is not completely understood; however, hydrofluoric acid is a strong acid that has been shown to dissolve, etch, or otherwise alter granites as well as some other types of stone.

Granite Appearance

The building's granite exterior surfaces currently are not uniform in color, as evidenced by light and dark mottled or blotchy areas, as shown in Fig. 1.

Figure 1 - *Typical mottled appearance of the
exterior granite surface*

This mottled or blotchy appearance first became evident approximately 40 to 50 years after the granite was installed, before recorded acid cleaning had been performed. Close observation of the current state of the building's facade revealed variation in the degree of mottling (surface deterioration). For documentation purposes, the deteriorated surfaces were categorized as follows and as shown in Fig. 2.

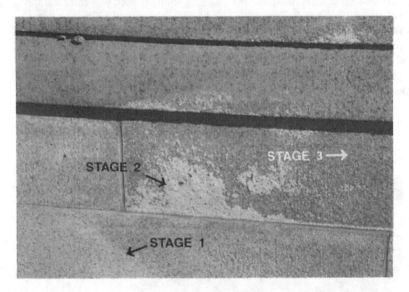

Figure 2 - *Categories of observed granite surface deterioration*

- Stage 1 - the original grooved, bush-chiseled surface appears as a white to light gray uniformly textured surface, slightly lighter in color than the adjacent stone surfaces.
- Stage 2 - the stone surface appears as bright white surface with an uneven granular texture, sometimes including discoloring stain deposit. The white surface material is softer than surrounding material and can be removed with a knife blade.
- Stage 3 - surface loss or exfoliation, the delamination of thin layers of stone material from exposed surface, of Stage 2 material results in exposure of deeper sound, unfinished granite mineral that has a rough, uneven, darker gray appearance. The maximum observed loss of material was approximately 3 mm (1/8 inch).

In his book, *Stone in Architecture*, E. M. Winkler described the following four stages of granite decay [1].

1. Fresh granite: Mineral constituents are unweathered. Feldspars and hornblende retain their glassy luster and original colors. The freshness of feldspars can also be checked with a pocket knife to demonstrate the hardness. The fabric appears unfractured.
2. Partially stained granite: Most mineral constituents still appear sound. Plagioclases are partially gritty and turning dull; biotite is slightly decomposed. There is partial staining along widening microcracks.
3. Completely stained granite: Plagioclases are partly decomposed to soft clay aggregates. There is staining of the entire of the entire rock material, which is intensely microfractured throughout.

4. Weakened granite: Slight weathering of potash feldspars; bleached quartz is
    microfractured. Open grain boundaries; intense microfracturing.

The three observed levels of stone surface deterioration corresponded well with
Winkler's stages 2, 3, and 4 of granite decay, indicating that the natural weathering of the
granite is having an effect on the surface appearance.

Additional discoloration of the surface of the granite appeared to be the result of the
deposition or introduction of an external material on the stone surfaces. Various types of
staining exist throughout the building's exterior, including accumulations of surface soil,
copper patina run-off, ferrous staining, and biological growth. As described above, Stage
2 (Winkler's Stages 3 and 4) surfaces appeared softer and less dense than the original
granite minerals; which would make them more absorbent and more susceptible to
staining and to accumulations of deposits.

Exfoliation

Changes in the appearance of the granite are partly the result of incipient exfoliation
and actual exfoliation.   Significant areas of granite surface have experienced exfoliation
and loss of original surface finish, as shown in Fig. 3. Exfoliation is often

Figure 3 - *Loss of granite surface at a window sill*

the result of natural weathering and is typical of crystalline igneous rocks such as granite
that are exposed to wide temperature changes, such as diurnal solar heating or cyclic
freezing and thawing, in the presence of moisture.

As part of natural weathering, exfoliation is a process in which thin scales of rock,
normally less than a centimeter thick, are successively stripped from the bare surface of a
rock mass such as a granite mountain or a granite building. Physical and chemical forces

that cause differential stresses in the mineral grains cause exfoliation. Differential expansion and contraction occur along perpendicular crystal axes of orthoclase, a common feldspar mineral in granite. Daily temperature cycling due to solar radiation results in constant expansion and contraction of this mineral. Water can eventually enter along grain boundaries opened by this volume change and cause the material to exfoliate during cyclic freezing.

Organic Growth

Once stone surface has began to exfoliate, water may collect behind the delaminated material. Plant life, an example of which is shown in Fig. 4, can also be supported by water that collects behind the incipient exfoliation. Plants can be a source for complex organic acids and can also accelerate the rate of deterioration.

Figure 4 - *Organic growth present behind incipiently exfoliated granite*

Exposure

The amount (depth) of surface deterioration varies greatly depending on the location of the stone on the building and exposure of the stone to moisture. For example, greater degrees of mottling and exfoliation were observed at areas where water can enter the stone from above, such as at parapets and watertables. Areas which are perpetually shaded exhibit higher degrees of exfoliation and surface loss, because these areas typically do not dry out completely. The most severe loss of surface is at locations subjected to water leakage from above, such as stone units situated below leaking gutters and failed waterproofing membranes, as shown in Fig. 5.

Figure 5 - *Heavily mottled granite surfaces below
a landing with a history of water leakage
problems*

Original Finishing

The original bush-chiseled finishing technique likely created a stone surface that more rapidly experienced the latter stages of granite decay than a honed or polished surface. The impact force of bush-chiseling physically alters the surface of the stone by formation of microfractures. Microfractures allow entry of water, and therefore increase the rate of chemical weathering of igneous minerals.

Previous Granite Cleaning

Chemical changes in the stone surface could have been indirectly induced during application of chemical cleaners. Chemical cleaners, such as strong acids, clean by dissolving certain surface contaminants and can dissolve granite surface mineral grains to which the contaminants are adhered. This dissolution can create microscopic voids in the freshly cleaned surface, increasing susceptibility to weathering deterioration, and may actually cause a more rapid build-up of dirt. In the case of hydrofluoric acid, dissolution of silicate minerals can lead to a "frosting" of minerals on the surface and along near-surface grain boundaries if the acid is applied to a surface that is absorptive. Shortly after cleaning in which frosting occurs, an initial whiter appearance may be present. However, over time this could contribute to a mottled appearance of the stone.

The cleaning performed in 1964, reportedly using hydrofluoric acid, likely dissolved stone minerals and has led to accelerated deterioration of the stone. On certain granite units at the building, a pattern of Stage 2 alternation and dirt accumulation exists that resembles an uneven wash pattern such as would be created by acid cleaning with an acid soaked rag. This pattern is shown in Fig. 6.

Figure 6 - *Pattern of deterioration and dirt accumulation resembles an uneven wash pattern such as would be created by cleaning with an acid soaked rag. Note how the pattern extends from stone to stone*

Field and Laboratory Studies

Petrographic, X-ray diffraction, and scanning electron microscope (SEM) studies were conducted on granite samples exhibiting exfoliation. The studies revealed that changes in the aesthetic appearance (mottling) of the granite are primarily the result of alteration of the mineral structure of the granite surface, and secondarily, from deposition of foreign material on or under the surface of the granite. Altered surfaces are more susceptible to staining, which amplifies the mottled appearance of the surface. Alteration of the mineral structure is known to occur as a result of natural weathering, but deterioration can also be the result of exposure of the granite minerals to strong acids, such as hydrofluoric acid. These studies showed that discoloration (mottling) is a surface phenomenon that has not adversely affected the body of the stone. Evidence of internal disruption of the body of the granite was not detected.

Petrographic and X-Ray Diffraction Studies

Field petrographic studies were performed, including examination of representative areas of the exterior granite with a field microscope. Information gathered through field studies was supplemented by laboratory petrographic examination, scanning electron microscope (SEM), and X-ray diffraction studies performed on samples in the laboratory.

Thin sections of granite were made from cored granite samples for use in laboratory petrography. The samples removed included granite that exhibited exfoliation, surface mottling, noticeable discoloration, and staining, as well as granite unaffected by visible deterioration. The interior of the stone represented by all cores was found to be petrographically similar. No direct evidence was found of internal disruption of the granite.

Three samples were studied by X-ray diffraction techniques, including samples consisting of naturally weathered and exfoliated granite. In areas unaltered by exfoliation, the granite was found to consist of quartz, feldspars, and mica.

X-ray diffraction studies of exfoliated stone revealed the presence of hydroxides or other compounds of potassium, aluminum iron, and silicon. This indicates that natural chemical alteration of granite to clay-type structures is occurring. Clay formation is increased by the ready availability of water, increasing the rate of stone deterioration. The correlation of a mottled appearance with natural weathering of the stone was confirmed by SEM studies, as discussed below.

SEM Studies

Scanning electron microscope (SEM) studies were conducted using an SEM equipped with an energy-dispersive X-ray analyzer to identify the elemental composition of material samples. Photomicrographs of the exposed granite surfaces and a freshly fractured surface were also examined and compared.

Four granite samples were evaluated by the SEM studies. The studies confirmed the results of petrographic studies: that the discoloration or mottling of exposed granite is caused by differential weathering of different components in the granite. SEM studies revealed that lighter-colored, "white" regions contain white quartz particles with characteristic smooth surfaces, while the "dark" regions are typically depressed locations containing highly-laminated structures of mica or feldspar. Weathering of the stone results in a surface of hilly (on a microscale) laminated structures, as shown in Fig. 7. As opposed to a less laminated un-weathered surface structure as shown in Fig. 8. The laminated structures permit a build-up of dirt deposits and also are responsible for different effects of light, which contribute to the surface color variations and discoloration.

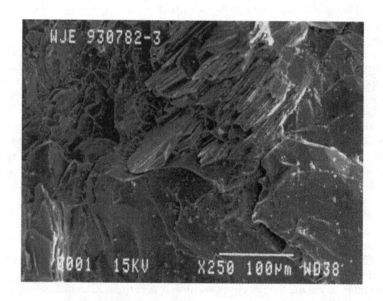

Figure 7 - *Photo from 250 times magnification SEM study of weathered granite surface. Note the hilly laminated structures*

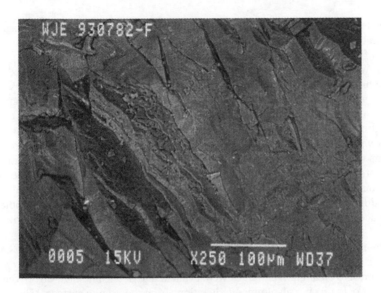

Figure 8 - *Photo from 250 times magnification SEM study of fractured(unweathered) granite surface*

Field and laboratory studies showed that mineral alteration of the exterior granite at the building is the result of chemical and physical changes of the stone at its exposed surface. Chemical alteration of the granite occurred when primary igneous minerals such as feldspars were changed to softer, secondary clay minerals through hydrolysis. Over time, variations in tooling of an exposed stone surface, as well as fractures or other natural imperfections in the granite, result in differing degrees of water penetration into the stone matrix. Because the rate of mineral hydrolysis (clay formation) is increased by the presence of water, differing degrees of water penetration into the granite equate to variations in the rate of surface weathering. The primary effect of the altered material is the change in appearance to the surface of the stone.

Surface Treatment And Cleaning Studies

Observation of the in-situ condition of the stone, supplemented with laboratory studies, revealed that the mottled appearance of the stone surface is due to alteration of the granite surface materials. Mineral alteration of granite is a result of natural weathering; however, the rate of granite alteration at the subject building was most likely accelerated due to cleaning with highly acidic cleaners. The study also indicated that the mineral alteration was a surface phenomenon; granite material below the surface appeared unaffected by deterioration.

It currently is believed that removal of the altered material would be beneficial to the service life of the stone. The softer, more absorptive altered material will hold moisture against the unaffected stone below, increasing the rate of hydrolysis. Additionally, biological growth is present below the alteration material (the growth is not visible until the altered material is removed). The growth can be a source for complex organic acids which accelerate the surface deterioration.

Several different techniques were evaluated to address the removal of mineral alterations, as well as staining and dirt accumulations. Microabrasive techniques and chemical techniques were studied for removal of surface dirt and mineral alterations present on the granite. Various refinishing techniques were studied to determine their effectiveness in redressing and refinishing the granite surface. The granite selected for cleaning exhibited altered stone, soiling, and staining.

A primary goal for the cleaning of the granite surface is to remove staining or dirt accumulations without damage to the granite, providing granite surfaces with a relatively uniform appearance after treatment. To achieve a relatively uniform appearance, the altered stone material (Stage 2 mineral formation described previously) needs to be removed in addition to staining or dirt accumulations. The chemical techniques studied removed surface soiling, but were not effective in removing the altered stone material.

Abrasive Cleaning Studies

Several abrasive cleaning techniques were evaluated to determine their effectiveness in removing not only dirt but also mineral alterations from the granite surface. The techniques tested all project an abrasive medium at low pressure using compressed air. A number of variables, such as media type, air pressure, and flow rate can be adjusted depending upon the substrate type and desired results. The abrasive techniques included the following:

- **Pelletized carbon dioxide pellets. (Pelletized Carbon Dioxide)** - Pelletized carbon dioxide cleaning uses compressed air to accelerate frozen carbon dioxide (CO_2) or "dry ice" pellets to a high velocity. When the pellet strikes the substrate to be cleaned, impact (kinetic) energy and rapid heat transfer (thermal shock) between the pellet and the substrate cause the frozen pellet to shatter and vaporize. As the solid carbon dioxide changes into gas, its volume increases up to 800 times in volume (thermal-kinetic effect). Reportedly, a combination of kinetic energy, thermal shock, and thermal-kinetic effect removes coatings or contaminants from the substrate surface, without damage to the substrate. The carbon dioxide dissipates into the air.
- **Polyurethane sponge with embedded small abrasive particles. (Sponge System)** - The sponge system uses compressed air to accelerate a sponge medium to a high velocity. The sponge medium is an open cell, water based polyurethane sponge to which abrasives are bonded. When the sponge strikes the substrate to be cleaned, the sponge flattens out. Impact of the abrasives removes contaminants from the substrate. Reportedly, contaminants are contained by the sponge as it reshapes after impact, reducing airborne dust. A variety of sponge media is available. Reportedly, 85 to 90 percent of the sponge media can be recycled and reused.
- **Fine inert mineral powder. (Microabrasive Powder)** - The wet microabrasive powder cleaning system consists of a fine inert mineral powder mixed with air and water and then applied at very low pressures through a controlled nozzle. The system projects the medium at a low pressure using a rotating vortex. The impact of the microabrasive removes the contaminants from the surface. The use of water during application and for rinsing cuts down on airborne dust.

The microabrasive powder and sponge techniques were effective in removing alteration mineral and surface dirt. Examples of areas cleaned with these techniques are shown in Fig. 9. The pelletized carbon dioxide was not as effective as the other treatments in removing dirt and was not effective in removing mineral alteration.

Several test areas cleaned by these physical abrasive techniques were examined using a field microscope. These areas included samples performed with the microabrasive powder system and with the sponge system with 80 and 220 grit sponge.

Figure 9 - *Three samples of trial cleaning of the granite surface. The sample to the left was the microabrasive powder method. The other samples were the sponge system*

Based on the microscopic examination, both the microabrasive powder and sponge techniques removed the vast majority of surface soil. No obvious mineral alteration remained on cleaned surfaces where each cleaning technique was applied. The abrasives used are harder than the altered minerals but softer than the unaltered granite minerals. Because of this, none of the underlying, unaltered surfaces cleaned with the various abrasive techniques suffered any damage that could be detected microscopically.

Redressing and Refinishing Studies

For those granite areas that exhibit exfoliated surfaces, the solid, unaltered stone surface profile below the altered stone is highly variable in texture and appearance. This rough unaltered stone surface, exposed by microabrasive cleaning, will require refinishing or retooling in certain areas to provide an even profile and appearance. Trial refinishing techniques were performed at selected sample areas. These techniques included honing of the altered surface using a power circular disk grinder with a 16-grit abrasive wheel, and redressing of the surface with a pneumatic bush-chisel, with and without prior honing. The results of these techniques are shown in Fig. 10.

Honing of a window sill with a power circular grinder with a 16-grit abrasive wheel was evaluated using a field microscope. This technique provided a smooth finish without visible microfractures. However, this finish does not match the original bush-chiseled finish surface.

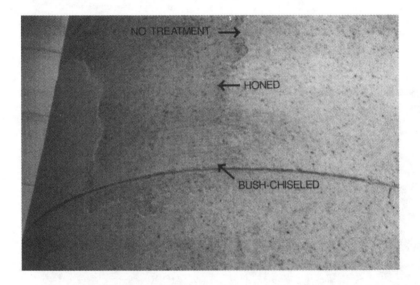

Figure 10 - *Samples of trial granite refinishing techniques*

Bush-chisel retooling of the surface provides a surface finish that matches the original bush-chiseled finish; however, this will result in formation of surface microfractures. The presence of these microfractures will accelerate the rate of weathering relative to a smooth or polished surface; however, this would provide a surface that will weather similarly to the original bush-chiseled finish.

Honing of the granite surface prior to retooling with the bush-hammer did not result in a visible difference in finish appearance. However, deeply pitted exfoliated areas required honing prior to bush-chiseling to provide a uniform matching finish.

The surface treatment samples at the subject building will continue to be monitored for a year before large scale implementation. During that time, accelerated weathering studies will be performed to anticipate long term effects of the treatments.

Organic Growth Removal

The microabrasive techniques were effective in removing organic growth residue from the surface of the granite. Because the organic material is softer than the microabrasive medium, the organic growth was easily removed from the areas tested.

The organic growth residue was removed more easily than the alteration surface mineral and with comparable effort as typical surface soil.

Conclusions

The granite studied, which has been in place for more than 80 years, is a medium grained white granite, consisting primarily of quartz, feldspar, and mica minerals. This granite which has a highly textured bush-chiseled finish, has exhibited visible surface changes over time and currently has a highly variable appearance. Petrographic, X-ray diffraction, and scanning electron microscope (SEM) studies revealed that the uneven appearance and exfoliation of the exterior granite studied is due to alteration of the granite surface minerals to clay minerals and is expected to continue to develop. Mineral alteration is the result of natural weathering, likely accelerated by strong acidic (hydrofluoric acid) cleaners used in 1960s; water leakage at specific locations; and organic growth. The original, highly textured bush-chiseled finish has likely played a significant role in the development of mineral alteration. Loss of granite thickness from mineral alteration was as much as 3 mm (1/8 inch).

Removal of the soft alteration minerals, dirt, and organic materials, combined with redressing of the stone at severely exfoliated areas, can mitigate the uneven appearance of the granite. These treatments also may mitigate or slow mineral alteration. Microabrasives readily remove the soft alteration minerals and leave unaltered underlying granite minerals intact, localized chemical cleaning was not found to be effective. Surface treatments should be preceeded by protecting granite from extreme water exposure, such as repairing waterproofing membranes and joint treatments, if deteriorated.

As granite facades weather and age it can be expected that certain similarly structured granites on other buildings across the country will require that the granite be cleaned or refinished to address mineral alteration. The techniques used should be carefully studied to determine the long term effects of the cleaning process on the material. Strong acids are still commonly used as cleaners because of their immediate impact on the surface appearance of stone; however, the long term impact on stone surfaces can be detrimental.

The effect that mineral alteration and subsequent refinishing will have on overall granite performance is not well known. There may be significant structural effects for thin stone veneer granite panels that that undergo similar mineral alteration as that experienced by the granite studied. Surface losses of 3 mm (1/8 inch) on a 30 mm (1 3/16 inch) thick stone panel results in a 20 percent loss of strength, based upon section properties. Designers should consider this and the effect of the stone finish upon the natural weathering and potential surface loss of building stone that is anticipated to remain in-place for long time spans.

References
[1] Winkler, E. M., *Stone in Architecture; Properties Durability,* Springer-Verlag, NewYork, New York, 1997, pp. 213-214.

Seymour A. Bortz,[1] and Bernhard Wonneberger[2]

Review of Durability Testing in the United States and Europe

Reference: Bortz, S. A. and Wonneberger, B., **"Review of Durability Testing in the United States and Europe,"** *Dimension Stone Cladding: Design, Construction, Evaluation, and Repair, ASTM STP 1394*, K. R. Hoigard, Ed., American Society for Testing and Materials, West Conshohocken, PA, 2000.

Abstract: There are criticisms that durability (accelerated weathering) test procedures have no relationship to natural weathering. The fact is that stone can vary from quarry to quarry, within a single quarry, and within a single quarry block. Therefore, it is important to test the specific supply of stone for a large building project. Stone used successfully on a similar project in the past may not have the same physical or mechanical properties for a current project. Durability testing can provide comparative information that can determine stones that are more susceptible to erosion or deterioration from natural weathering.

The purpose of this paper is to review various durability test procedures used in Europe and the United States. The Europeans are exploring separate test procedures which are appropriate for specific types of stones, while the Americans in the United States are studying a single test method that can be carried out to a standard procedure. The European systems rely on saturation coefficient and porosity, while some utilize a freeze-thaw test. The British have also studied separate test procedures that are specific for limestone, sandstone, slate, granite and marble. The French and Belgians have attempted to relate compression, capillary coefficient, sonic modulus testing and wear resistance to durability. There is wide diversity between the durability test procedures preferred by the French and Belgians then preferred by the British. The Americans rely to a great extent on freeze-thaw testing to determine durability. At present, the Americans have published more data than the Europeans regarding comparisons between durability testing and natural weathering. Based on the analysis in this paper, it may be possible to find a common thread for the development of a standard test for all stones or separate tests for individual types of stone.

Keywords: stone, durability, European test systems, United States test systems, natural weathering, accelerated weathering

---

[1] Senior Consultant, Wiss, Janney, Elstner Associates, Inc., 330 Pfingsten Road, Northbrook, IL 60062.

[2] Senior Architect, Wiss, Janney, Elstner Associates, Inc., 330 Pfingsten Road, Northbrook, IL 60062.

Introduction

Durability can be defined as the quality of a material to resist wear and decay and continue to be useful after an extended period of time and usage. For the purpose of this paper, we are interested in the method durability of stone can be measured in the laboratory and extend the results to its long-term use on a structure. Technological changes have led to widespread use of thin stone cladding for both low and high-rise buildings. However, there appears to be some confusion in the stone industry with regard to the necessity of stone testing and the selection of appropriate tests to determine the durability of stone. For strength, porosity, and absorption, the American Society of Testing and Materials (ASTM) procedures are used both in the United States and Europe. However, while a wide variety of tests are being used to assess the durability of stone, no standardized test has yet been accepted. For this reason, there is a need for a standardized durability test procedure.

In the past, when stone was used in small thick units as a masonry surface against a backup wall, a surface loss of 1/8 in. (3 mm) or 1/4 in. (6 mm) was negligible. However, similar surface loss for a 1-1/4 in. (30 mm) thick stone, reduces the thickness by 10% to 20%. The change in flexural strength is dependent on the square of the thickness of the stone and, therefore, the same loss in thickness can reduce the resistance to bending between 20% to 40%.

All stones weather and change with time. The characteristics of the stone and the severity of the environment it must withstand are factors that control the rate of weathering. Some architects and stone consultants depend on the service record of stone without testing; however, because stone is a naturally variable material, examples exist in which stone failures occurred where this has been the criteria for acceptance[1]. Thus, durability testing should be required for medium and high-rise buildings.

The European nations have developed various tests for determining stone durability. Their philosophy has been that a single test capable of addressing all of the various mechanisms of weathering will not be possible and, therefore, the assessment of durability will need to be based on a series of tests. In the United States, a single durability test procedure is under development that is based on the environment to which the stone will be subjected. Until recently, the Europeans have directed most of their durability testing efforts using sandstone and limestone[2]. The Americans have been studying durability using granite, marble, sandstone, and limestone.

Durability Testing in Europe

It has been common practice to assess durability of dimension stone in Europe by observing the reaction of similar dimension stone to exposure on existing (exemplar) buildings. This method has several difficulties. One is that it is difficult to assure the quality of the stone used in any particular building is the same as that currently available from the same quarry. Another is that it is difficult to assure the environmental exposure presented to the stone in the existing building is sufficiently similar to the exposure presented to the stone in the new building. Attempts are made to avoid these difficulties by performing laboratory durability tests with the stone. A comparison of French,

Belgian, and British durability test methods for limestone is given in the following review[3].

The present French system for the assessment of the suitability of a limestone for use in any particular exposure requires the measurement of porosity, a capillary coefficient, freeze-thaw testing, or by inference from the values of porosity and absorption coefficient *(24 hr soak ÷ 5 hr boil)*. The Belgian system is similar to the French in that emphasis is placed on freeze-thaw resistance with also an emphasis on the need to rely on exemplars before making a final decision on the durability of the stone to be used. The assessment of freeze-thaw resistance requires measurement of the saturation coefficient and a parameter related directly to pore structure. This is the diameter of the pores at 10% saturation[4]. The degree of saturation referred to is the degree to which mercury penetrates the structure of the stone under a given pressure. Because a 10% penetration of mercury is equivalent to a 90% penetration of water, the size of the marginal pores at this degree of saturation of mercury determines the ease with which the material becomes more than 90% saturated with water. Thus, the pore diameter may be an indication of the risk of freeze-thaw damage. The Belgians have found empirically that if the marginal pores have a diameter greater than (2.5 mm), the risk of damage is negligible. This method of assessment is not applicable to stone with a porosity lower than 5% or to a stone with a porosity greater than 50%. In the former case, the risk of damage is very low and in the latter case, the stone is too porous for external use.

The laboratory assessment of durability in Britain has come to be based almost entirely on the results from a salt crystallization test that has been developed over many years[5]. The justification for this test is that the deterioration of limestone (which is usually caused by freeze-thaw, attack by acid rain, or by crystallization of contaminating salts) is basically a result of crystallization attack. Freeze-thaw damage is regarded to be similar to damage from crystallization of salts because it occurs when ice crystallizes from water. The initial chemical reaction between calcium carbonate crystals (limestone and marble) and acid rain (oxides of sulfur) produces calcium sulfate hydrate. The crystallization and recrystallization of this salt causes more damage than the initial reaction. Different types of limestone decay at different rates, because the damage is dependent more on pore structure of the stone than on initial composition. The pore structure of limestone can vary from block to block even if the composition does not vary significantly. The results obtained using the crystallization test correlate well with the known behavior of limestone during natural weathering. At the present time, little information is available regarding the use of this test procedure to assess the durability of stone types other than limestone and marble.

Since the British have found the crystallization test so successful in assessing the durability of limestone and marble, they have abandoned the development of a freeze-thaw test[6]. However, in the *"Guide to the Selection and Testing of Stone Panels for External Use"* that is published by the Center for Window and Cladding Technology at the University of Bath, England, there is a section on *"Aged Strength Testing"*[7], which states flexure strength tests should be conducted prior to aged strength testing and after 50, 100, 200 and 300 thermal cycles of between -4°F and +150°F (-20°C and +70°C).

The Center for Window and Cladding Technology has also produced a table which recommends a series of durability tests that take into account the available knowledge from other published works and foreign standards, Table 1. This table lists all of the stones that might be used on the exterior of a building.

Table 1 – *European Test Methods for Determining Stone Durability*[8]

Stone Type	Petrographic Description	Water-Absorption	Porosity	Saturation Coefficient	Acid-Immersion	Salt Crystallization	Freeze-Thaw	Wetting/Drying	Thermal Stability
Granite	X	X							
Limestone	X	X	X	X		X	X		
Sandstone	X	X	X	X	X	X	X		
Marble	X	X							X
Slate	X	X			X		X	X	

Various test standards have already been produced by certain European countries that are related to durability testing of stone. In the future, CEN (Comite European de Normalization) has noted they will produce European Standards similar to those that ASTM has produced for the United States.

Durability Testing in the United States

In the United States there has been an effort to find a test procedure that will assess the durability of stone under natural weathering conditions[9]. Weathering and deterioration of thin building stone is a complex process that has not yet been completely documented. Normal geological deterioration processes are at work on existing buildings and, therefore, many of the methods of geological examination of weathering can be used to study changes in thin stone. Data determined using these examination methods can be compared with actual weathering behavior on existing buildings.

In addition to the ongoing durability test studies in the United States, a stone exposure test wall was constructed at the National Bureau of Standards (NBS) in 1948, now located at the National Institute of Standards and Technology (NIST) in Gaithersburg, Maryland near Washington, DC as a long-term project to study the action of various natural weathering agents affecting stone[10, 11]. The wall was constructed of many different types of stone from various locations across the United States. No detailed examination of this wall has been performed, however, the ASTM Dimension

Stone Committee (C-18) has observed the wall several times in recent years. Various stones are showing considerable erosion, even in the Washington, DC environment. This indicates some stone types are more susceptible to deterioration from natural weathering than other stone types.

Experimental work has been performed in the United States to develop a durability test procedure that will provide good data with regard to natural weathering of stone. One of the earliest attempts at standardizing a method was the adoption of the ASTM Test Method for Combined Effect of Temperature Cycles and Salt Solution on Natural Building Stone (C 218, discontinued 1965). Results of some comparative tests using this procedure are shown in Table 2. Two groups of standardized bars of marble were designated #100 and #101 and tested at two separate laboratories. One group of specimens was tested at the Illinois Institute of Technology Research Institute (IITRI) laboratories in Chicago, Illinois, and the other group was tested at the NBS laboratories near Washington, DC. The test consists of selectively exposing the stone to a gypsum solution and measuring changes in length. The greater the expansion, the less durable the stone. Note the good agreement between the laboratories in testing standardized bars of two different marbles. Although this test appeared to be effective in predicting marble behavior, it did not appear effective for other types of stone. The test method was discontinued because of this discriminatory aspect. However, as noted earlier, the Europeans have found the test to be effective for limestone.

Table 2 – *Percent linear expansion of marble
as a function of exposure to gypsum solution*

Cycles	IITRI #100	NBS #100	IITRI #101	NBS #101
10	0.05	0.03	0.09	0.08
20	0.08	0.07	0.14	0.12
30	0.12	0.09	0.18	0.16
40	0.6	0.14	0.23	0.19
50	no reading	0.17	no reading	0.21
60	0.23	0.21	0.31	0.26
70	no reading	0.25	no reading	no reading
80	0.34	0.30	0.37	0.33

In 1958, the Armour Research Foundation (ARF) established a cyclic freeze-thaw test procedure for marble, Table 3. This test procedure has also been effective for durability studies related to limestone and granite. Attempts have been made in this procedure to provide treatments that simulate all the environmental conditions (physical and pollution) that have been indicated to effect the weathering of stone.

A stone durability test method has been developed in the United States that subjects the stone to a cycle of operations representing the actions of the different weathering agents at an accelerated rate. An analysis of the test results can be performed that compares the properties of a material having unknown accelerated weathering behavior with the corresponding properties of materials of similar composition and structure whose normal weathering behavior is known. The test procedure can be adjusted for different climates and exposures.

Table 3 – *Accelerated weathering test procedure*

1. 1/2 hour water soak at room temperature
2. 1 hour drying at 170°F (77°C)
3. 1 hour fly ash abrasion at 30 psi
4. 2 hour acid dip, 0.01 molar H_2SO_3
5. 1 hour salt dip, 5% NaCl
6. 1/2 hour forced air drying, room temperature
7. 1 hour water soak at room temperature
8. 16 hours at -10°F (-23°C)

Note: Infrared and ultraviolet irradiation during 1 through 7

Before the test procedure is started, the test specimens are evaluated for dynamic Young's Modulus of Elasticity (sonic modulus) using the ASTM Test Method for Fundamental Transverse, Longitudinal and Torsional Frequencies of Concrete Specimens (C 215). The sonic modulus testing is repeated at designated intervals during the freeze-thaw cycling to provide a nondestructive method of indirectly monitoring the changes in flexural strength of the specimens.

Figures 1 and 2 are plots of marble and granite subjected to this treatment showing the loss in actual flexural strength compared with number of cycles of the durability test. Table 4 lists in detail the changes that occurred during the durability test using marble. Performing the test up to 30 cycles was initially established because it was noted that the loss of properties in the stone appeared to stabilize after this number of cycles.

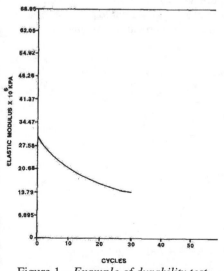

Figure 1 – *Example of durability test results for marble.*

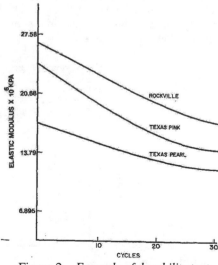

Figure 2 – *Example of durability test results for granite.*

Table 4 – *Results of a 30 cycle durability study*

Marble Type	Modulus of Rupture, kg/cm^2		
	Initial	After 30 cycles	Change %
1	238.6	221.4	7.22
2	108.5	36.2	66.62
3	131.4	109.0	17.07
4	151.1	106.0	29.83
5	168.7	155.1	8.04
6	83.7	63.1	24.62
7	122.4	70.4	42.50
8	55.8	44.9	19.42
9	140.3	67.4	52.00
10	200.0	119.8	40.00
11	162.3	95.4	41.00
12	119.5	52.5	56.00
13	98.6	44.9	54.00
14	196.8	150.2	24.00
15	164.9	134.1	16.00

The comparison of natural weathered marble is detailed in Figure 3 that charts the sonic modulus test data determined from the specimens. These specimens were exposed on the roof of an ARF building for 8 years. Similar changes for the natural weathered marble are determined when comparing these curves to changes observed for the stone exposed to the durability test procedure described in Table 3. At the time of these comparisons, granite and limestone were not experimentally exposed to controlled natural weathering. However, this limited data did exhibit considerable promise for a durability test procedure that provides simulated information regarding the natural weathering behavior of stone.

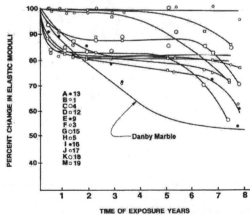

Figure 3 – *Natural weathering test results for 12 different domestic marbles.*

Based on these early studies, it was noted that a correlation existed between the changes in flexural strength and sonic modulus of elasticity of a stone specimen. The changes in absorption varied greatly and apparently followed no pattern.

A second experiment was initiated which consisted of subjecting the marble to 11 cycles in air between +170°F (+77°C) and -10°F (-23°C). Table 5 lists the results of this experiment. These results indicate heating and cooling had the greatest effect on the marble properties to the exclusion of the other environmental conditions. These results confirmed the preliminary hypothesis that bonds between marble crystals tend to weaken because of differential thermal expansion, thus lowering the flexural strength.

Table 5 – *Changes in sonic modulus at 4 and*
11 cycles of heating and cooling in air

Marble Type	Decrease in Sonic Modulus, %	
	4 cycles	11 cycles
Dovelle	22.93	27.47
Ozark T.	16.54	19.70
Silvetto	9.64	14.77
Cedar T.	27.32	34.91

After these studies were completed it was decided to simplify the procedure, expand it for use with other types of stone, and try to establish a real time exposure for the procedure. The number of cycles was extended to 300, which is comparable with the ASTM Test Method for Resistance of Concrete to Rapid Freezing and Thawing (ASTM C 666, Procedure A). In addition, the samples were exposed to a weak (4 pH) sulfurous acid solution on the finished face to simulate acid rain. The samples were then cycled between -10°F (-23°C) and +170°F (+77°C) in an automated chamber at the rate of four cycles per day. Thus, the controlling factors of the weathering rate are the average rainfall and the pH of acid rain.

Recently, for reasons of cost, the number of cycles for the test procedure was reduced to 100. It was determined that this cycle reduction was acceptable because the greatest changes generally occur in the first 50 cycles for most types of stone. Data for both 100 and 300 cycles is presented for this discussion.

In order to record and correlate the weathering change of stone, a comparison study is necessary between stone under natural weathering conditions and laboratory conditions. An appropriate accelerated weathering test procedure can be determined through the use of the steps provided by Sereda & Litran[12] and Schaffer[13], Table 6. It is noted the results should be reported in as much detail as possible with clear statements of the assumptions made and their implications for the reliability of service life predictions.

Table 6 – *Recommended steps for determination of an*
appropriate durability test procedure for stone

Step 1.   Performance requirements
Step 2.   Characterization of material
Step 3.   Possible degradation mechanisms
Step 4.   Postulate methods of causing accelerated weathering
Step 5.   Performance requirements for predictive service life tests
Step 6.   Long-term tests under service conditions
Step 7.   Compare degradation obtained in service and accelerated tests
Step 8.   Determine performance criteria for accelerated tests
Step 9.   Determine product service life
Step.10.   Report the data

There have been concerns that a durability test procedure has no relationship to natural weathering and the test has no meaning for building projects in warmer climates. With regard to the latter concern, heating and cooling, acid rain, and pollutants still affect the properties of stone in warmer climates. Therefore, it has been noted that the test procedure can be modified to cycle between +5°C and +77°C (+40°F and +170°F) in order to provide information regarding the performance of the stone subjected to environmental factors other than freezing and thawing.

With regard to the former concern that the durability test procedure has no relationship to natural weathering, studies are currently in progress comparing sonic modulus and strength test results between stone subjected to natural weathering and the durability test procedure. One such study was performed 35 years ago. Twelve domestic marbles were placed on the roof of a building located immediately south of the main business district in Chicago. The marbles were monitored quarterly using sonic modulus testing. Figure 3 shows the results of this work, including the results for Danby marble, indicated as "I" on the graph. A current study has granite, marble, and limestone specimens exposed to natural weathering on the roof of a WJE building in Northbrook, Illinois, Figure 4. Figures 5 through 7 show the sonic modulus curves that have been determined after 4 years of exposure. These tests will be extended over a 10-year period.

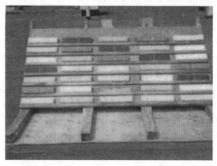

Figure 4 - *Stone test specimens exposed to natural weathering on roof.*

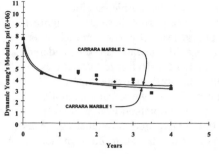

Figure 5 – *Natural weathering studies of marbles*

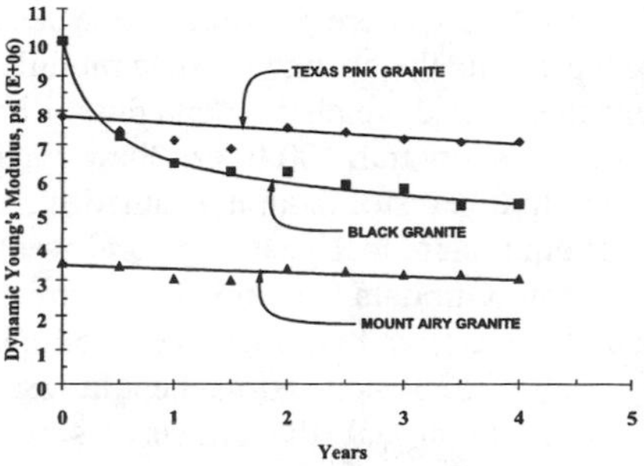

Figure 6 - *Natural weathering studies of granites*

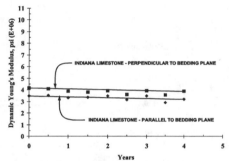

Figure 7 – *Natural weathering studies of Indiana limestone*

The changes in properties are due to differential expansion and contraction of the individual calcite crystals, and some dissolving of the calcite. Figure 8 consists of sonic modulus curves for different types of limestone subjected to the durability test procedure. The Massangi and Valders dolomitic limestones show no basic effect, while the Indiana limestone has a slight downturn trend at the end of 100 cycles.

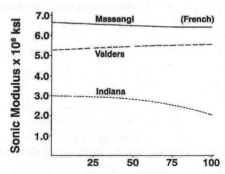

Figure 8 – *Accelerated durability test results for three different types of limestone*

Recently, tests were performed on a second set of Danby marble specimens. Figure 9 presents the change in sonic modulus determined during these tests. Figure 10 presents the natural weathering and durability test curves superimposed on each other. These curves show that 100 freeze-thaw cycles of durability testing can be considered equivalent to 8 years of natural weathering. Therefore, 12 to 16 freeze-thaw cycles would be equivalent to 1 year of natural weathering in a northern temperature environment. Our data from this work, and similar additional work using naturally weathered stone from buildings, were compared with data obtained from durability testing of attic stock stone (stone kept in reserve, but not exposed to weathering). This work indicated that real-time effects on stone properties can be estimated from laboratory tests.

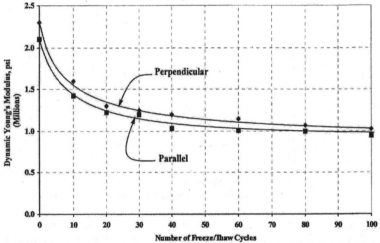

Figure 9 – *Accelerated durability test results for Marquis Gray Danby Marble*

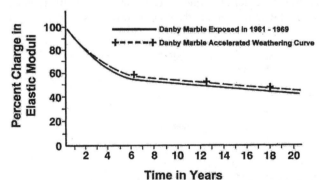

Figure 10 – *Natural weathering results for Marquis Gray Danby Marble*

Figure 11 shows the change in sonic modulus that occurred when granite was subjected to the 4 pH sulfurous acid bath regime previously discussed. Acid exposure apparently has little or no effect on the granite. However, the temperature change does appear to cause differential expansion that breaks the bond between the mineral crystals and, therefore, lowers the strength.

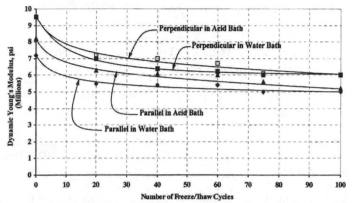

Figure 11 – *Accelerated durability test results for Rockville Beige Granite*

Conclusion

The Europeans have been studying various test procedures that will allow comparisons of durability between different varieties of the same class of stone. However, no attempts have as yet been made to correlate results of these test procedures with real time natural weathering. ASTM Committee C-18 in the United States has been exploring methods to utilize a single standard durability test procedure that will provide an estimation of life expectancy of a stone under natural weathering conditions. Data has been accumulated between stone exposed to the American durability test procedure and similar stone exposed to natural weathering that is indicating a correlation does exist.

References

[1] Mialco, B., et al, "Guide to the Selection and Testing of Stone Panels for External Use," Center for Window and Cladding Technology, University of Bath, Claverton Down, Bath, England BA27AY (10BN1874003092), October 1997, p. 15.

[2] Ross, K. D. and Butlin, R.N., "Durability Tests for Building Stone." Building Research Establishment Report, 1989, p. 8.

[3] Honeyborne, D. B. "The Building Limestone of France," Building Research Establishment Report, 1982, pp. 12-16.

[4] "Centre Scientifique et Technique de la Construction: Pierres blanches naturelles, Note d'Information Technique," 80. CST, rue de la Violette 5, 1000 Brussels, Belgium, July 1970.

[5] Ross, K. D. and Butlin, R.N., "Durability Tests for Building Stone." Building Research Establishment Report, 1989, p. 3.

[6] Ross, K. D. and Butlin, R.N., "Durability Tests for Building Stone." Building Research Establishment Report, 1989, p. 16.

[7] Mialco, B., et al, "Guide to the Selection and Testing of Stone Panels for External Use," Center for Window and Cladding Technology, University of Bath, Claverton Down, Bath, England BA27AY (10BN1874003092), October 1997, p. 45.

[8] Mialco, B., et al, "Guide to the Selection and Testing of Stone Panels for External Use," Center for Window and Cladding Technology, University of Bath, Claverton Down, Bath, England BA27AY (10BN1874003092), October 1997.

[9] Bortz, S. A. and Wonneberger, B., "Durability Testing of Thin Stone," *Rock Mechanics*, Proceedings of the 35th U.S. Symposium, 1995, pp. 373-378.

[10] Kessler, D. W. and Anderson, R. E., "Stone Exposure Test Wall," BMS Report 125, September 20, 1951.

[11] Stuteman, E. and Clifton, J. R., "Stone Exposure Test Wall at NIST, Degradation of Natural Building Stone," *Geotechnical Special Publication* No. 72, July 1977.

[12] "Durability of Building Materials and Components," *STP 69*, Sereda & Litran, Editors. American Society for Testing and Materials 1980, pp. 23-27.

[13] Schaffer, R. J. "The Weathering of Natural Stones," His Majesty's Stationery Office, London, 1932, pp. 99-105.

Design of Stone Cladding Systems

Edward A. Gerns,[1] Bernhard Wonneberger,[2] and Michael J. Scheffler[3]

Design and Selection of Exterior Granite Pavers

Reference: Gerns, E. A., Wonneberger, B., and Scheffler, M. J., **"Design and Selection of Exterior Granite Pavers,"** *Dimension Stone Cladding: Design, Construction, Evaluation, and Repair, ASTM STP 1394*, K. R. Hoigard, Ed., American Society for Testing and Materials, West Conshohocken, PA, 2000.

Abstract: Over the past several years, thin granite pavers have become commonly used in exterior pavement construction. One- to three-inch-thick granite slabs that are usually more than one foot square are often used in new building deck and plaza construction. Granite pavers are often set on thin-set mortar, a flexible sand and gravel bed, or pedestal supports located at the corners of each paver. This paper provides information and guidance for architects and engineers on the selection of granite types and support systems that are appropriate for use in various pavement applications. It also provides an example of an initial selection of paver thickness for a typical size granite paver. Factors described that are to be taken into account for stone selection include stone strength and durability, safety factors, tolerances, the flexibility and typical detailing of the support system used, type and frequency of service loads anticipated by the designer, and anticipated weathering exposure and environment.

The paper is intended to provide designers topics to consider for initial granite pavement design, including sizing pavers, prior to the designers more detailed evaluation and analysis. Information herein can be useful in helping designers quickly determine whether a granite pavement system is appropriate and which support system is best suited for the site conditions present.

Keywords: granite, stone, pavers, design, plazas

[1] Senior Architect/Engineer, Wiss, Janney, Elstner Associates, Inc., 120 N. LaSalle Street, Chicago, IL 60602
[2] Senior Architect/Engineer, Wiss, Janney, Elstner Associates, Inc., 330 Pfingsten Road, Northbrook, IL 60062
[3] Consultant, Wiss, Janney, Elstner Associates, Inc., 330 Pfingsten Road, Northbrook, IL 60062

Natural stone granite claddings are widely used in architectural applications. However, because granite tends to be more durable and exhibit less distress than other stones such as sandstone and marble, it has received less attention than those stones in terms of evaluation and repair. In particular, long-term weathering of granite has been studied and documented less than that of other natural stones such as marble, which have experienced notable weathering-related problems when used as an exterior veneer cladding in certain climates. Often, consideration of the long-term effect of weathering is not considered when selecting granite for construction, as weathering effects on granite occur slowly relative to the human time frame.

Plazas have been an integral part of architectural expression for thousands of years. Though their function has varied, the understanding of the need for open space relative to the built form has long been understood as a way of accentuating and dramatizing the built form. In ancient times, plazas were used as gathering spaces as well as for religious ritual. During the Middle Ages, the need for open space to serve as relief to the increasing density of the medieval city further emphasized the need for plazas. The industrial revolution created three significant changes that impacted plaza design. New building systems produced taller and larger buildings, further increasing the density of cities. Architects as well as governing bodies began to understand the need for mandating plazas to reduce density. These new building systems resulted in the incorporation of plazas into designs with new and unusual design parameters and, therefore, new support systems evolved. Finally, the invention of the automobile resulted in new loading considerations. No longer were plazas only used by pedestrians and horses, but horizontal and vertical design loads became an order of magnitude larger than they had historically been. Today, the incorporation of plazas as an integral part of an architectural design has become very common. Frequently, the design of the plaza is not given the same level of thought as the rest of the building even though it may be subjected to some very extreme environmental conditions. Typically plazas have a very short life expectancy. If proper attention is not paid to critical design issues, unsightly cracking of the paving system and premature deterioration are inevitable.

Stone Properties

Numerous paving materials are available for designers to choose. Among the most common are stone, precast concrete and brick. Each material has specific characteristics that must be considered. For the purposes of this paper, stone will be discussed; primarily granite.

Stone is a naturally occurring anisotropic brittle material. "Anisotropic" means the material has different mechanical properties in different directions to the grain, rift or bedding plane. As such there is potentially significant variability in the material both physically and aesthetically. Localized discontinuities, strength variability based on orientation and wet/dry behavior and aging strength characteristics all should be considered in material selection. Among the physical properties that must be considered, the most important include porosity, absorption, hardness, compressive and flexural strength. Absorption provides a general indication of the durability of the stone that can be determined through testing using methods as recommended in the ASTM Test Method for Absorption and Bulk Specific Gravity of Dimension Stone (C 97). Compressive and flexural strength are necessary to assess the structural capacity of a particular system and can be evaluated through testing using methods as recommended in the ASTM Test Method for Compressive Strength of Dimension Stone (C 170) and the ASTM Test Method for Flexural Strength of Dimension Stone (C 880), respectively. These properties can vary depending on the orientation of the applied load and if the specimens are tested wet or dry.

Support Systems

Among the issues that must be considered by the designer, perhaps the most critical is the method of support for the paving system. Four options exist, each with advantages and disadvantages. They include sand set systems, mortar set systems, pedestal systems and bituminous set systems.

Sand Set System

The oldest method of supporting pavers is the use of a sand bed. This system has been used for thousands of years. Relatively small and thick pavers (12 in. x 12 in. [30.5 cm x 30.5 cm] or less and 3 to 4 in. [7.6 to 10 cm] thick) are set into a well draining bed of sand as illustrated in Fig. 1. Traditionally a layer of gravel, or more recently a drainage mat, is also included to facilitate drainage. Joints are also filled with sand. This system is capable of supporting very large loads, but has limitations for pedestrian traffic due to the uneven walking surface. Shifting of pavers can occur as sand in the system washes out from between and below the paving units. Maintenance of the system is generally minimal, however sand does need to be added to the joints on a regular basis. The use of larger, thinner pavers can result in cracking and tipping problems, as will be discussed later. The arrangement of the pavers should be considered depending on the loading. Horizontal forces can result in shifting of the pavers depending on the pattern. A herringbone layout is the most effective pattern to resist shifting due to the interlocking of the individual units.

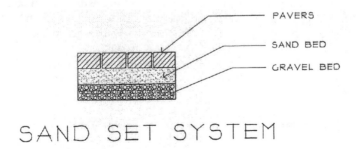

SAND SET SYSTEM

Figure 1

Mortar Set System

Traditionally, the most common method of supporting plaza pavers is on a sand/cement mortar bed as illustrated in Fig. 2. Typical mixes for the mortar bed are 1:3 or 1:4 portland cement to sand mix. The mortar bed may or may not be reinforced depending on the loading conditions. For this system to function properly, the paver must be fully bonded to the mortar bed. Several factors contribute to the proper installation and performance of this system; they include stiffness of the mortar mix, paver size and installation techniques. A mortared system can be designed bonded or unbonded to the supporting structure. If the system is unbonded, reinforcement should be provided in the mortar to achieve adequate strength of the system. An unbonded system is typically characterized by a membrane between the mortar bed and the supporting structure. The membrane allows the paving surface to move independently of the structure. In a bonded system, the mortar is applied directly to the structure and is intended to act compositely with the structure.

One common form of distress that is typical of mortar supported paving systems in cold climates is freeze-thaw deterioration. As water enters the system from the joints and to a lesser extent through the paver itself, expansive forces caused by freezing water and subsequent thawing often results in a loss of bond between the mortar and paver.

Another form of distress is differential thermal movement between the paver and mortar. The paver and mortar setting bed can have highly differing coefficients of thermal expansion. Extremes of exposure or temperature can create large forces between components of the system. If large enough stresses develop at the interface, debonding may result.

Several techniques exist to improve the performance of the mortared systems. The incorporation of modified latex mortar admixes can improve the bond between the pavers and the mortar. Also, a slurry bond coat below the paver and setting bed can further enhance bond and, therefore, performance. Providing proper slope at the paver surface to quickly direct rainwater toward the drains is also very important. If these additional steps are included and properly executed, the mortared system has the potential to carry higher loads without cracking the pavers and is less susceptible to freeze thaw deterioration.

If installed properly, a mortar set system is capable of carrying very high loads. Very few mortar set systems, however, are immune to freeze-thaw damage-- particularly in cold climates.

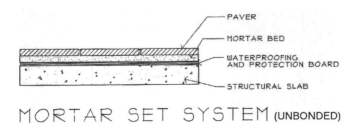

MORTAR SET SYSTEM (UNBONDED)

Figure 2

Pedestal System

Within the past twenty years, the use of pedestal support systems has become more popular. The use of pedestals has been very common in Europe for many years. In the United States, however pedestals supporting precast concrete pavers were formally more common in protecting roofs, but the ease of constructability, longevity and maintenance have made them more attractive to building owners and architects for plaza surfaces. Paver units are typically supported at the corners by high-density polyethylene or vulcanized rubber pads of various configurations and adjustment capabilities (see Fig. 3). Some systems, such as circular telescoping pedestals, actually function as forms for small concrete columns when significant depth of the support is required. Additional support for pavers can be achieved when more pedestals are set at the edges or center of the paver, however, it is critical these additional supports are accurately positioned to carry equal loads with the other supports. Joints between pavers, supported by pedestals, are typically left open to allow water to drain to the waterproofing membrane below and to allow for easy removal and replacement of pavers. Open joints, however, require that the space below the pavers be cleaned out as part of routine maintenance. Usually cleaning is only necessary at the drains if proper slope is provided to the drains at the waterproofing membrane level.

The limitation of pedestal systems is the load capacity. For pedestrian traffic, pedestals are usually adequate. However, vehicular traffic is generally not recommended.

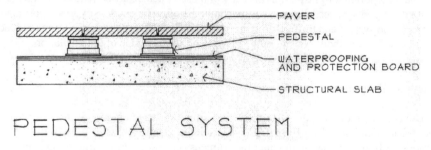

PAVER

PEDESTAL

WATERPROOFING AND PROTECTION BOARD

STRUCTURAL SLAB

PEDESTAL SYSTEM

Figure 3

Bituminous Sand System

The most recent development in paver support is the use of a bituminous sand setting bed as illustrated in Fig. 4. Bond between the paver and setting bed is achieved by a neoprene tack-coat. The long-term performance of these systems however is not well known. The leaching of the oils from the bituminous constituents into the paver can result in staining. As with mortar set systems, performance is dependent on the degree of bond between pavers and the setting bed and providing proper slope to the drains at the paver surface.

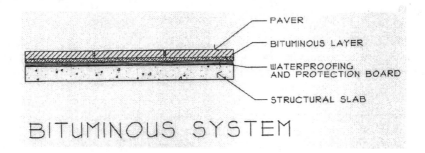

Figure 4

Design Considerations

The selection of an appropriate support system is governed by many factors. The most critical include; load capacity, available depth, paver size and manufacturing tolerance, maintenance and initial and life cycle costs.

The incorporation of insulation into any of these systems may be required if the plaza is over a conditioned space. The insulation should be of sufficient density to support loads imposed by the system and traffic without crushing. The waterproofing membrane will act as a vapor barrier and therefore should be placed on the warm side of the insulation. In these situations, the insulation can serve as a protection board for the membrane.

Fabrication Tolerances

Depending on the support system selected, dimensional tolerances of the stone may impact the installation. The National Granite Building Quarriers Association (NBGQA) prescribes a ±1/16 in. variation in panel face dimension, and ±1/4 in. variation in panel thickness for panels thicker than 1 5/8 in. These and other fabrication tolerances vary significantly depending on the size of the stone, fabrication process and finish. Tighter thickness tolerances may be required for a pedestal system to minimize shimming. This is of particular concern if the same pedestal will support different stones. Further, the treatment of plan variation and edge squareness is essential if proper joint width is to be maintained. Specified tolerances should be carefully considered and may be relaxed, resulting in some cost savings, if there is no significant impact on the performance of the system.

Structural Design Considerations

There are three approach methods for the design of pavement systems. Selection of an appropriate method is dependent on the parameters of a particular project. The methods include:

1. Design based on past experience. It is important for the designer to understand that the paving system is dependent on subsurface bearing and the environment. Therefore, a system that has previously worked may not be appropriate for other locations.
2. Design based on past experience and laboratory testing. This method is often used when new materials are being introduced into a system with significant historical precedence.
3. Mathematical models. This technique can be useful when enough information is available to create an appropriately accurate model. Assumptions made by the designer can dramatically affect the results and often do not fully consider installation-related issues that affect the performance and durability of the system.

The loads expected on the paving system usually govern the thickness of any type of paver. The ability to accurately predict the expected magnitude and frequency of loading is critical to the performance of the systems. Generally, the governing load condition is a point load applied by vehicles and usually is based on the intended use of the plaza. The magnitude of the load is a function of the accessibility of the plaza as well as the intended function of the plaza space. The expected range for vehicle loading can vary greatly. One further consideration for vehicle loading is the use of cranes or man lifts for maintenance, which may be performed from the plaza level. Often the effect of an extended boom can place substantial loads on a particular wheel of the vehicle. Design for a method of load transfer or redistribution in these situations is perhaps more economical then allowing these loads to dictate the entire design. Heavily loaded zones of a plaza could also be predefined and separated from the other sections of the plaza with bollards or other physical means. A combination of support mechanisms may become desirable in these situations.

Depending on the type of material to be used as a wearing surface, the stone's strength and appropriate factor of safety can be used to select a preliminary thickness for a particular paver size. Factors of safety vary greatly depending on the type of material to be specified. As an example, granite stone requires a factor of safety of 3 when designing for bending which is not related to connections[1]. However, in the case of a paver, the failure of the system is more of a maintenance issue rather than a life safety issue. Safety factors are used to account for variation of the material, aging and load variation and predictability. The factor of safety selected will dictate the percentage of breakage that should be expected unless the loads are very predictable[2]. The following factors of safety are generally used for flexural design of different types of stone:

Table 1 – *Recommended flexural design safety factors
for various types of stone.*

Stone Type	Flexural Design Safety Factor
Granite	3
Marble [3]	5
Limestone and [4] Sandstone	8

A pedestal system should have a more predictable behavior than a mortared system. A mortared or bituminous system is more dependent on installation quality; therefore, modeling its performance is difficult.

Once an appropriate thickness has been selected for a particular size and support condition, one additional structural factor should be considered. Estimation of the traffic that will use the pavement over its design life is an important factor in the structural design of pavement of any type. The Portland Cement Association (PCA) suggests that a load frequency factor be applied to the allowable stress in a paver[5]. The number of repetitions is based on the full service life of the plaza. The factor, as shown in Table 2, varies between 1, for a single load application, to almost 2 for 400 000 load cycles.

Table 2 – *Recommended additional safety factors for load repetitions.*

Number of Repetitions	Additional Safety Factor
400 000	1.96
130 000	1.82
32 000	1.67
8 000	1.54
2 000	1.43
490	1.33
120	1.25
30	1.18
1	1.00

For a particular paving material, the ultimate strength of the material should be divided by the safety factor accounting for aging and material variation and the safety factor accounting for repetitive loading. This result is the allowable stress for the material.

Structural Design Example

All paving materials are susceptible to flexural stresses, even when they are installed over rigid setting bed materials such as mortar or bituminous sand. Load that is applied to the stone paver will cause a shortening of the setting bed, depending on the physical properties of the setting bed. The modulus of elasticity and Poisson's ratio of the setting bed influences the amount of shortening that result. The stone tile will bend as the shortening occurs at the location of the applied load while less shortening occurs at the other areas under the same paver unit where the applied load does not exist. The amount of bending and flexural stress that results is dependent on the elasticity of the setting bed. For instance, stone pavers installed over sand setting beds will be subjected to higher flexural stresses than when installed over more rigid grout setting beds.

The potential for cracking of the stone is increased further if the modulus of elasticity of the stone paver is greater than the modulus of elasticity of the mortar setting bed. The modulus of elasticity of a mortar setting bed can be about 100 000 psi (689 500 KPa) while the modulus of elasticity of granite can be as high as 10 000 000 psi (68 950 000 KPa). Therefore, compression and shortening of the mortar setting bed will induce higher flexural stresses in the stone because of the great difference in stiffness from that of the stone.

The graphs presented below provide a comparative analysis of paver support systems. Figure 5 depicts a 24 in. (61 cm) square pedestal supported paver for three different paver thicknesses. Figure 6 depicts a 24 in. square granite stone paver with a modulus of elasticity of 5 000 000 psi (34 475 000 KPa) that is supported by various types of 1 in. thick setting beds for two different paver thicknesses. Analysis of the both systems are based on plate bending and assume the materials are isotropic and within the elastic limits of the stone. Load in both analyses is based on a 6 in. square area and a 1,000 lb. (454 kg) applied load. As can be seen in the graph of Fig. 6, the resulting stress of the paver on a sand setting bed can be about three times higher than the resulting stress of the same type of paver on a mortared setting bed. As previously noted, mortar setting beds can deteriorate in freeze-

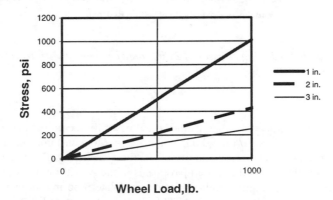

Figure 5 - *Estimated stress in 24 in. square paver on a pedestal supported system.*

thaw environments, perhaps to the consistency of sand. Therefore, the stiffness of the setting bed will also be reduced. The resulting stresses in the stone paver can also increase to levels that are as high as stresses that results from a sand setting bed.

Increasing the depth of the setting bed can also cause greater shortening of the setting bed when under load. Therefore, increased depth of the setting bed will also result in higher stresses in the pavers.

Any discontinuities of support for the stone paver will also create flexural stresses within the stone unit when loads are applied to the surface. The flexural stresses created by bending over discontinuities or unevenness in the setting bed can be greater than the flexural strength of the stone and result in cracking. The larger the stone paver, the greater the potential for cracking. Long, slender pavers are even more susceptible to cracking than wider, long paver because of their smaller section properties.

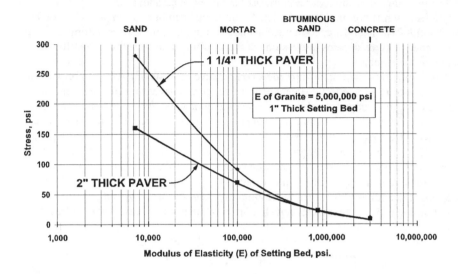

Figure 6 - *Calculated resulting stresses of 24 in. square paver on various setting beds.*

Other Considerations

Several other non-structural issues should be addressed for the proper performance of a paving system. Proper slope, 1/4 in. (0.635 cm) in 12 in. (30.5 cm) minimum, is recommended for brick pavements by the Brick Institute of America (BIA) in Technical Note 14, September 1992, as well as for all pavements in the ASTM Guide for Use of High Solids Content, Cold Liquid-Applied Elastomeric Waterproofing Membrane With Separate Wearing Course (C 898) and the ASTM Guide for Design of Built-Up Bituminous Membrane Waterproofing Systems for Building Decks (C 981). This recommended minimum slope should be provided at the paving surface and at the waterproofing level. If the aesthetics of a particular design requires the plaza surface to be flat, telescoping pedestal supports can be used that can be set at various angles to adjust for slope at the waterproofing membrane level beneath the pavers.

Drains that are integrated into the system should be bi-level to allow for drainage at the paver level as well as the waterproofing level. Cleaning of the drains should be included as part of the routine maintenance schedule. Single level drains with dome strainers can often be used beneath pavers that are supported on a pedestal system.

Expansion joints should be provided at intervals that are appropriate for the material used for pavers. Joints between pavers should accommodate thermal expansion but need not extend through the entire system. Expansion joints between paving sections, particularly in full mortar systems should extend through the entire depth of the system.

For mortar set brick pavement the BIA states (Technical Note 18, January 1991) that to account for differential movement between paving elements for a 100° F (38° C) temperature change, and moisture expansion, thermal expansion and freezing expansion of brick units an expansion joint spacing of 16 ft. (4.8 m) is adequate. Since granite does not undergo significant moisture or freezing expansion the spacing for mortar set granite systems can be greater. A typical granite/mortar set pavement system that experiences a 100° F temperature change and which uses 1/2 in. (1.27 cm) wide joints may be able to satisfactorily accommodate expansion with joints spaced at 30 ft. (9.1 m). This depends on the granite's thermal expansion characteristics and expected temperature change, and joint filler and sealant movement capabilities. Commonly used sedimentary and metamorphic stones can have expansion characteristics almost twice that of granite and, therefore, would typically require closer spacing of expansion joints.

Expansion from freezing water can loosen sand set pavers both vertically and laterally. Further deterioration and debonding occurs when entrapped water is expelled by wheel loading on the pavers.

Tractive forces, resulting from vehicular movement, may need to be addressed when considered joint width and paver movement. Though these are typically more of a factor for roads rather than plazas, enough play must exist between paving units so crushing does not occur from the horizontal load applied during the braking action of vehicles.

A waterproofing membrane should be included in the paving system over occupied spaces. The membrane could be a sheet product or liquid applied. Regardless of the type, it is critical that a protection sheet be included to prevent damage to the membrane during installation of the paving system.

Careful attention should also be given to the edge detailing of plazas. When the plaza is adjacent to a building or other fixed element, an expansion joint should be provided at those locations. Other edges may require restraint to prevent the pavers from migrating and water from entering the system.

Regardless of the type of paver selected, the wearing surface must have a coefficient of friction that will minimize the likelihood of slippage. According to the ASTM Test Method for Static Coefficient of Friction of Polish-Coated Floor Surfaces as Measured by the James Machine (D 2047), a minimum coefficient of friction (COF) equal to 0.5 is traditionally considered to provide non-hazardous walkway surfaces, while the American Disabilities Act (ADA) recommends a minimum COF of 0.6. It must be recognized that even if these values are met in the initial installation of a paving system, the COF can become reduced as the surface wears. Thus the need to roughen the surface may be required in the future as a result of wear. For interior stone paving surfaces, floor sealers are specially formulated to provide an adequately high COF for the floor surface. It should be noted that these are minimum standards and based on dry conditions. Obviously, when conditions are wet or contaminants, such as oil, are left on the wearing surface, the likelihood of slipping may be increased.

The proper design of a plaza is obviously not an exact science. Guidance for several key factors of paver design has been provided. However, as with many aspects of construction, common sense and experience are perhaps the most important ingredient to assure long-term performance of a plaza.

References

[1]   National Building Granite Quarriers Association, Inc., "Specifications for Architectural Granite," Washington DC, 1999, p. 5.

[2]   Bortz, S. A., Wonneberger, B., "Probabilistic Safety Factors," *Stone through the Ages*, Marble Institute of America, Volume 45, 1990, p. 8-19.

[3]   Marble Institute of America, *Dimension Stone Design Manual,* Columbus, Ohio, 1999, Marble p. 48.

[4]   Indiana Limestone Institute of America, Inc., *Indiana Limestone Handbook,* Bedford, Indiana, 20th edition, 1998, p. 17.

[5]   Portland Cement Association, "Thickness Design for Concrete Pavements," Concrete Information Booklet, Chicago, p. 31.

David G. West[1] and Marc Heinlein[2]

Anchorage Pullout Strength in Granite: Design and Fabrication Influences

---

Reference: West, D. G. and Heinlein, M., "**Anchorage Pullout Strength in Granite: Design and Fabrication Influences,**" *Dimension Stone Cladding: Design, Construction, Evaluation, and Repair, ASTM STP 1394*, K. R. Hoigard, Ed., American Society for Testing and Materials, West Conshohocken, PA, 2000.

Abstract: For the past 10 to 15 years, significant emphasis has been placed on evaluation of the bending strength of stone panels used for thin veneer cladding. However, failures of stone cladding on buildings are more commonly due to problems with the anchor and/or anchorage design or installation than with the bending strength of the granite panel. Judging from the calculations submitted by engineers designing stone cladding systems, many designers of stone cladding panels and anchoring systems are unaware of the issues addressed in this paper.

This paper reports the results of a series of tests according to ASTM Test Method for Strength of Individual Stone Anchorages in Dimension Stone (C1354) using two granites and an assortment of edge anchors. These tests examined possible causes for the variation in anchorage pullout loads. Situations examined included:
a) variation for a single stone type tested with the same anchor configuration.
b) variation for a single stone type tested with different anchor types and configurations.
c) variation between different stone types tested with the same anchor configuration.
The results indicate that the most significant source of variation in anchorage pullout strengths of edge anchors is the thickness of stone material resisting the pullout load. Other sources of variation include the depth of embedment of the anchor, and the geometry of the anchor bracket and anchor cutout in the stone, but these were lower in magnitude.

The conclusions presented in this paper provide a basis for more appropriate consideration of the anchor pullout capacity in stone panels during design. They also provide a basis for possible revision of ASTM C1354 to reflect the key findings of this research.

Keywords: cladding, granite, dimension stone, design, anchor, anchorage, pullout, kerf

---

[1]Hyder Consulting, Level 13, 601 Pacific Highway, St Leonards NSW 2065, Australia
[2]Corived Srl, Via Marella 19, 55045 Pietrasanta (LU) Italy

Background

The widespread use of thin stone veneer cladding grew in conjunction with the development of fabricating techniques that permitted the sawing of thin slabs of marble and travertine in the 1960s, and then granite in the late 1970s.

Fixing techniques were developed to accommodate the thinner and larger slabs of stone which architects and builders were using, but in some cases, these did not take into account the full range of service conditions. As a result, there have been a number of significant failures of stone cladding, and many less prominent (or smaller scale) failures.

One of the consistent themes of these failures is that problems with the fixing system are almost always a contributory cause to failure, if not the primary cause. Failures of stone panels themselves due to high wind loads appear to be non-existent to date.

The focus on the bending strength of stone panels to the detriment of the anchorage design has been criticised by others for at least fifteen years.

Chin, Stecich and Erlin [1] outlined design issues for the use of thin stone veneers. In addition to the wide-ranging review of the topic covered by them, Chin, Stecich and Erlin proposed a formula for calculating the stress in stone kerfs due to anchors. This formula allowed for stress concentration due to the radius at the base of the kerf slot, as well as for variable points of engagement of the lateral load. It appears that the formula was derived for continuous anchors in a continuous kerf slot. Subsequently, Stecich, Chin and Heidbrink [2] revised this formula by modifying the stress concentration constant.

McCabe [3] described the approach to basic stone anchor design, including sample calculations that addressed the need to consider the load at the anchorage point. He proposed an approach for calculating the allowable surface area for individual fixings inserted into stop-end kerf slots.

Clift and Bayer [4] stated that most stone cladding failures can be attributed to poor anchorage design, and thus efforts to improve performance of stone cladding should be directed to the details and criteria associated with fixings.

Lewis [5, 6] described the issues involved in stone anchorage design, including significant emphasis on the need for testing of anchorages as individual specimens and on full-sized panels. He promulgated some basic concepts for stone anchorage design. These were addressed in significantly greater detail in Lewis [7].

A procedure for testing full-sized panels of stone cladding was published in 1991 as ASTM Test Method for Structural Performance of Exterior Dimension Stone Cladding Systems by Uniform Static Air Pressure Difference (C1201). This provided a basis for standardising full-sized panel tests involving the stone panel, the anchors and the backup support system.

The ASTM Guide for Design, Selection, and Installation of Exterior Dimension Stone Anchors and Anchoring (C1242) was first published in 1993. There have been several revisions since original publication. This document provides detailed information on types of stone anchoring systems and good detailing practice, as well as identifying details that should be avoided. The current version has some shortcomings with regard to testing recommendations, but these should be addressed by revisions currently under ballot by Committee C18.

An important reference for assessing the design of stone anchorages is ASTM Test Method for Strength of Individual Stone Anchorages in Dimension Stone (C1354), first published in 1996. This describes a standard approach to conducting fixing pullout tests from stone specimens. This standard is becoming more widely used as the basis for evaluating stone cladding designs.

There is a German standard for determining the pullout load at a dowel hole, and the draft European standard prEN 13364:1998 Natural Stone Test Methods - Determination of Breaking Load at Dowel Hole is currently under ballot. Both of these methods are limited to dowel hole anchorages, and utilise a 6 mm stainless steel dowel cemented into a 10 mm diameter hole.

An increasing number of project specifications for stone cladding are incorporating requirements for anchor pullout testing in specimens of the stone to be used on the building, but understanding of the significance of the results is still developing.

Existing Data

During the preliminary phase of the research leading to this paper, existing anchorage pullout test data for a range of fixing details were reviewed. These fixing details included:
a)   kerf brackets of varying lengths in continuous and stop-end kerf slots.
b)   dowels of varying diameters in kerf slots and drilled holes.
c)   rear anchors.

This review showed that the pullout loads for edge anchors were typically lower than those for rear anchors. It also showed that there was considerably more variation in pullout loads for kerf anchor details than for any other type of fixing detail for which data was available.

Experimental Procedure

Aims – On the basis of the review outlined above, it was decided to test edge anchors, with a specific emphasis on kerf anchors, and to examine the variation in pullout loads caused by different kerf anchorage cutout details and different lengths of engagement of anchors.

Test Method – Tests were carried out following the procedure in ASTM C1354.

Materials – Two granites were selected for testing:
a)   Mondariz granite is a fine to medium grained grey-beige colored granite from the Vigo region in northwest Spain.
b)   Impala Black granite is a fine grained dark grey granite from South Africa.

Table 1 — *Bending strength of granites*

Material	Modulus of rupture (ASTM C99)
Mondariz granite	13-14 MPa
Impala Black granite	17-20 MPa

Selection of these materials was based on availability, and on general consistency of appearance, physical properties and the lack of any pronounced rift or texture other than in the plane of the slabs. Consideration was also given to obtaining materials with strengths in different parts of the typical strength range for granites used as cladding. Bending strength properties for these materials are given in Table 1.

Specimens – Forty specimens measuring 300 mm x 300 mm were prepared from slabs of 30 mm nominal thickness for each material. One face of the slab was polished, and the rear face was gangsawn. An anchorage cutout was fabricated into each of the four sides of each specimen using diamond tools. Four types of cutout were prepared (Figure 1) as follows:

a)   continuous kerf slot
b)   200 mm long stop-end kerf cutout
c)   100 mm long stop-end kerf cutout
d)   6 mm diameter drilled hole

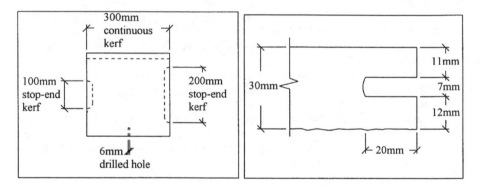

Figure 1 – *Specimen configuration*   Figure 2 – *Dimensions of anchor cutout*

Tests were carried out on both the front and rear kerf legs of kerfed specimens, but only to the rear face of specimens with drilled holes. Five specimens were tested in each combination of anchor, anchorage and conditioning regime. Sets were replicated on the Mondariz granite by using both front and rear kerf legs with the same anchor and conditioning regime. As the front and rear kerf legs on most Mondariz specimens were different thicknesses, this provided useful data on the effect of kerf leg thickness on the pullout capacity. A range of measurements was made on each specimen, before and after testing (Figure 2).

Anchors – The basic types of anchor used (Figure 3) were as follows:

a)   extruded aluminum kerf bracket, cut to length (300 mm, 100 mm, 50 mm & 25 mm).
b)   as for (a) but with strips of a neoprene bearing pad between kerf anchor and granite.
c)   extruded aluminum kerf bracket with bulb, cut to length (300 mm, 100 mm, 50 mm & 25 mm).
c)   stainless steel plate anchor with 6 mm diameter stainless steel dowel.

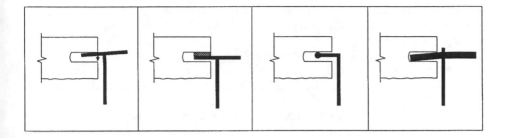

Figure 3 – *Kerf anchor types*

Conditioning – The majority of specimens were soaked in water at 22°C for a minimum of 48 hours and a maximum of 120 hours. Some specimens of Mondariz granite were dried in a humidity-controlled oven at 65°C and allowed to cool to 22°C within the oven prior to testing.

Test Rig – The tests were performed on a bench mounted universal testing machine with a load cell capacity of 10 kN. Load values were displayed on a digital readout with peak value memory.

Specimens were supported by the anchor, which was bolted in position and adjusted to be parallel to the loading knife edge prior to each test, and a continuous knife edge able to rotate in one direction (Figures 4 and 5). A range of measurements of the position of the specimen in the test rig were taken or checked for each specimen.

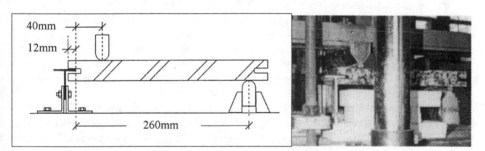

Figure 4 – *Testing arrangement*   Figure 5 – *Testing rig*

Test Execution – Specimens were positioned in the test rig, and a small preload applied to ensure the specimen was oriented parallel to the loading knife edge. Load was applied at a constant rate so as to reach failure with a 100 mm long bracket in approximately 2 minutes. A similar rate was used for all specimens, resulting in varying test durations depending on the strength of the anchorage with different lengths of anchor bracket. Measurements of the position of the specimen in the test rig were checked during the loading phase. The relationship between the anchor and the granite specimen was monitored visually during loading.

Results – The pullout load at failure for each specimen was determined in accordance with equation (1), which is the formula given in ASTM C1354.

$$\text{Anchorage pullout load} = (\text{test machine load} \times A) / \text{span} \tag{1}$$

where A =   span less the distance between anchor support point and loading knife edge

span   =   distance between anchor support point and supporting knife edge

A normalized failure load was calculated for each specimen using equation (2).

$$\text{Normalized load} = \frac{\text{Anchorage pullout load}}{(\text{thickness of kerf leg under load})^2} \tag{2}$$

The normalized load is not a load, strictly speaking, as it has units equivalent to stress. However, because the geometry of the support point and bracket under test has not been fully considered, this value should not be used for comparison purposes except where test conditions are essentially identical. It was determined in order to permit comparison of the ultimate pullout loads between different anchor configurations irrespective of variation in the thickness of the kerf leg under load. Comparisons between the pairs of values given in the tables throughout the following section show that variation in kerf leg thickness results in little significant difference between normalized loads for the same anchor and specimen configuration.

The results are presented in tables throughout the following section. Unless otherwise indicated, throughout this paper the mean pullout load at failure and standard deviation for each set of 5 specimens have been given, along with a mean value and standard deviation for normalized load for each set of 5 specimens. The results are presented in the format {mean ± standard deviation}. Where two sets of values are given in a single cell of a table, this denotes that two sets of tests for this condition were completed, typically with differing thicknesses of kerf leg.

Observations – Deflection of the anchor occurred to some extent during testing of most specimens. With the extruded aluminum kerf anchor, this meant that the load was ultimately applied at the outer end of the kerf leg (Figure 3a). When a neoprene bearing pad was inserted, this theoretically provided a more distributed load over the outer half of the kerf leg (Figure 3b). When the extruded aluminum kerf anchor with bulb was used, the load was applied to a point approximately midway along the kerf leg (Figure 3c). In some cases, the deflection of the anchor was so substantial that some bearing at the outer end of the kerf leg also occurred, although this was not frequent.

The stainless steel dowel anchor deflected in every test, such that the load was applied to the outer end of the kerf or drilled hole (Figure 3d).

Specimens with kerf anchor details failed instantaneously, as did specimens with dowels in kerf slots. Those specimens with dowels in drilled holes failed progressively, with a sequence of small spalls from the rear face of the specimen. The peak load was sometimes achieved at the first failure, but sometimes immediately prior to the second or third spall. There was substantial deflection of the stainless steel dowel associated with these progressive failures.

Discussion

The data set generated by carrying out nearly 400 anchorage pullout tests on two types of granite is substantial, and this paper does not attempt to present all of the findings. Instead it concentrates on the issues of greatest importance to designers of stone anchorages.

Comparison Between Dry and Wet

Seven sets of Mondariz specimens were tested in both dry and soaked conditions, using a range of anchor configurations. The results are given in Table 2 and Figure 6. These results show little significant difference between dry and soaked ultimate pullout loads for this material.

Table 2 — *Comparison between dry and soaked specimens, Mondariz granite*

Anchor configuration	Dry specimens		Soaked specimens	
	Failure load (N)	Normalized load	Failure load (N)	Normalized load
continuous kerf,	3173 ± 343	13.1 ± 1.4	2803 ± 371	12.2 ± 1.5
50 mm bracket	1395 ± 267	13.5 ± 2.2	1418 ± 163	13.0 ± 1.6
continuous kerf,	3591 ± 255	16.6 ± 1.4	3500 ± 193	17.1 ± 0.7
100 mm bracket	1929 ± 173	17.5 ± 1.8	2369 ± 193	18.4 ± 1.4
continuous kerf,	5176 ± 956	26.8 ± 2.5	4667 ± 840	24.6 ± 1.6
300 mm bracket	2995 ± 643	29.1 ± 4.7	2670 ± 222	25.0 ± 1.8
200 mm stop-end kerf,	2785 ± 594	12.2 ± 1.2	2647 ± 510	12.6 ± 1.9
50 mm bracket	1237 ± 45	13.1 ± 0.8	1390 ± 286	13.0 ± 1.7
200 mm stop-end kerf,	4594 ± 454	18.6 ± 0.6	4382 ± 482	18.1 ± 1.5
100 mm bracket	1781 ± 200	18.8 ± 1.9	1677 ± 249	17.6 ± 2.5
100 mm stop-end kerf,	2881 ± 651	13.9 ± 1.5	2704 ± 602	13.3 ± 1.3
50 mm bracket	1738 ± 110	15.5 ± 1.0	1650 ± 182	14.6 ± 1.7
drilled hole,	2737 ± 119	11.8 ± 0.6	2815 ± 371	11.2 ± 0.9
6 mm diam. pin	1910 ± 199	15.3 ± 1.1	2067 ± 255	18.3 ± 3.0

Based on these results, the majority of tests were performed with the specimens in the soaked condition, as per the recommendations of ASTM C1354, in order to maximise the variations of anchor configuration which could be tested.

Comparison Between Types of Granite

Results for both types of granite are presented for a range of anchor configurations in Tables 5, 6 and 7 and Figure 7. These show that there is a substantial difference in ultimate pullout load between the Mondariz and Impala Black granites.
The normalized pullout loads for a given anchor configuration in the Impala Black are in the range of 40-70% greater than the normalized pullout loads for the Mondariz.

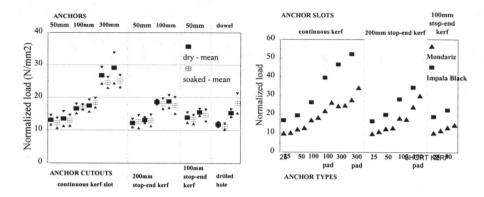

Figure 6 – *Anchorage pullout loads
dry vs soaked*

Figure 7 – *Anchorage pullout loads
granite types*

This proportional difference compares favorably to the 40% proportional difference in modulus of rupture between the two materials. It is therefore reasonable to conclude that the bending strength of the granite is a major determining factor in the pullout load capacity of an anchorage in the edge of a granite panel. Subject to understanding the other factors acting, it therefore should be possible to develop a model to accurately predict the pullout strength of a given stone anchorage design.

Effect of Kerf Leg Thickness

The influence of the thickness of the kerf leg under load can be seen in all of the results given in this section. Significant differences between failure loads for two sets of tests using the same anchor configuration are typically not matched in the normalized loads for those sets of tests. This is highlighted in Table 3 and Figure 8.

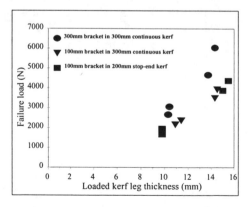

Figure 8 – *Anchorage pullout loads: influence of kerf leg thickness*

Table 3 — *Effect of loaded kerf leg thickness, Mondariz granite*

Anchor	Front kerf leg			Rear kerf leg		
	Failure load (N)	Thick (mm)	Normalized load	Failure load (N)	Thick (mm)	Normalized load
300 mm bracket, continuous kerf	2670 ± 222	10.3	25.0 ± 1.8	4667 ± 840	13.7	24.6 ± 1.6
300 mm bracket, continuous kerf, bearing pad	3066 ± 268	10.4	28.3 ± 2.7	6046 ± 587	14.3	29.6 ± 3.0
100 mm bracket, continuous kerf	2369 ± 193	11.4	18.4 ± 1.4	3500 ± 193	14.3	17.1 ± 0.7
100 mm bracket, 200 mm stop end kerf	1677 ± 249	9.8	17.6 ± 2.5	4382 ± 488	15.5	18.1 ± 1.5
100 mm bracket, continuous kerf, bearing pad	2166 ± 193	10.9	18.4 ± 1.5	3938 ± 406	14.5	18.6 ± 0.8
100 mm bracket, 200 mm stop end kerf, bearing pad	1959 ± 268	9.8	20.6 ± 3.1	3885 ± 518	15.0	17.2 ± 1.1

These results highlight the critical importance of recording the kerf leg thickness and reporting this value in conjunction with the failure load. While ASTM C1354 requires the reporting of this information, it is not clearly specified, and thus many test labs fail to include this information on reports. Indeed, perhaps consideration should be given to requiring that the failure load be normalized against the nominal thickness for the kerf leg under test.

The results obtained indicate that the pullout load of a kerf anchor is roughly proportional to the square of the loaded kerf leg thickness.

For a typical kerf slot detail in a granite panel for curtain walling, where:
a)   the 30 mm thick granite panels have a thickness tolerance of ± 2 mm;
b)   the kerf slot is nominally located in the center of the panel section;
c)   the kerf slot position is fixed from the front face of the panel to a tolerance of ± 0.5 mm;
d)   the kerf slot width has a tolerance of ± 0.5 mm;
then the rear kerf leg thickness could vary from 9 mm to 15 mm in thickness, and still conform to specified tolerances (Figure 9). This would mean that there could be variation of up to +56% or –44% in the failure load for test specimens with the rear kerf leg varying from the nominal design dimension. That is, designs based on a nominal 12 mm thickness of the rear kerf leg could have panels with pullout capacities equivalent to 60% of the nominal design capacity, even if that nominal design load was verified by testing. It is unlikely that many designers currently take this into account when designing kerf anchors for granite panels, other than through the safety factor.

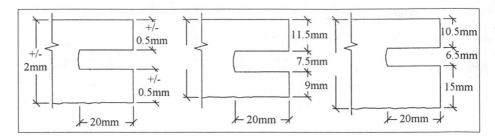

Figure 9 – *Variations in rear kerf leg thickness due to fabrication tolerances*

Comparison Between Kerf Anchor Bracket Types

Table 4 and Figure 10 contain results for several sets of specimens tested with different configurations of kerf anchors, as listed below:

a)   extruded aluminum kerf bracket with flat bearing against kerf leg, but under load, the bracket deflected, resulting in point loading on the end of the kerf leg cantilever

b)   kerf bracket as in (a) but with neoprene bearing pad along full depth of engagement of kerf bracket in kerf slot

c)   extruded aluminum kerf bracket with bulb bearing against midpoint of kerf leg

d)   kerf bracket as in (c) but with neoprene bearing pad along full depth of engagement of kerf bracket in kerf slot

Table 4 — *Comparison between kerf anchor types, Mondariz granite*

Anchor	Continuous kerf specimens		Long kerf specimens	
	Failure load (N)	Normalized load	Failure load (N)	Normalized load
100 mm bracket with flat bearing	3500 ± 193	17.1 ± 0.7	4382 ± 488	18.1 ± 1.5
	2369 ± 193	18.4 ± 1.4	1677 ± 249	17.6 ± 2.5
100 mm bracket with bearing pad	3938 ± 406	18.6 ± 0.8	3885 ± 518	17.2 ± 1.1
	2166 ± 193	18.4 ± 1.5	1781 ± 268	20.6 ± 3.1
100 mm bracket with bulb kerf	4306 ± 926	21.9 ± 2.1	6110 ± 233	24.1 ± 0.9
	2880 ± 291	26.4 ± 3.4	2842 ± 166	30.1 ± 2.6
100 mm bracket with bulb kerf & bearing pad	3384 ± 500	17.2 ± 1.5	n.d.	n.d.
	2001 ± 172	19.0 ± 1.7		

These results confirm the expectation that kerf anchors which have a bulb to permit transmission of the load closer to the base of the kerf leg give a higher pullout load than kerf anchors with flat bearing which results in transmission of the load at the end of the kerf leg. This finding is consistent with engineering theory. Checking of the results obtained in these tests against the predicted values based on the position of the respective anchor types showed that the magnitude of the difference is less than is predicted by that theory. This may be due to deflection of the kerf anchors with a bulb, with resultant additional load contribution at the end of the kerf leg.

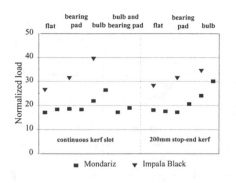

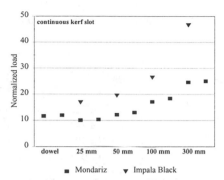

Figure 10 – *Anchorage pullout loads*
anchor type and engagement
(100 mm long)

Figure 11 – *Anchorage pullout loads*
continuous kerf slot
(varying bracket lengths)

Results for specimens tested with a neoprene bearing pad were similar irrespective of the kerf anchor type (with or without bulb). There is only a slight increase in pullout load for specimens tested with a neoprene bearing pad compared to flat kerf specimens. Furthermore, where a bulbed kerf was also tested with a neoprene bearing pad, the results were similar to specimens tested with a flat kerf bracket. These results suggest that where kerf slots are filled with elastomeric sealant, as has been common in curtain wall construction, the form of the kerf bracket is not critical, as the load is unlikely to be transmitted by the bulb (if present) on the end of the kerf bracket.

This means that sealant filled kerfs designed using bulbed kerf brackets and with calculations based on load transfer towards the base of the kerf leg may be under-designed.

Another issue of concern arising from these results is the provision of information on the position of the kerf anchor in the kerf slot during testing. ASTM C1354 requires that this information be reported, but it is not clearly specified, and thus many test labs fail to include this information on reports.

Comparison Between Different Bracket Lengths in Continuous Kerf

Five different lengths of bracket were tested in a continuous kerf slot. The results for these bracket lengths are given in Table 5 and Figure 11 for both types of granite.

These results show a significant difference in ultimate pullout load depending on the length of the bracket engaged in the continuous kerf slot. As would be expected, there is an increase in pullout load with increasing length. However, the differences between the 6 mm dowel, 25 mm bracket and 50 mm bracket are not substantial.

Similar patterns of results were obtained for varying anchor bracket lengths in the 200 mm and 100 mm stop-end kerfs.

Table 5 — *Comparison between different bracket lengths in continuous kerf slot*

Anchor	Mondariz granite		Impala Black granite	
	Failure load (N)	Normalized load	Failure load (N)	Normalized load
300 mm bracket	4667 ± 840 2670 ± 222	24.6 ± 1.6 25.0 ± 1.8	4086 ± 492	46.6 ± 3.5
100 mm bracket	3500 ± 193 2369 ± 193	17.1 ± 0.7 18.4 ± 1.4	2860 ± 491	26.4 ± 2.5
50 mm bracket	2803 ± 371 1418 ± 163	12.2 ± 1.5 13.0 ± 1.6	1965 ± 109	19.5 ± 0.9
25 mm bracket	1916 ± 228 1105 ± 51	10.1 ± 0.9 10.4 ± 0.4	1864 ± 161	16.9 ± 0.7
6 mm dowel	2652 ± 195 1359 ± 101	11.7 ± 0.5 12.0 ± 0.6	n.d.	n.d.

Comparison Between Different Lengths of Kerf Slot

Three different lengths of kerf slot, plus a drilled hole, were tested during this project. The pullout load capacities for a given type of bracket in each type of kerf slot are compared in Tables 6 and 7 and Figures 12 and 13.

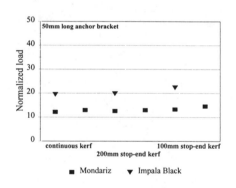

Figure 12 – *Anchorage pullout loads varying cutout length (50mm bracket length)*

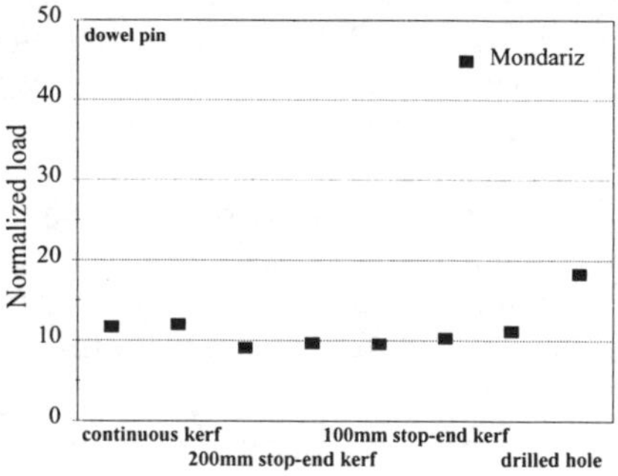

Figure 13 – *Anchorage pullout loads varying cutout length (dowel pin)*

These results show that there is little difference in ultimate pullout load for a given type of anchor bracket, irrespective of the type of kerf slot.

There is a slight trend of increasing ultimate pullout load as the length of the kerf slot approaches the length of the anchor bracket. However, this is slight, and may simply be an artifact of the tests carried out. It was noticeable, though, that for the stop-end kerfs, as the length of the anchor bracket approached half of the total length of the slot, then the failure face would extend to follow the shape of the kerf slot itself. This indicates that the optimum length of stop-end kerf may be one with a straight bottom edge just longer than the length of the bracket, or in more practical terms, the length of the bracket plus bracket installation tolerances.

Table 6 — *Comparison between different lengths of kerf slot - 50 mm bracket*

Kerf type	Mondariz granite		Impala Black granite	
	Failure load (N)	Normalized load	Failure load (N)	Normalized load
Continuous kerf	2803 ± 371 1418 ± 163	12.2 ± 1.5 13.0 ± 1.6	1965 ± 109	19.5 ± 0.9
200 mm stop-end kerf	2647 ± 510 1390 ± 286	12.6 ± 1.9 13.0 ± 1.7	2279 ± 164	19.9 ± 1.3
100 mm stop-end kerf	2803 ± 371 1418 ± 163	13.3 ± 1.3 14.6 ± 1.7	2524 ± 458	22.4 ± 2.3

Table 7 — *Comparison between different lengths of kerf slot - 6 mm diameter dowel*

Kerf type	Mondariz granite		Impala Black granite	
	Failure load (N)	Normalized load	Failure load (N)	Normalized load
Continuous kerf	2652 ± 195 1359 ± 101	11.7 ± 0.5 12.0 ± 0.6	n.d.	n.d.
200 mm stop-end kerf	1938 ± 103 929 ± 77	9.1 ± 0.7 9.7 ± 0.2	n.d.	n.d.
100 mm stop-end kerf	1821 ± 210 1184 ± 100	9.6 ± 0.5 10.3 ± 0.5	n.d.	n.d.
Drilled hole	2815 ± 371 2067 ± 255	11.2 ± 0.9 18.3 ± 3.0	2869 ± 205 2198 ± 186	18.9 ± 1.5 28.0 ± 2.9

Conclusions

Testing of a variety of kerf bracket configurations and a range of cutout details on two types of granites has provided data showing that:

a) the thickness of the loaded kerf leg is critical to analysis of pullout load results obtained from ASTM C1354 anchorage testing;

b) there is a relationship between pullout load results and the bending strength properties of the granites tested;

c) increased distance of the point of contact of the kerf anchor from the base of the kerf slot results in a decrease in the magnitude of pullout load results;

d) bulbed kerfs embedded in sealant probably have similar pullout load capacity to flat kerf anchors embedded in sealant;

e) there is an increase in pullout load capacity with increase in length of kerf brackets inserted into a continuous kerf slot;

f) the relationship between length of kerf bracket in a continuous kerf slot and the pullout load capacity is not directly linear; and

g)   there is surprisingly little variation in pullout load capacity for a given anchor type inserted into different lengths of kerf slot.

Acknowledgments

The authors acknowledge the significant assistance provided by Italian stone fabricators Campolonghi Srl and Lapidei Srl in fabricating the test specimens used in the research leading to this paper.

References

[1]   Chin, I. R., Stecich, J. P. and Erlin, B., "Design of Thin Stone Veneers on Buildings," *Proceedings of the Third North American Masonry Conference*, The Masonry Society, June 1985. Also published in *Dimensional Stone*, Sept./Oct. 1986, pp.45-57.

[2]   Stecich, J. P., Chin, I. R. and Heidbrink, F. D., "Testing for Thin Stone Veneers on Buildings," *Exterior Claddings on High Rise Buildings*, Chicago Committee on High Rise Buildings, Fall Symposium, 1989. Also published in 2 parts in *Dimensional Stone Magazine*, Nov. 1992, pp.28-35,51 and Feb. 1993, pp.18-27.

[3]   McCabe, J. T., Jr., "Basic Stone Anchor Design," *Dimensional Stone*, Nov. 1988, pp.22-26.

[4]   Clift, C. D. and Bayer, J. A., "Stone Safety Factors: Much Ado About Nothing?," *Dimensional Stone*, Jan./Feb. 1989, pp.38-40.

[5]   Lewis, M. D., "Stone Anchorage Design: An Installer's Perspective," *Dimensional Stone Magazine*, Apr. 1992, pp.24-29,59.

[6]   Lewis, M. D., "Stone Anchorage Design: Fundamental Principles," *Dimensional Stone Magazine*, July 1992, pp.24-26.

[7]   Lewis, M. D., Modern Stone Cladding - Design and Installation of Exterior Dimension Stone Systems. *ASTM Manual 21*, American Society for Testing and Materials, Philadelphia, 1995.

Investigation and Restoration of Existing Stone Cladding Systems

Kurt R. Hoigard[1] and George R. Mulholland[1]

Repair Methods for Stone Facades

Reference: Hoigard, K. R. and Mulholland, G. R., **"Repair Methods for Stone Facades,"** *Dimension Stone Cladding: Design, Construction, Evaluation, and Repair, ASTM STP 1394*, K. R. Hoigard, Ed., American Society for Testing and Materials, West Conshohocken, PA, 2000.

Abstract: The dimension stone industry has made significant progress in the last 40 years toward improving the quality and longevity of stone cladding. Material standards have been updated, new tests have been developed, design guides have been published, and a myriad of technical papers have been written discussing everything from connection design to full panel mock-up testing. Despite all of this new information, buildings still get built with, or develop, dimension stone cladding "problems". This paper discusses practical methods for addressing some of the more common repair issues.

The repair methods presented were developed by the authors for application on a variety of consulting projects, primarily involving marble and granite. Repair methods are discussed for addressing minor chips, spalls, partial missing pieces, cracks, and defective or ineffective anchorages. Guiding concepts behind the repairs are presented, and photographs of actual installations are used for demonstrative purposes.

Keywords: dimension stone, anchor, spall, crack, repair, cladding

Introduction

Despite the advances made over the last 40 years in the design, fabrication, and installation of thin dimension stone cladding systems, the authors routinely encounter buildings in need of stone repairs. Whether due to long-term deterioration, accidental damage, or fabrication and installation defects, most repair projects have certain common elements, including the types of distress requiring repair and a desire on the part of at least one party (Owner, Contractor, or other) to avoid complete stone replacement. This paper discusses practical methods developed by the authors for addressing some of the more common repair issues encountered. The repair methods presented were developed for application on a variety of projects, primarily involving marble and granite. Repair methods are discussed for addressing minor chips, spalls, partial missing pieces, cracks, and defective or ineffective anchorages.

---

[1]Principal and Senior Engineer, respectively, Raths, Raths & Johnson, Inc., 835 Midway Drive, Willowbrook, IL, 60521.

Repair Materials

Before discussing the specifics of various repair types a brief discussion of common repair materials is in order. As with conventional design, appearance, strength, durability, and ease of use are the driving factors in the selection of repair materials. Achieving the right balance between these factors can be a challenge since in some ways they can be mutually exclusive. The material with the best initial appearance may not be durable; an easy-to-install material may be aesthetically unacceptable.

The repair of marble and granite facade panels primarily involves the use of matching stone, stainless steel anchor hardware, and epoxy adhesives and fillers. Colored portland cement-based mortars of various types are often encountered in limestone and sandstone restoration, but are beyond the scope of this paper.

Matching Stone

The obvious use for replacement stone on a repair project is to provide replacement pieces. Matching stone can also be used to replace a portion of a broken stone panel, provide "plug" material for hiding anchor pin installations, or when crushed, act as a coloring aggregate in bonded patches. Sources for matching stone include the original quarrier (if still operating), salvage yards, and other non-restorable pieces from the subject building. Occasionally, matching stone will not be available. In these cases a close match may be available from another producer. The color plates provided by the Marble Institute of America [1] are a good source for identifying materials with similar appearances.

Anchor Hardware

Supplemental anchor installations are common elements in stone cladding repair projects and are frequently encountered in conjunction with partial or complete stone replacement, and crack and spall repairs. In all cases, the authors recommend the use of stainless steel for its corrosion-resistant properties and relatively high nobility against cathodic corrosion from contact with dissimilar metals.

Stainless steel anchor hardware usually takes the form of bent bars or rods (Figure 1). Many other configurations are available from specialty producers, including made-to-order

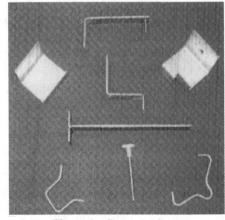

Figure 1 - *Stone Anchors*

pieces in any size or shape. Increases in material lead time should be assumed when custom-fabricated parts are specified in lieu of standard shapes.

Epoxy Adhesives and Fillers

The authors have found carefully selected epoxy-based materials well suited for stone cladding repair work. Uses include adhesive installation of supplemental anchors, structural bonding of stone cracks and chips, as a cosmetic filler for chip and spall repairs and to "hide" supplemental anchor installation holes. Epoxies are extremely durable two-component hardening polymer systems. Most have mixing ratios of one part resin to one or one-half part hardener. Available viscosities range from very low (water-like) to high (paste-like). Epoxies may be filled or unfilled, indicating the presence or absence of an inert filler to reduce cost and modify material properties. In filled products the filler is frequently rock flour, which offers the two-fold benefit of reducing cost and improving the thermal compatibility of the material with stone and concrete by reducing the thermal coefficient of expansion.

A common misconception is to assume that any two-part hardening polymer is an epoxy. Polyester resins, for example, are two-component hardening polymer systems requiring the mixing of only a few drops of hardener to cure a relatively large amount of resin. Poor thermal compatibility with stone, combined with a high level of brittleness, makes polyester resins poorly suited for exterior stone repairs. This problem is compounded by the fact that several companies market polyester-based products for stone use. The authors have identified the use of polyester resin as the root cause of several expensive facade failures.

Desirable epoxy properties vary with each application. In general, fast initial set is important for supplemental anchor installations and chip repairs, whereas a slower set can prove beneficial for crack repair. While base color has almost no importance for anchor installations, visible work such as chip, spall, and crack repairs require materials with lighter base colors that can be tinted to match the stone. High viscosity "knife grade" epoxies work well for most vertical or overhead applications except small crack repairs, where low viscosity is needed for the epoxy to penetrate sufficiently. Similarly, materials incorporating rock flour filler are best for most work except small crack repairs, where the requirement for low viscosity precludes their use.

Two of the most important epoxy properties are thermal coefficient of expansion and deformation temperature. As with most polymers, the structural properties of epoxies change with temperature, typically expanding, losing strength, and becoming softer as the temperature increases. Repairs to exterior cladding stones must, therefore, take into account the thermal coefficient of expansion for the stone being repaired and the ambient temperature range for the building locale, as well as surface temperature increases from solar gain, and compare them to performance data provided by the epoxy manufacturer. As a guide, the authors have measured south-facing surface temperatures as high as 140°F (60°C) on light colored stones, and 180°F (82°C) on dark stones. Concrete and masonry back-up structures, on the other hand, rarely exceed 120°F (49°C).

Chips

Chips are small pieces of stone broken off from the main piece of cladding material. Typically less than 1 in^2 (6.5 cm^2) in surface area, they frequently occur around the perimeter of cladding pieces as a result of handling or impact damage. In practice, the repair of a chip is essentially the filling of the divot left by the removal of the chip. Three choices are available for the filler: the original chip, sealant, or an epoxy filler.

In some cases the actual stone chip may be available, particularly if the damage was due to post-construction impact, in which case the chip may still be adhered to the cladding panel perimeter sealant. Recovered chips may be re-attached to the parent stone panel by adhesive bonding. For this purpose the authors recommend using a knife grade epoxy tinted to match the stone. When properly executed this type of repair can be virtually undetectable.

Edge chips located above the third floor can frequently be addressed simply by filling with the same material used to fill the joints between adjacent cladding panels (typically elastomeric sealant). In this case the sealant joint simply becomes slightly wider locally (Figure 2). While readily visible at close range, this type of repair is usually difficult to identify from any significant distance.

Figure 2 - *Chip filled with sealant*

When the original stone chip is unavailable, and sealant filling is unacceptable for aesthetic reasons, excellent chip repairs can be accomplished by filling with epoxy tinted and finished to match the stone. For marble, veining can be reproduced by using multiple tints. The visual texture of granite can be reproduced by tinting the epoxy to match the base stone color and adding crushed stone pieces of the size and color to match the secondary minerals. Abrasive tools of various types can reproduce finishes ranging from thermal (use a rough cut diamond grinder) to high polish (use progressively finer diamond matrix rubber polishing pads).

Supplemental Anchors

The authors have found a variety of conditions requiring the installation of anchors to supplement those already present on stone cladding panels. Some of the more common of these include: honeycombed concrete at stone anchor locations on precast concrete wall panels, deteriorated anchors or back-up materials, spalls at anchor locations, and stone cracks located such that the resulting stone pieces are not independently stable under design loads.

While stainless steel anchor hardware is available in a wide variety of shapes and configurations, including smooth and threaded rods, bent bars, flat bars (for battens), welded tees, and headed anchors, the authors find threaded rods with or without disk-shaped heads to be the most versatile for supplemental anchor installations. Both types of installation require drilling holes through the face of the stone panel. Regardless of stone type, the authors strongly recommend using only wet cut diamond coring equipment to drill the required holes in order to avoid damaging the surrounding stone and weakening the anchor installation. Percussion drills should never be used.

The driving factors governing the choice between straight threaded rods and headed anchors are stone shear strength and panel thickness. Thin

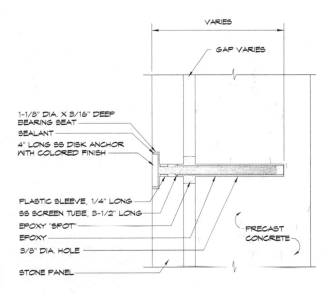

Figure 3 - *Headed supplemental anchor*

panels (less than 1 inch or 2.5 cm thick) and weak stones frequently require the use of a headed anchor in order to generate sufficient wind pull-off strength without failing the stone in a punching shear mode. The aesthetics of headed supplemental anchor installations can be improved by milling a recessed seat into the stone, thereby allowing the anchor head to be installed flush with the surrounding stone (Figure 3). In this type of installation the effective stone thickness lost to the milled seat can be countered by a slight increase in head diameter.

In addition to wind suction, supplemental anchors may also need to resist gravity and wind pressure loads. Each installation needs to be evaluated on a case-by-case basis. Stone clad precast panels are generally constructed with the stone separated from the concrete back-up by no more than a thin sheet of plastic and do not require supplemental anchors to provide wind pressure restraint. Hand-set stone on masonry back-up usually incorporates a cavity directly behind this stone, and therefore requires supplemental anchors to provide restraint for both wind suction and wind pressure. The authors have found that small diameter threaded rods inserted into epoxy-filled screen tubes can meet this requirement by using the threaded rod to resist wind suction loads and the hardened epoxy "post" formed by the screen tube to resist wind pressure loads (Figure 4). Depending on the component geometry, these concepts can also be used on unitized curtain wall systems.

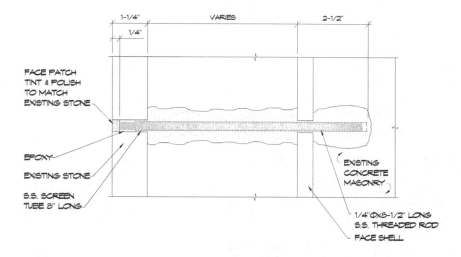

Figure 4 - *Concealed supplemental anchor*

Supplemental anchors installed through face-drilled holes can be effectively "hidden" by careful attention to surface repairs at the drilled hole (assuming a headed anchor is not used). By leaving the anchor rod recessed approximately ¼ inch (0.6 cm) from the surface, surface restoration can be accomplished by the means previously discussed for chip repairs. Stone plugs cut from similar material can be bonded in place with tinted epoxy, or a matrix of tinted epoxy and crushed stone can be used as a filler and finished to match the surrounding stone (Figure 5).

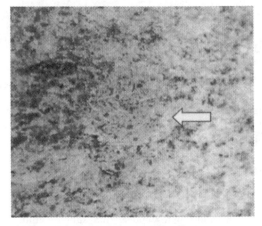

Figure 5 - *Epoxy filler with crushed stone conceals a supplemental anchor in thermally finished granite (life size as shown)*

Spalls

For the purposes of this paper, spalls are pieces of stone, larger than chips, dislodged from the finished surface of a stone panel. This type of damage is most frequently found at anchor locations and can result in loose pieces of significant size requiring re-attachment to the parent stone. A good way to repair spalls is to bond the dislodged piece to the parent stone with knife grade epoxy adhesive. Depending on the size of the spall, pins or stitching dogs (U-shaped pins) should be considered in order to provide mechanical attachment to the parent stone and act as a back-up to the epoxy adhesive bond.

Spalls associated with existing anchor locations need to be assessed for the cause of the spall. Corrosion of the anchor, undersized anchors, expansive anchor grout [2], and unexpected loadings such as swing stage impacts can all cause spalls (Figure 6). The authors recommend considering all spall repairs as cosmetic only and not reliable for transferring wind or gravity loads. Supplemental anchors designed to provide the restraint lost by the spalled anchor should be installed near all anchor-related spalls.

Figure 6 - *Stone kerf spalls due to expansive anchor grout*

Cracks

The purpose of stone panel crack repair is three-fold: restore structural integrity to the damaged piece, keep water out of the building cavity, and improve the appearance of the damaged stone. Although the authors have been able to achieve crack repairs with flexural strengths equal to those of the original undamaged panels, stability assessment of the individual stone pieces associated with the crack is highly recommended. The attachment of individual pieces to the building should be sufficient to withstand code-prescribed loads with adequate factors of safety. If the pieces to be repaired are not independently stable, supplemental anchorages should be installed prior to executing crack repairs (Figure 7).

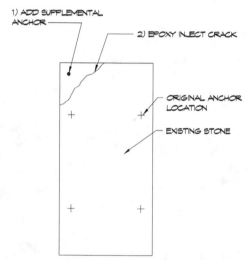

Figure 7 - *Unstable stone piece, add supplemental anchor to stabilize stone piece before crack injection procedures begin*

Cracks can appear anywhere within a stone panel, but may need to be addressed in differing manners dependent upon location. Most stone cracks are small, having widths from 0.002 to 0.008 inches (0.05 to 0.20 mm). However, cracks wider than 0.015 inches (0.38 mm) may be encountered. The repair material type and the specific repair process needed are dependent upon the size of the crack, the color of the stone, the location of the stone panel on the building, the location of the crack within the stone panel, and the type of back-up structure present.

Although matching the repair material's color to the existing stone is sometimes difficult, the authors feel it is good practice to match colors as closely as possible. In a practical sense, the aesthetics of stone crack repairs located above the third floor are less critical than those near street level.

The authors have used two different approaches to repair stone cracks: epoxy injection, and rout and fill. Epoxy injection is recommended for use on small, non-contaminated stone cracks. Rout and fill repairs are recommended when epoxy injection cannot be used. Such cases include stones with colors that cannot be readily matched with low viscosity epoxies, large cracks, and cracks contaminated with materials that would inhibit proper bonding of an injected epoxy. Since the color of epoxies which can be pumped is typically limited to dark tones, the application of epoxy injection is typically used on stones which are darker in color.

Epoxy Injection

The epoxies used for crack injection are typically low in viscosity and require a means of limiting the loss of epoxy out the back side of the panel being repaired. In general, this means selecting the spacing of injection ports and the viscosity of the injected epoxy to promote lateral epoxy migration between injection ports before significant spillage out the back side of the crack occurs. Laboratory testing by the authors indicates port spacing of one to two times the stone thickness usually works well.

The epoxy injection crack repair procedure begins by placing thin strips of masking tape perpendicular to the crack at a center-to-center spacing of one to two times the stone thickness along the length of the crack. A surface dam is created by spreading a thermoplastic resin over the length of the crack. Before the surface dam material hardens, the masking tape is removed, providing injection port locations along the length of the crack (Figure 8). After the surface dam material has hardened, the crack is then injected with a low viscosity epoxy under pressure, starting from one end of the crack and working toward the other end. The epoxy should be pumped at one port location until the epoxy is visible at the next port. Close monitoring of the volume of the injected material helps detect excessive back side spillage. Once the crack is full and the epoxy has hardened, the surface dam material can be scraped, peeled, or chipped off the stone face (Figure 9). Typically, buffing the epoxy-filled crack is not required.

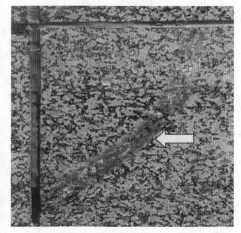 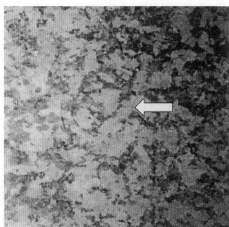

Figure 8 - *Thermoplastic resin with epoxy injection ports*

Figure 9 - *Completed epoxy injection crack repair*

Rout and Fill

The rout and fill crack repair method (Figure 10) incorporates the use of a diamond grinder and a trowel grade epoxy tinted to match the surrounding stone. Since the original crack within the stone is not always perpendicular to the stone surface, care must be taken to ensure the grinder bit/blade follows the crack through the depth of the stone (Figure 11). The crack is routed to a depth of approximately 75 percent of the stone thickness and the routed joint is cleaned. Masking tape is placed over the entire length and trimmed to the edges of the routed crack, exposing the area to be filled while leaving a protective mask on the stone surface. Duct tape is then placed over the

Figure 10 - *Rout and fill crack repair*

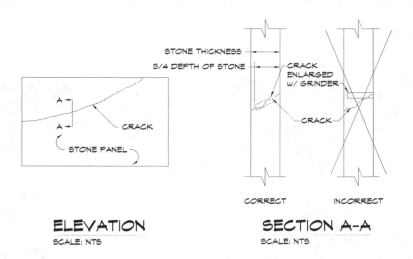

ELEVATION
SCALE: NTS

SECTION A-A
SCALE: NTS

Figure 11 - *Rout and fill crack repair, grinding procedures*

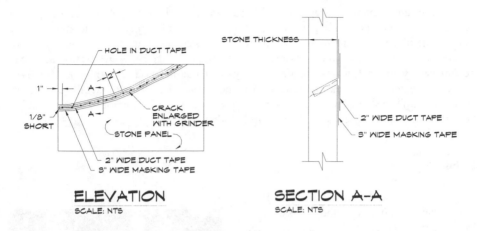

Figure 12 - *Rout and fill crack repair, "injection" procedures*

masking tape and punctured with an awl at a 2 inch (5.1 cm) spacing along the length to create "ports" (Figure 12). Trowel grade epoxy tinted to match the color of the stone is placed in empty caulk tubes and "injected", using a standard caulk gun, through the holes in the duct tape to fill the routed area. The process is carried out from one end of the crack toward the other, with the epoxy injected through one port until it is observed at the next port. The active injection port is then sealed with tape and injection starts again at the next port. Once the entire crack is filled, the duct tape should be removed and the epoxy troweled flush with the masking tape, which should be removed after epoxy has set, but not cured. After full cure is achieved the exposed epoxy filler can be finished to match the surrounding stone.

Partial Missing Pieces

In some cases the authors have encountered stone panel cracks running outside of the anchor locations, resulting in loss of the detached piece before repairs could be made. Two options are available for repair under these circumstances: replace the entire piece, or replace the missing portion. If partial replacement is desired, the fractured area of the existing piece of stone must be trimmed off, leaving a clean and true edge to which a repair piece can be mated. A repair piece to replace the missing portion (frequently called a dutchman) needs to be cut so that it will abut the freshly cut surface on the existing stone. As discussed previously, sources for the dutchman include other damaged stones on the same building, or replacement stone from various sources including the original quarry, a similar stone from another quarry, or stone salvaged from another building.

The same general concepts used for spall and crack repairs apply to the attachment of the dutchman to the building and completion of the joint between the dutchman and the main stone piece. Depending on size, the dutchman can be pinned to the main stone or independently anchored to the back-up structure. The interface between the two pieces can be finished by application of knife grade epoxy to the mating surfaces (similar to a spall) or it can be treated as a crack and repaired by epoxy injection or rout and fill techniques. Alternately, if the shape and size of the repair piece permit, a sealant joint can be installed between the two pieces, making them entirely independent.

Laboratory Testing

Since each building stone facade varies in material type and strength, stone anchorage, and material back-up, applicable repair types and the design capacities of those repairs will vary from project to project. Supplemental anchors and crack repairs offer the greatest number of permutations. As previously discussed, supplemental anchor capacity is affected by stone strength and thickness, the size of the cavity between the stone and the back-up structure, and the type of back-up material. Crack repairs are primarily affected by stone strength and aesthetic issues.

In order to address the variations discussed above, the authors recommend using laboratory testing to determine design capacities for proposed repairs. The flexural strength of the original stone is best determined through the methods prescribed by ASTM Standard Test Method for Flexural Strength of Dimension Stone (C 880). Similar testing on specimens cut from laboratory trial crack repairs can be used to assess the crack repair strength relative to the original stone strength (Figure 13).

Figure 13 - *ASTM C 880 test apparatus*

Supplemental anchorage strengths can be determined by performing tests similar to the ASTM Standard Test Method for Strength of Individual Stone Anchorages in Dimension Stone (C 1354). For these tests, field conditions of stone type, thickness, and back-up structure arrangement are simulated as closely as possible. The proposed supplemental anchorages are then installed according to the proposed repair specifications and procedures, and then tested to failure.

Mock-ups

Before commencing any significant stone repair project the authors strongly suggest performing sample installations (called mock-ups) of all of the various repairs required. The purpose of mock-ups is three fold: they provide the Design Professional an assurance that the Contractor has the correct materials and equipment to perform the installations according to the repair specifications; they give the Contractor a chance to become familiar with the repair materials and the specification requirements; and, when accepted, they provide aesthetic standards for the rest of the project. The authors prefer to have each workman that will be performing the repair work participate in the mock-up installations (Figures 14 and 15). The mock-ups should be installed at the project site on stones that are easily accessible, but out of sight from normal traffic (loading dock, rear elevation, roof, etc.), and should be maintained for the duration of the project.

The authors have attended numerous mock-up installations for each type of repair mentioned in this paper, with varied initial success. It is imperative the Design Professional insist the Contractor follow the specified procedures during the mock-up, since minor deviations in repair installation methods can have detrimental effects. For this reason, even experienced repair contractors should be required to go though the mock-up installation process.

Figure 14 - *Supplemental anchor mock-up, coring countersink hole for supplemental anchor head*

Figure 15 - *Supplemental anchor mock-up, drying of anchor hole*

Summary

The authors have found that stone repair in lieu of stone replacement is a viable option for many buildings exhibiting damage to stone facade components. Periodic review of in-place repairs over the last ten years has demonstrated successful performance of the repair methods described herein. Key items associated with successful stone repairs include:
1. Understanding the construction of the facade in question
2. Understanding the cause(s) of the damage being repaired
3. Paying careful attention to repair method and material selection
4. Testing of proposed repairs
5. Preparation of detailed repair plans and specifications
6. Execution of in-place repair mock-ups

Additionally, field inspection of the repair work during installation is recommended as a means of ensuring the repair methods and materials proven by the testing and mock-up processes are incorporated into the actual repair work.

References

[1]   *Dimension Stones of the World, Volumes 1 and 2*, Marble Institute of America, Farmington, Michigan, USA, 1990.

[2]   Hoigard, K.R., November 1999, Portland Cement and Gypsum - An Expansive Combination, *RRJ Insight*, Issue No. 13, PP 3-4, http://www.rrj.com.

Ian R. Chin[1]

Common Causes of Failures of Stone Claddings on Buildings

Reference: Chin, I.R., **"Common Causes of Failures of Stone Claddings on Buildings,"** *Dimension Stone Cladding: Design, Construction, Evaluation, and Repair, ASTM STP 1394*, K. R. Hoigard, Ed., American Society for Testing and Material, West Conshohocken, PA, 2000.

Abstract: Stone claddings on buildings are often chosen by building owners and designers for their natural aesthetic effect, their historically proven weathering durability, and their inherent low maintenance costs. However, these attributes are quickly eliminated when failure of the stone cladding occurs.

Investigations by the author, of distressed granite, limestone, and marble claddings on over 20 buildings have revealed that the common causes of failures in stone claddings on these buildings include the following:

1. Failure of the stone cladding connections in 45 percent of the buildings due to:
   a. Inadequate structural design of the connections.
   b. Corrosion of embedded metals.
   c. Failure to accommodate anticipated construction tolerances.
   d. Incompatible contacting materials.
2. Reduction in the strength of the stone due to exposure to the weather in 40 percent of the buildings.
3. Water leakage into the interior of 15 percent of the buildings due to:
   a. The absence of a flashing and weephole system or of an internal gutter and drainage system in the stone cladding.
   b. Ineffective flashing and weephole system or ineffective gutter and drainage system in the stone cladding.

Based upon the knowledge gained from the investigations, these common causes of failures in stone claddings are discussed, and recommendations to avoid failures in stone claddings on buildings are presented for consideration.

Keywords: failures, stone cladding, connections, corrosion, bowing, marble, granite, limestone

[1]Vice President, Principal and Chicago Unit Manager, Wiss, Janney, Elstner Associates, Inc. (WJE), 120 North LaSalle Street, Suite 2000, Chicago, Illinois 60602.

Introduction

The early use of stone for construction of structures utilized large blocks of stone and depended on the size of the stone blocks to provide structural support and stability. The pyramids (circa 2723 - 2563 B.C.) which are estimated to contain approximately 2000000 blocks of limestone, each weighing approximately 5600 lbs (2540 kg) [*1*]; and the Parthenon (447-432 B.C.) with its 4 ft (1.2 m) thick stone walls and 6 ft-2 in. (1.9 m) diameter, solid stone columns [*2*] are examples of the early use of stone in structures.

During the Mediaeval (9th to 15th century) and Renaissance periods (15th to 16th century) the early use of solid blocks of stone in walls gave way to stone-faced walls consisting of random stone rubble set in a mass of mortar between inner and outer faces of stone ashlar [*3*].

With the advent of skeleton frame construction in the late 1800s, the use of thick load bearing walls gave way to thinner non-load-bearing walls. The early non-load-bearing walls were often constructed with of 4-in. (102 mm) thick stone panels anchored to a clay masonry back-up wall.

The use of rational design principles for masonry in the 1960s combined with improved stone fabrication equipment and techniques resulted in the start of the use of 1-1/4 in. (30 mm) thick stone panels anchored to a back-up wall of masonry, concrete, or metal framing.

In the late 1980s, stone faced composite panels, consisting of 1/16 in. (1.5 mm) thick panels adhered to 3/8 in. (10 mm) honeycombed aluminum core began to be used on the exterior walls of buildings.

Based upon the above history of the use of stone in exterior walls on buildings, the thickness of stone in exterior walls on buildings has been reduced from approximately 4 ft (1.2 m) to 1/16 in. (1.5 mm) over the last 5000 years with the most dramatic decrease from approximately 4 in. (102 mm) to 1/16 in. (1.5 mm) occurring during the last 40 years.

The use of these thin stone veneers in exterior wall cladding systems on buildings has resulted in types of failures in the stone claddings that did not occur in the thicker stone walls. This condition occurred because the use of thin stone claddings places greater reliance on design and on the physical properties of the stone than before for their successful performance, and failures often occur whenever the design, the construction, and/or the stone material of the cladding system is inadequate.

Over 20 major buildings with failed stone claddings have been investigated by the author. These buildings vary in height up to 82 stories tall with the majority being around 40 stories tall. The stone cladding on these buildings consisted of granite (25 percent), limestone (40 percent), and marble (35 percent).

The investigation of the failed stone cladding on these buildings has revealed the causes of the failures to be as follows:

1.   Failure of stone cladding connections in 45 percent of the buildings.
2.   Reduction in strength of stone in 40 percent of the buildings.
3.   Water leakage in 15 percent of the buildings.

A discussion of these failures and recommendations for consideration on how to avoid these types of failures in stone claddings on buildings are presented in this paper.

Failure of Stone Cladding Connections

The variables of a stone cladding system that most impact the cost of the system and the cost of the overall building are its weight and thickness. Consequently, designers of stone cladding systems either devote most of their attention on the flexural behavior of the stone panels under wind load to establish the minimum thickness of the panels or specify an aesthetically acceptable stone of a certain thickness without any rational engineering design. This design approach is often misdirected because a large percentage of stone cladding failures occur at connections and flexural failure of stone cladding is rare; and because the design of the stone cladding connections where a large percentage of the failures occur becomes secondary to the establishment of the thickness of the cladding. Consequently, this design approach has contributed to the failure of the stone cladding connections on several buildings.

The common causes of the failure of stone cladding connections include:
- Inadequate structural design of connections.
- Corrosion of embedded metals.
- Failure to accommodate construction tolerances.
- Incompatible materials in connection system.

Connection Failure Due to Inadequate Structural Design

Inadequate structural design of stone cladding connections occur when improper structural design methods, improper design loads, inadequate safety factors, improper stone material properties, and/or improper details are utilized in the design. When these conditions are considered in the design, as discussed below, the failure of stone cladding connection will be minimized.

Structural Design - The design of stone cladding connections should be based upon ASTM C 1242 "Standard Guide for Design, Selection, and Installation of Exterior Dimension Stone Anchors and Anchoring Stations" [4]. A commonly used connection in stone cladding is a steel tab inserted into a kerf cut in the stone panel. Failure of this type of connection has occurred on several buildings. The strength of this connection is affected by the depth of the kerf, the thickness of the stone left after the kerf is cut, the radius of the inside corner of the kerf, the location where the load is applied to the kerf, and the strength of the stone. These conditions are often taken into account by designers except for the effect of the radius of the kerf which will have stress concentrations under wind loads which will significantly increase the stresses in the stone at the connections. Because the effort required to measure the radius of kerfs is considerable, it is quicker to confirm the design of kerfs in stone panels by testing in accordance with ASTM C 1354 "Standard Test Method for Strength of Individual Stone Anchorages in Dimension Stone" [5]. Load testing of untested, complex or multiple use stone cladding connections should also be performed to verify the design of the connection.

Design Loads - The design loads on the typical stone cladding are wind or seismic loads and the weight of the cladding. The design wind load and the design seismic load must comply with the requirements of the governing building code. The design wind load should include the higher than typical wind loads that occur at the corners and at the upper regions of the façade, as required by the building code. For buildings of unusual geometric shapes or for buildings on site locations that warrant special considerations, wind tunnel testing of the building should be performed to determine the wind loads and wind load distribution [6].

Safety Factors - Stone is a product of nature. The properties of stone are, therefore, not consistent and will vary from stone quarry to stone quarry and between different locations in the same quarry. Consequently, the recommended design safety factor of stone has traditionally been significantly higher than man-made construction materials such as steel, aluminum and concrete. The following industry recommended safety factors are recommended to be used to design stone cladding systems on buildings:

1. Structural Steel Elements: 1.33 to 2.5 per the American Institute of Steel Construction, Inc. [7]. Typically, 2.0 when used as gravity supports for limestone cladding, per the Indiana Limestone Institute of America, Inc. [8].
2. Aluminum elements: 1.20 to 1.95 per the Aluminum Association [9].
3. Granite Veneer: 3.0 for granite panels, 4.0 for all anchorage assemblies per the National Building Granite Quarries Association, Inc. [10].
4. Marble Veneer: 5.0 per the Marble Institute of America, Inc. [11].
5. Limestone Veneer: 8.0 per the Indiana Limestone Institute of America, Inc. [12].

Stone Material Properties - the final design of the connections for stone claddings on buildings should be based upon the physical properties of the actual stone material supplied for the specific project. Preliminary design of the stone cladding and its connections may utilize "historical" or "book" properties of the selected stone material published by stone trade associations or by the stone supplier. However, the properties of the actual stone material supplied for the project should be confirmed by testing. If the testing reveals that the properties of the stone supplied or is to be supplied for the project is less than the "historical" or "book" properties, upon which the preliminary design is based, then such stone material should be rejected or the design modified if possible.

Stone Connection Details - The selection of stone connection details should be based upon ASTM C1242 "Standard Dimension Stone Anchors and Anchoring Systems" (4). Stone cladding connection details that utilize a "blind anchorage technique" to blindly place an anchor that is attached to the cladding across the air space behind the cladding into grout pockets in concrete or masonry back-up walls are difficult to construct properly. Failure of blind anchorage stone cladding connections have occurred due to bond failure between the anchor and grout and to difficulties in constructing the blind anchorage connection. Stone cladding connections that utilize the blind anchorage technique have proven to be a very risky procedure. Connections that utilize positive mechanical anchors are more dependent than connections that depend on bond.

Connection Failure Due to Corrosion of Embedded Metals

When steel corrodes it expands up to about five to ten times its original size. When steel that is embedded in stone panels corrodes, forces resulting from the confinement of the corrosion by the stone will crack and fracture the stone. To prevent this type of failure from occurring in stone claddings on buildings, metal elements that are embedded in or are otherwise in direct contact with the stone should be of stainless steel. Other metals such as galvanized steel and aluminum may be used if they are protected from moisture, chlorides, and galvanic action.

Connection Failure Due to Failure to Accommodate Construction Tolerances

Improper connections that have caused failures of stone claddings have also occurred as a result of the failure of the contractor to construct the specified connection in accordance with the design requirements; and as a result of the failure to recognize and accommodate the differences in tolerance between the structural frame of the building and the stone cladding. The failure to design or construct stone claddings to accommodate structural frame and cladding tolerances has resulted in significant field shimming, cutting, and/or other modifications to the specified connection details that have caused the connection to fail.

Stone claddings are usually designed to be constructed in close proximity to the structural frame of the buildings. The stone cladding has its own fabrication and construction tolerances; and each structural system (concrete, steel, etc.) also has its own but different manufacture, fabrication, and construction tolerances. The combined tolerances of the stone cladding and of the structure of the building should be taken into account in the design to avoid tolerance related cladding problems.

A minimum horizontal adjustment capability of about 1 in. (25 mm) inward and outward for concrete framed buildings; and of about 2 in. (51 mm) inward and 1 in. (25 mm) outward for steel framed buildings is generally required in stone cladding connections to accommodate the cumulative in/out tolerances of the cladding and the structure [*13*]. Stone cladding connections should, therefore, be designed so that they can be adjusted within this general clearance requirement as well as about 3/8 in. (10 mm) upwards and downwards to accommodate general vertical elevation tolerances.

Connection Failure Due to Incompatible Materials

There are several frequently used construction materials that have a proven track record for durability whenever they are used by themselves. However, some of these materials are not compatible with each other and their use in a stone cladding connection system that places them in contact with each other can result in failure of the connection, as described below.

Stone and Epoxy - Epoxy is sometimes used to bond connection support liners to the back of stone panels, to join pieces of stone together in a prefabricated assembly, to set recessed metal inserts or reinforcement into stone panels, and to seal cracks in stone panels. Epoxy and stone are not thermally compatible. Laboratory tests performed by Wiss, Janney, Elstner Associates, Inc. (WJE) have revealed that the approximate coefficient of thermal expansion and contraction of an epoxy with less than 50 percent filler is 28×10^{-6} in. per in. per degree F (50×10^{-6} mm per mm per degree C). The published coefficient of thermal expansion of granite, limestone, and marble is as follows:

Granite: (6.3 to 9.0) 10^{-6} in. per in. per degree F [14](11 to 16) 10^{-6} mm per mm per degree C)

Limestone: (2.4 to 3.0) 10^{-6} in. per in. per degree F [15] (4 to 6) 10^{-6} mm per mm per degree C)

Marble: (3.69 to 12.3) 10^{-6} in. per in. per degree F [16] (7 to 22) 10^{-6} mm per mm per degree C)

Therefore, for a given change in temperature, the epoxy tested will expand or contract approximately four times that of granite and marble and approximately 10 times that of the limestone.

Forces resulting from the confinement of this differential movement between epoxy and stone has resulted in the following types of cladding distress:

a.   Debonding of connection support liners.
b.   Cracking of stone panels at connections.
c.   Debonding of joints between sections of stone.
d.   Cracking of stone panel away from connections.

The use of epoxy in stone cladding connections and joints should, therefore, be avoided. In addition, epoxy will discolor when it is exposed to the exterior and adversely affect the appearance of the stone cladding.

Stone and Gypsum Based Mortar - Gypsum based mortar are sometimes used in stone connection kerfs at the top of stone panels to eliminate pockets in the kerfs where water can accumulate and freeze. Gypsum based mortar is often selected for this purpose because it sets up quickly. However, unlike stone, when gypsum based mortars are exposed to moisture they expand and the forces that develop from confinement of this expansion by the stone can cause cracks and fractures to develop in the stone at the connection kerfs. The use of gypsum based mortar in stone cladding connection kerfs should be avoided.

Reduction in Strength of Stone

On five of the buildings investigated, the stone cladding was of 1-1/4 (30 mm) thick white marble panels and the panels failed because the marble had lost significant strength due to exposure to the weather after being on the building for about 10 to 16 years. On these buildings the distress in the panels included connection failures, cracking of the panels, and/or bowing of the panels.

One of these buildings is located in Chicago, Illinois, (latitude approximately 42°, north). For this building, laboratory accelerated weathering testing of samples of the marble panels that had been on the building for about 16 years and of original "attic stock" replacement marble panels stored in a heated room in the building revealed that the weaker panels on the building had lost approximately 75 percent of their original flexural strength after 16 years of exposure to the weather and that they will lose up to a total of 85 percent of their original flexural strength after another ten years on the building [17]. The laboratory testing also revealed that marble panels on the building with the largest bow also had the largest strength loss due to exposure to the weather.

The laboratory accelerated weathering testing of the marble panels included ASTM C880 flexural strength tests performed on specimens before, during, and after 300 cycles of exposure to temperature cycles of -10° F (23° C) to 170° F (76° C) at a rate of three cycles per day while being immersed tension face down in 1/4 in. (6 mm) deep solution of 0.01 molar sulfurous acid.

Evaluation of the test results indicate that approximately one hundred cycles of this laboratory accelerated test is equivalent to an exposure of about 12 years of actual weathering in Chicago, Illinois, or in other geographic locations with similar climatic conditions.

In-situ testing of approximately 50 panels on the building revealed that due to the strength loss of the marble panels, the pull-off strength of the marble panel connections had also been reduced to the extent that under design wind loads their safety factor was less than one.

The potential for the reduction in strength of marble as well as granite, limestone, and sandstone was reported by D. W. Kessler in 1919. According to Kessler, in 1875, the Ordinance Department of the United States Army placed 20 in. (508 mm) long granite, limestone, marble, and sandstone specimens in water at temperatures of 32° F (0° C), and 212° F (100° C), measured their length, and performed compression tests on the specimens. This testing revealed that after this heating and cooling in water, the marble specimens had a permanent increase in length and the compressive strength of all of the specimens was reduced as follows [18]:

- Granite: 16.3 percent
- Limestone: 41.2 percent
- Marble: 53.8 percent
- Sandstone: 33.1 percent

Although limestone and sandstone have the potential to lose strength in the range that marble does, distress conditions due to this strength loss have primarily occurred in modern marble claddings because the thickness of modern limestone and sandstone claddings on buildings are significantly thicker than the 1-1/4 in. (30 mm) thickness of modern marble claddings.

However, failure of thin stone panels that were reinforced with reinforcing bars set into grooves that were cut in the back of the panels has occurred. The panels were reinforced to increase their strength. They failed as a result of corrosion of the mild steel reinforcing bars that were used to reinforce 1-1/4 (30 mm) thick panels of a highly veined marble and by expansion of the epoxy that was used to set the reinforcing bars to reinforce 3 in. (76 mm) thick limestone panels.

To minimize the detrimental effects of strength loss of granite, limestone, and marble on buildings, all parts of the cladding system must be carefully designed. In addition, detailed testing of the specific stone fabricated and supplied for building should be performed prior to their installation to confirm that the properties of the actual stone supplied for the building are consistent with the properties upon which the design is based.

Water Leakage

Stone claddings on buildings are fabricated and/or constructed with joints that are exposed to the weather. These joints are "sealed" with sealant, mortar, or gaskets. Rainwater is expected to penetrate the stone claddings through mortar joints and through weathered sealant joints and gaskets. To prevent this water from leaking into the interior of the building and causing damage to interior finishes and discomfort to the occupants, a secondary line of defense, such as a flashing and weephole system or an internal gutter and drainage system should be incorporated into the stone cladding to collect and drain the water harmlessly to the exterior.

The major causes of water leakage into the interior of buildings with stone claddings are:

1. The absence of a flashing and weephole system.
2. Ineffective flashing and weephole system due to:
    a.   Lack of end dams.
    b.   Flashing recessed inward from face of cladding
    c.   Holes and tears in flashing
    d.   Improper splices in flashing
3. Ineffective internal gutter and drainage system due to poor joints in the system.

To minimize water leakage into the interior of buildings with stone claddings, the stone cladding should have a properly designed and constructed flashing and weephole system and/or internal gutter and drainage system. In addition, water testing of a full-scale mock-up of the stone cladding system should be performed to verify the water tightness of the cladding and its flashing system. The water testing should be performed before and after creating "weathering" slits in the sealant and the gaskets in the joints of the stone cladding to verify that the flashing system and/or internal gutter system is effective in preventing water leakage into the interior of the building.

Another cause of water leakage into the interior of buildings is uncontrolled condensation that forms on the back face of the stone cladding on buildings in northern climates. During cold weather, condensation will form when the temperature of the back face of the cladding is at or below its dew point temperature. If this condensation is not controlled, it can leak onto and damage interior finishes.

To minimize water leakage into the interior of buildings due to condensation, the stone cladding system should be adequately insulated and contain a properly designed and constructed vapor barrier. In addition, metal windows and curtain wall mullions should contain properly designed and constructed thermal beaks. A full scale mock-up of untested, complex, or multiple use cladding systems should be tested prior to construction to verify that condensation will not develop on the back face of the cladding under design conditions.

Conclusions

The common causes of failures of stone claddings on buildings as occurred in the 20 major buildings with distressed stone claddings investigated by the author are:

1. Failure of stone panel connections due to:
   a.   Inadequate structural design of the connections.
   b.   Corrosion of embedded metals.
   c.   Failure to accommodate construction tolerances.
   d.   Incompatible contacting materials.
2. Reduction in strength of stone due to exposure to the weather.
3. Water leakage into the interior of the building due to:
   a.   The absence of a flashing and weephole system or of an internal gutter and drainage system in the stone cladding.
   b.   Ineffective flashing and weephole system or ineffective gutter an drainage system in the stone cladding.

These common causes of failures in stone cladding in buildings can be minimized when emphasis is placed on the performance of proper connection design; the performance of proper, timely, and germain material testing; and the use of a flashing and weephole system or an internal gutter and drainage system in the stone claddings.

References

[1]   Conservation of Building and Decorative Stone, Volume 1, John Ashurst and Francis G. Dimes, Eds., Butterworth - Heinemann, London, England, 1990, p.. 19.

[2]   Fletcher, B., A History of Architecture, University of London, The Athlone Press, 1975, p. 213-219.

[3]   Feilden, B.N., Conservation of Historic Buildings, St. Edmundsbury Press Ltd., Bury St. Edmunds, Suffolk, England, 1982, p. 62.

[4]   Minimum Design Loads For Buildings and Other Structures, ANSI/ASCE 7-95, p. 15, American Society of Civil Engineers, New York, New York.

[5]   "Specification for Structural Steel Buildings" in Manual of Steel Construction, Allowable Stress Design, Ninth Edition, pp. 5-48 and 5-49, American Institute of Steel Construction, Inc., Chicago, Illinois, 1989.

[6]   "ILI Technotes - Safety Factors" in Indiana Limestone Handbook, 19th Edition, p. 121, Indiana Limestone Institute of American, Inc., Bedford, Indiana.

[7]   "Specifications for Aluminum structures - Allowable Stress Design," p. 1-A-22, in Aluminum Design Manual, The Aluminum Association, Washington, DC, 1994.

[8]   Specifications for Architectural Granite, p. 5, The National Building Granite Quarries Association, Inc., Barre, VT, 1996.

[9]   Dimension Stone Design Manual III, p. 0004.04, Marble Institute of America, Inc., Farmington, Michigan, 1991.

[10]   "ILI Technotes - Safety Factors" in Indiana Limestone Handbook, 19th Edition, p. 120, Indiana Limestone Institute of American, Inc., Bedford, Indiana.

[11]   Ballast, David Kent, AIA, Handbook of Construction Tolerances, McGraw-Hill, Inc., New York, NY, 1994, p. 282, 314.

[12]   Building Design and Construction Handbook, Fourth Edition, Frederick S. Merritt, Ed., McGraw-Hill Book Company, Inc., p. 4-21.

[13]   Indiana Limestone Handbook, 19th Edition, p. 8, Indiana Limestone of America, Inc., Bedford, Indiana.

[14]   Dimension Stone Design Manual III, p. 0004.01 Marble Institute of America, Inc., Farmington, Michigan, 1991.

[15]   Proceedings of Seminar on Recladding of the Amoco Building in Chicago, Illinois, November 1995, Chicago Committee on High Rise Buildings, Chicago, Illinois, Report No. 15, P. 3-5.

[16]   Kessler, D.W., Physical and Chemical Tests on the Commercial Marbles of the United States, No. 123, Technologic Papers of the Bureau of Standards, Department of Commerce, Washington Government Printing Press, 1919, p. 28.

Joseph P. Solinski[1]

Thin Stone Veneer / Study and Remediation

Reference: Solinski, J. P., **"Thin Stone Veneer/Study and Remediation,"** *Dimension Stone Cladding: Design, Construction, Evaluation, and Repair, ASTM STP 1394,* K. R. Hoigard, Ed., American Society for Testing and Materials, West Conshohocken, PA, 2000.

Abstract: Thin stone veneer panels have been used in exterior wall cladding systems for many years. The advent of computerized engineering has enabled designers to devise systems that are structurally sound, lightweight, and cost effective. Unfortunately, even with all the engineering evaluation, component detailing, and testing, stone cladding has been installed improperly on many buildings despite sound theoretical analysis. Condition surveys and maintenance reviews have detected installation deficiencies within thin stone veneer systems that have cost building owners millions of dollars to remedy. Two case studies involving stone veneer systems are presented, outlining the problems found and the solutions used in remediation.

Keywords: stone veneer, exterior wall, travertine, granite, cladding, condition survey, defects, liner blocks, solutions, expanding polyurethane foam, remediation

Introduction

Thin stone veneer facades (1.91 cm to 6.35 cm) have grown in popularity in building construction since the early 1960s. Technological advances in structural design, stone fabrication, adhesives, and fastenings allow the designer and engineer to specify thinner, lighter stone panel systems. However, as panels get thinner, installation quality control and adherence to details becomes more and more critical. It becomes the responsibility of the installer to follow the proper methodology and use the appropriate materials designed and engineered for the project. Sometimes field modifications exist in order to address unforeseen conditions and should not be assumed to be adequate, unless properly engineered or tested. Two buildings, erected in the 1980s, are profiled as case histories within this paper, one with a travertine cladding and one with a granite cladding. Both buildings underwent extensive renovations to correct the installation defects.

[1]President, Stone & Glazing Consulting and Construction Consulting Laboratory, International, 1601 Luna Road, Carrollton, TX 75006.

Case History #1

The exterior wall of this 12-story downtown office building is comprised of alternating horizontal bands of dark gray glass and travertine stone panels. The building was erected in 1982.

The travertine panels (2.23 cm thick, 152.4 cm wide by 86.4 cm tall) were restrained from lateral wind loads by anchoring the panels to the floor slab edge with a copper wire and grout-anchoring method, [1]. The weight of the panels was supported with two 15.2 cm x 15.2 cm travertine liner blocks that were installed at quarter points on the lower portion of each panel. The liner blocks were set on a continuous steel angle attached to the building structure. Each liner block was glued to the backside of the panel with epoxy adhesive and secured with two 5 mm diameter stainless steel dowel pins.

In 1997 our consulting firm was commissioned by a prospective buyer to survey the exterior wall. During this limited condition survey an unstable travertine panel on the seventh floor was noted. This 110 kg spandrel panel was loose and it could be moved by hand with minimal effort. The discovery of this loose panel prompted a more extensive survey of the stone veneer on the exterior wall. The survey consisted of performing stage drops around the perimeter of the building and reviewing each travertine panel. Each panel was tapped with a rubber mallet to verify the panel stability. The observations were recorded on a survey sheet and later compiled on a summary sheet, (Figs. 3 and 4). The final tabulations revealed 79% of the panels were loose on at least one corner and most were loose in three or four corners. Sixteen panels were found to be unstable and they had to be immediately stabilized. A common symptom of the unstable panels was differential alignment. This misalignment is often assumed to be an installation variance, however, differential alignment may also be a symptom of stone anchor failure and requires investigation to identify the reason for the alignment difference (Figs. 1 and 2).

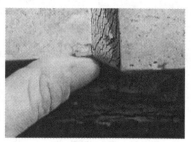

Figures 1 and 2: *Vertical translation of the travertine panels.*

Through investigation as described above, it was determined that the stone liner blocks, which support the gravity load of the panel, were debonding from the back side of the travertine panels, forcing the wind supporting wire anchors to also support the gravity load, (Figs. 5 and 6). During the study, the stainless steel dowel pins attaching the liner blocks to the back of the stone panel were found to not effectively penetrate the panel to provide a fail-safe assembly (Figs. 7 and 8). The combination of added load, years of exposure to water penetration, and temperature variations were also contributing factors in the release of the liner blocks.

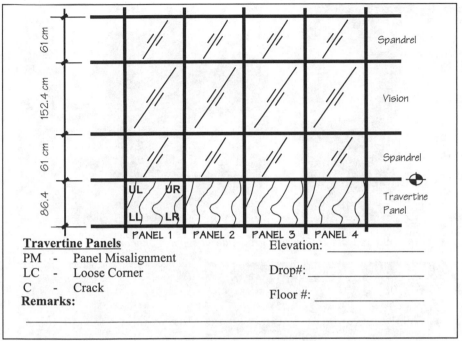

Travertine Panels

PM - Panel Misalignment

LC - Loose Corner

C - Crack

Remarks:

Elevation: _____

Drop#: _____

Floor #: _____

Figure 3: *Example of a Travertine Panel Survey Sheet. This form was used during the condition survey to document the current status of the travertine panels.*

	Panel Column Numbers				Floor Level
Corner	1	2	3	4	
UL	X	X	X	X	
UR	X	X	X	X	Twelfth Floor
LL		X	X		
LR	X	X			
Totals	**3**	**4**	**3**	**2**	
UL	X	X	X	X	
UR	X	X	X	X	
LL	X	X	X	X	Parapet
LR	X	X	X	X	
Totals	**4**	**4**	**4**	**4**	

Total UL (Upper Left)	72
Total UR (Upper Right)	71
Total LL (Lower Left)	52
Total LR (Lower Right)	56
Total Findings for East Elevation	251

Figure 4: *Example of the Travertine Project - Loose Panel Summary Chart (Partial summary shown for general information only. Note: "X" denotes loose corner of panel found during inspection).*

Figures 5 and 6: *Copper wire and grout lateral support anchors, [1].*

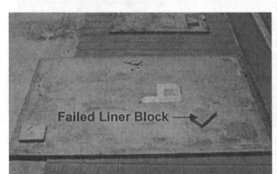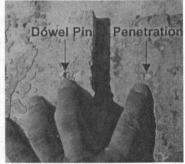

Figures 7 and 8: *Liner block release from the back of the travertine panel.
Note the negligible penetration of the dowel pin into the back
of the stone panel in the right Figure.*

Several options to stabilize the stone veneer were presented to the owner, including removal and reattachment. Because of the expense and tenant disruption associated with a project of this magnitude, the owner chose to proceed with a remedial design that was least invasive to the tenant. The design used aluminum plates at the vertical edges of the stone panels and was called the batten plate stabilization method. This method proved to be 50% more cost effective as compared to removal and reattachment.

The batten plate stabilization method would support the gravity load of the panel and restrain outward load during high winds. The aluminum batten plate would be fastened into the concrete perimeter beam by embedding internally threaded inserts and anchoring them into the concrete with high strength epoxy. Engineering calculations and laboratory testing verified the structural integrity of the design (Figs. 9 thru 14).

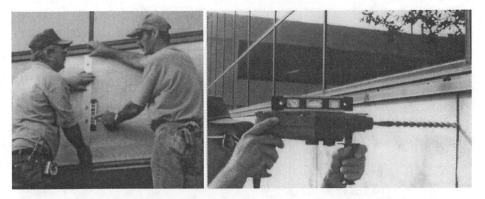

Figures 9 and 10: *After testing the structural integrity of the batten plate in laboratory conditions, field installation provided verification of the feasibility on jobsite conditions. A template was made to provide accurate locations when drilling into the slab perimeter beam. Holes were drilled through the panel joint into the beam to accept the internally threaded insert.*

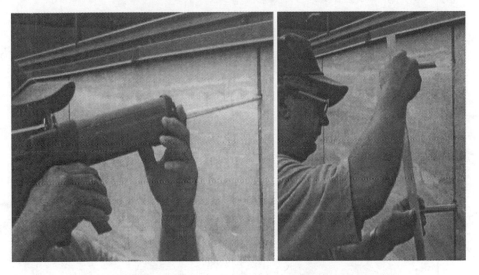

Figures 11 and 12: *Structural epoxy was injected into the hole, calibrating the amount of material for each application. The threaded inserts were attached to the batten plate. The backside of the batten plate was caulked with silicone sealant and the assembly was guided into the holes and onto the travertine panel. The perimeter edge of the plate was sealed to the panel. This sealing operation eliminated the removal of the original decayed sealant and provided a watertight assembly.*

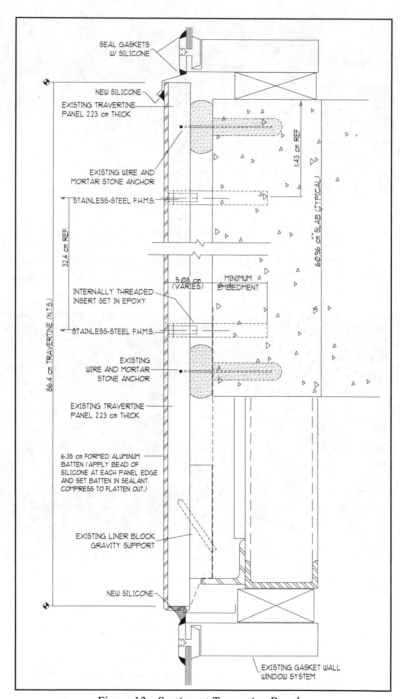

SEAL GASKETS
W/ SILICONE

NEW SILICONE

EXISTING TRAVERTINE
PANEL 2.23 cm THICK

11.43 cm REF.

60.96 cm SLAB (TYPICAL)

EXISTING WIRE AND
MORTAR STONE ANCHOR

STAINLESS-STEEL F.H.M.S.

32.4 cm REF.

5.08 cm
(VARIES)

MINIMUM
EMBEDMENT

INTERNALLY THREADED
INSERT SET IN EPOXY

STAINLESS-STEEL F.H.M.S.

86.4 cm TRAVERTINE (N.T.S.)

EXISTING
WIRE AND MORTAR
STONE ANCHOR

EXISTING TRAVERTINE
PANEL 2.23 cm THICK

6.35 cm FORMED ALUMINUM
BATTEN (APPLY BEAD OF
SILICONE AT EACH PANEL EDGE
AND SET BATTEN IN SEALANT.
COMPRESS TO FLATTEN OUT.)

EXISTING LINER BLOCK
GRAVITY SUPPORT

NEW SILICONE

EXISTING GASKET WALL
WINDOW SYSTEM

Figure 13: *Section at Travertine Panel*

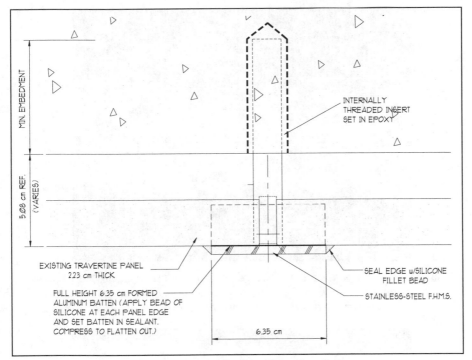

Figure 14: *Plan at Travertine Panel*

Because the appearance of the building exterior would be changed by the application of the aluminum battens, several finish options were presented to the owner. One option was to contrast the light colored travertine by painting the batten caps black to match the finish of the adjacent curtain wall frames. Another option was to conceal the battens by painting the aluminum battens to match the travertine stone veneer panels. Each concept was simulated in a computer model and with an on-site mock up at the building. The property owner chose to have the battens painted to blend into the travertine panels.

Mock-ups of various painting techniques were devised to replicate the travertine's natural appearance. These samples were then sent to a painting manufacturer of high performance exterior wall coatings and a pattern was established using a layering technique of three different colored paints. The result was a realistic match to the travertine panel and the batten strips effectively disappeared into the facade. The renovation was structurally sound, cost effective, and executed without major change to the original aesthetics (Figs. 15 and 16).

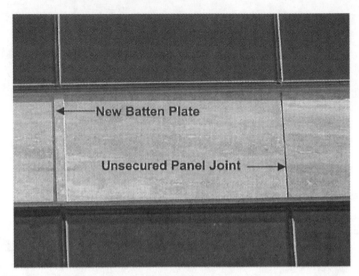

Figure 15: *The new batten plate is located on the left side and the unsecured panel joint is located on the right. Note how the custom paint allowed the batten strip to blend into the travertine panel.*

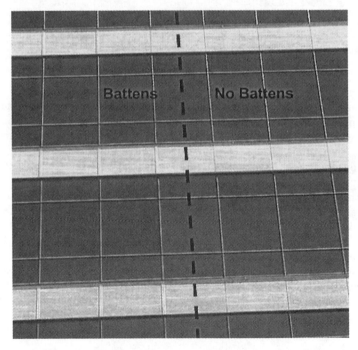

Figure 16: *The left side of the photograph has the batten plates attached to the panels. The right side has not been addressed.*

Case History #2

The exterior wall of this 22-story downtown office building is comprised of granite clad precast panels with punched opening windows on the tower portion and handset granite panels on the lower three levels of the building. The building was erected in 1987.

During a waterproofing renovation in 1995, panel misalignment was noted in the lower level stone veneer. This observation was followed by a panel releasing from the wall after the waterproofing contractor cut the decayed sealant from the panel perimeter. The 153 cm wide by 92 cm high, 125 kg panel dropped from the third floor level to the platform stage immediately below injuring the worker. The waterproofing program was put on hold and a survey of the panels was performed (Fig. 17).

Figure 17

The majority of the panels in immediate question were the face panels above the window soffit areas. Because the lower edge of the panels was exposed, (Fig. 18),the installer chose to use a liner block to support both the gravity load and windload. All of the lower level panels were conventional handset 3 cm granite panels. Panels were set using both kerf clip anchors and liner blocks.

Figure 18

Visual exterior inspections using a powered platform stage from the upper levels and binocular observations from the ground floor level was performed to identify panels that appeared to be out-of-plumb, skewed, or panels that had uneven sealant joints around the perimeter. A majority of the face panels above the window soffit areas revealed misalignment in the bottom edges of the stone veneer. By comparing the bottom edge of two panels juxtaposition, a slight offset was evident (Figs. 19 and 20). Although distress in sealant is another key indicator of panel movement, it should not be relied upon due to the possibility of previous caulking renovation work.

 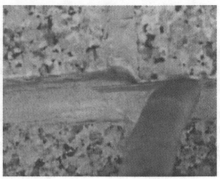

Figures 19 and 20: *While performing the visual survey of the exterior, stone panels were found with slight differences in the elevation of the lower corners. Anomalies such as these should be noted during facade reviews and prudently analyzed to determine if the difference in alignment is based upon poor setting techniques in the original installation or shifting of the panels due to anchor support failure.*

Because the hidden stone anchorage was suspect, the panel supports were in need of review. Panel removal was considered, but found to be costly due to the number of panels in question. In order to expedite the review and keep the costs to a reasonable level an alternate approach was implemented. An orthoscopic fiber optic borescope is typically used in the medical field, but with its ability to view the interior cladding cavity, it becomes a valuable tool in cladding review. The orthoscopic borescope was used to review the anchor conditions of the stone panels by cutting a 10 mm hole in the exterior caulking and inserting the 90-degree angle viewing scope. Approximately 200 panels were reviewed and photographed. Panel survey sheets were developed to document the existing conditions, without panel removal (Fig. 23). The defects identified with the borescope ranged from debonded liner blocks, broken kerfs, enlarged kerfs, excessive shims, rotated anchor clips, to anchor clips not engaged in the kerfs, (Figs. 21 and 22).

Figures 21 and 22: *The borescope photographs above are examples of defects identified during the survey. The left photo shows a debonded broken liner block and the right photo shows an enlarged kerf with a thin back leg on the stone liner.*

Panel # __

View of Panel from Exterior

Remarks:

☐   West

☐   East

☐   South

Left Liner

Right Liner

_____
_____
_____
_____
_____
_____

Epoxy
Epoxy Dab on Side
No Epoxy
Partial Epoxy
Crack In Epoxy

Clips
Excessive Shims
Bent Clip
Rotated Clip
Loose Nut
Corroded Fastener
Clip Not Engaged

Liners
Travertine
White Marble
Dowel Pin Exposed

Kerfs
Broken Kerf
Enlarged Kerf

Figure 23: *Example of the Granite Panel Survey Sheet.*

The data from granite panel survey sheets were summarized on a defect matrix, (Fig.26). The borescope survey provided data that persuaded the renovation team the stone panels had to be removed and retrofitted. Upon removal of the stone panels, many unanticipated defects were also exposed. Some installation defects considered outrageous when first discovered, were eclipsed by even worse defects. (Figs. 24 and 25).

Figures 24 and 25: *As the stone panels were removed many variations of the liner block application were discovered. The left photograph shows the liner pins did not appropriately penetrate the back of the stone. The right photograph shows an unconventional pin bending method of liner attachment.*

Panel Number	Elevation	LINERS		KERFS		Excessive Shims	CLIPS			EPOXY				REMARKS
		Travertine Liner	Marble Liner	Broken Kerf	Enlarged Kerf		Bent Clip	Rotated Clip	Clip Not Engaged	Epoxy Dab on Side	No Epoxy	Partial Epoxy	Crack in Epoxy	
1	East	X			X	X			X	X				
2	East	X			X	X			X					
3	East	X		X	X	X								
4	East	X			X									
5	East	X			X									
6	East	X		X	X									
7	East	X			X									
8	East	X			X					X				
9	East	X			X									
10	East	X			X									
11	East	X			X	X								
12	East	X			X									
1	West	X				X		X					X	Edge Misalignment
2	West	X											X	Edge Misalignment
3	West	X						X					X	Edge Misalignment
4	West	X						X						Edge Misalignment
5	West	X	X										X	Edge Misalignment
6	West	X						X					X	Edge Misalignment
7	West	X	X					X						Edge Misalignment
8	West	X						X						Edge Misalignment
9	West	X						X					X	Edge Misalignment
10	West	X						X					X	Edge Misalignment
11	West	X						X					X	Edge Misalignment
12	West	X						X						Edge Misalignment
1	South	X	X											
2	South		X							X				
3	South		X							X				
4	South		X							X				Loose Nut

Figure 26: *Granite Project Defect Summary Matrix   (Partial summary of data shown for general information only).*

During panel removal the existing liner blocks were found to be composed of either travertine or white marble. Both materials are much weaker than granite and should not have been used in this application, [2]. The typical 153 cm x 153 cm granite panels would transfer 86 kg of windload reaction to each liner block anchor. The windload and gravity support of the panels was accomplished with two 15.2 cm x 15.2 cm travertine or marble liner blocks set at quarter points of the lower portion of each panel. The liner blocks were typically glued to the backside of the panel with epoxy adhesive and secured with two 5 mm diameter stainless steel dowel pins. The stone panels were removed and each liner block was laboratory tested and found to have an average ultimate tensile strength of 23 kg. The 23 kg ultimate strength was compared to the allowable design load of 344 kg, (86 kg x 4.0 safety factor). The test results indicated the anchors were approximately 15 times under-designed. It appears the installers did not pursue verification of the structural integrity of the design from a design engineer.

New stone anchor supports were designed with an engineered and tested safety factor of five to replace the existing liner blocks. The new stone anchors were fabricated from stainless steel and were anchored to the backside of the granite panels with stainless steel expansion anchors specifically developed for stone anchor attachments. After the old anchors were removed from the panel the new anchors were installed. The reattachment of the stone panel required new kerf clip extrusions that permitted minimal shimming during installation (Figs. 27 and 28).

Figures 27 and 28: *The new stone anchor supports were fabricated from stainless steel and mechanically anchored to the backside of the stone panel with expansion type anchors specifically designed for use in stone. Aluminum extrusions were designed to fit the varying air space dimension, minimizing the use of shims.*

The upper portion of the building posed a significant yet different challenge. The sloped panels at the twenty-second level were also unstable and in need of repair. The shifting of the panels and the failed liner blocks made walking on the exterior side of the panels too dangerous for the workers and the public below (Figs. 29 and 30).

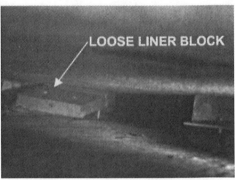

Figures 29 and 30: *The misalignment of the four stone panel corners caused concern in regards to the attachment of the sloped panels as shown on the left photograph. The parapet cap was removed and a visual inspection of the anchors revealed a liner block was no longer attached to the backside of the panel and was not providing the necessary structural support. The photograph on the right was taken with a zoom lens between the 5 cm gap from the backside of the stone panel and the topside of the precast panel. This defective anchor was approximately 1.8 meters from the top of the parapet.*

Safe access to the work became a primary focus in choosing a repair method. A tower crane approach was considered in order to provide the necessary safety precautions to mobilize and address the sloped panels. The glass atrium located above the lobby twenty stories below was a constant reminder of the need to provide a safe environment for the workers on the renovation crew.

An alternate plan was considered based upon a preliminary data shared by Kolbjorn Saether & Associates, an engineering firm located in Chicago, Illinois. The plan involved the use of expanding polyurethane foam. The structural grade polyurethane foam had recently been approved by Dade County officials to adhere clay tiles to roof structures. The material has a tenacious adhesive quality to all types of surfaces, even if they are slightly dirty. The foam has a compressive strength of approximately 0.35 kilogram/cm^2. The renovation theory was to inject the foam into the 5 cm gap and allow the foam to expand and fill the void behind the panels. This would not only temporarily stabilize the stone panels to the structure but also permit the workers to safely walk on top of the panels and drill pins through the stone veneer into the precast concrete underneath. The threaded rod pins were epoxied into the precast and bolted to the stone panels.

The foam application theory was laboratory tested using a sloped mock-up simulating the actual site conditions of the stone veneer. A plywood frame was fabricated and topped with clear acrylic to allow observation of the expanding foam. The clear acrylic was loosely fastened to 15 cm wood blocks to simulate the stone anchors.

The polyurethane foam is a two-part chemical curing material. Once the two components meet, a rapid expansion and curing of the material takes place. The material increases in volume approximately 20 times its liquid state. A custom mixing head was fabricated to fit the 5 cm gap between the stone and precast. This special head allowed the mixing operation to take place directly at the application location, 1.8 meters from the top of the parapet (Fig. 31).

Figure 31

The remedial contractor was allowed to practice on the mock-up several times in order to refine the techniques necessary to maneuver the apparatus and apply the foam. The protocol was also established in determining the quantity of material, the time between the application of the foam and the expansion time. If the material quantity or the timing were incorrect, a panel could be dislodged and fall from the building (Figs. 32 and 33). The foam was also tested for adhesive strength on existing stone panels, without cleaning the panels. The result was an average tensile strength of 1220 kg/m^2, compared to 684 kg/m^2 design load.

Figure 32 and 33: *The clear acrylic mock-up allowed the workers to view the application as shown on the left photograph. The right photograph shows the significant coverage of the material.*

Once the laboratory training was complete the contractor implemented the expanding foam stabilization. A string of lights were placed under the stone panels to illuminate the area during the successful application (Fig. 34).

Figure 34: *A string of lights was draped between the stone and precast along the work area. The lights not only allowed visual observations of the expansion of the foam, but have also acted as a gauge to verify the growth and direction of the rapidly expanding polyurethane foam.*

Conclusions

When stone veneer systems are properly engineered and detailed it is ultimately the responsibility of the contractor to install the system as designed. If field conditions do not match the intent of the drawings, the installer should take measures to ensure that corrective measures are properly engineered and tested. Ultimately it is the efforts of the construction team that should assure the longevity of today's construction.

Building owners spend millions of dollars every year repairing the defects resulting from inappropriate installations. Not only is remediation of these conditions a major expense, but also a high liability exposure. The result of a spontaneous panel release from a facade could be catastrophic.

The liability of an architect, engineer, or consultant's recommendation is high because the safety of the general public is dependent upon the façade components remaining secure. Therefore thorough investigations should be undertaken when reviewing exterior stone veneer applications. Prudent measures should be taken and proper documentation should be compiled in order to assess the condition of the exterior wall components. Innovative approaches must be used to resolve the challenges ahead, and fall within the economic boundaries of the property owner as long as the designs are well thought out, properly engineered, and tested.

Acknowledgments

Special thanks to my support staff and building owners and property managers that have challenged our firm with their demands and empowered us with their trust to address their cladding concerns.

References

[1]   Amrhein, J. E., and Merrigan M. W., *Marble and Stone Slab Veneer,* Masonry Institute of America, Los Angeles, CA, September 1986.

[2]   Lewis, M.D., *Modern Stone Cladding,* ASTM Manual Series: MNL 21, American Society for Testing and Materials, Philadelphia, PA, 1995.

R. Scavuzzo[1] and J. Acri[2]

In-Place Load Testing of a Stone Cladding Anchorage System

Reference: Scavuzzo, R. and Acri, J., **"In-Place Load Testing of a Stone Cladding Anchorage System,"** *Dimension Stone Cladding: Design, Construction, Evaluation, and Repair, ASTM STP 1394,* K. R. Hoigard, Ed., American Society for Testing and Materials, West Conshohocken, PA, 2000.

Abstract: Proper evaluation, simulation, and subsequent testing of the forces acting on a stone cladding anchorage system are critical elements in the overall success of the anchorage system design as it relates to serviceability, safety, durability, and aesthetics. In some cases, to accurately predict anchorage performance, the stone cladding system must be tested as a whole under service loading conditions to observe the total deflection of the entire anchorage system assembly, including anchors, studs, flashing, drywall, toggles, mounting screws, etc. Presented is a case study which incorporated in-place testing to simulate the combined dead load and wind load forces acting on a penthouse level mechanical screen wall on a multi-story building in the Denver-Metro area. Testing on a series of stone cladding anchorage systems was performed to help determine if design deflection criteria could be achieved.

Keywords: stone cladding, anchorage system, in-place load testing, anchorage performance

Introduction

The ASTM Standard Guide for Design, Selection, and Installation of Exterior Stone Anchors and Anchoring Systems (C 1242) provides a discussion of the design factors to be considered in the selection and use of attachment methods for exterior building stone. Consideration is to be given to the physical and material characteristics of the stone, design loads and safety factors, wind and seismic loads, building dimensional changes, and moisture control to name a few. The anchorage system being considered should be evaluated and selected based upon its ability to resist all applicable design factors. Additionally, the ASTM Guide includes a section discussing the "backup structure" which is defined as the means by which loads applied to the stone and anchors are transferred to the building's structure. The ASTM Guide states in part: "Whatever backup system is chosen, an understanding of the properties of that structure is

---
[1]Senior Engineer, CTC-Geotek, Inc., 155 S. Navajo St., Denver, CO, 80223.
[2]Consultant, Acri Stone & Tile Consulting, 17414 Louisiana, Aurora, CO, 80017.

prerequisite to the design of the cladding system. The design of the backup system should take into account gravity, wind, seismic, window, maintenance platform, shipping, and erection loads and the stone attachment means."

Presented is a case study which illustrates the failure of a stone cladding anchorage system due to the inability of the backup structure to resist the dead load and/or the wind load forces transferred to it from the stone cladding anchorage system as installed. In-place testing designed to simulate the combined dead load and wind load forces was performed on the stone cladding anchorage system as a whole to observe the total deflection of the multiple combinations of stud gauge weights, flashing and/or dry wall configurations, and toggle and mounting screws used. Testing was performed to help determine if design deflection criteria could be achieved.

Project Description

The case study subject building was a multi-story building in the Denver Metro area. Exterior facade of the penthouse level mechanical screen wall of interest consisted of granite panels having nominal dimensions of approximately 4.5 by 5.2 feet (1.4 by 1.6 m) and 1-3/8 inch (3.5 cm) thick. Dead weight of the stone panels was approximately 490 pounds (222 kg). The backup structure of the mechanical screen wall consisted of a metal stud system that incorporated both 18-gauge and 12-gauge studs covered with combinations of exterior grade drywall, thin gauge metal flashing, shims, and metal plates. Stone anchors having nominal dimensions of 2 inches (5.1 cm) in height with a 1-1/2 inch (3.8 cm) wide shelf and 3/16-inch (4.76 mm) thick were used. Stone anchor attachment was achieved via 1/4-inch diameter and 2-inch long (6.35 mm diameter, 5.1 cm long) self tapping screws or by 1/4-inch (6.35 mm) diameter toggle anchors. Due to observed failure of the stone cladding anchorage system during the installation process at numerous locations (i.e., suspected yielding of clip angles and/or pull-out of anchors), CTC-Geotek, Inc. was requested to perform in-place load testing on the multiple stone cladding anchorage system configurations.

In-Place Testing Program

An in-place testing program was established to evaluate the ability of the as-built stone cladding anchorage support system configurations to resist the combined dead load and tensile wind load forces. Based upon the anchor design incorporating two dead load anchors per panel, and a panel dead weight of 490 pounds (222 kg), each anchor was required to withstand a dead load of 245 pounds (111 kg). Wind loads for a typical panel having dimensions of 4.5 by 5.2 feet (1.4 x 1.6 m) were calculated by the design team to be 476 pounds (216 kg) on each anchor which was based upon a maximum wind load of -41 lb/ft^2 (-2 kPa). A safety factor of 1.5 was applied, resulting in each anchor being required to withstand a tensile load of 714 pounds (324 kg).

As opposed to applying a resultant force of 755 pounds (342 kg) to the anchor at the appropriate resultant angle, it was decided by the design team that the combined loading could be applied by loading the anchors to simulate the 245 pounds (111 kg) dead load and then pulling the anchor normal to the stud to simulate the 714 pounds (324 kg) wind load. A maximum deflection of 3/8 inch (9.5 mm) was designated as the in-place load testing acceptance criteria.

Field Testing

In-place load testing was performed on two stone cladding anchorage systems. Typical anchorage system configurations tested are as shown in the schematics provided in Figures 1 and 2.

The first series of in-place load tests were performed at two locations on the stone cladding anchorage system configuration schematic provided on Figure 1. As shown, the anchorage system consisted of an 18-gauge stud wall covered with a light gauge metal flashing. Anchorage to the stud was achieved via a 1/4 inch (6.35 mm) diameter 2-inch (5.1 cm) long toggle anchor. Due to the configuration of the wall at these locations, 5/8 inch (1.6 cm) metal shims were used in addition to the same thickness exterior grade drywall.

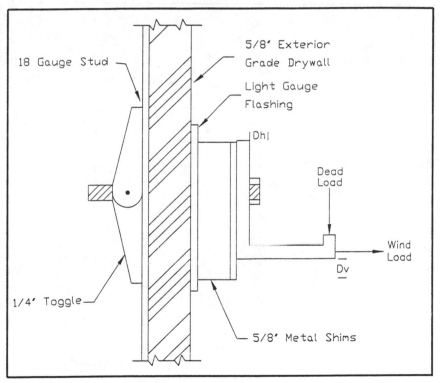

Figure 1 - *Stone Anchor Schematic (18-Gauge Studs)*

The anchorage system was subjected to application of combined dead and tensile (wind) loading. One-half of the reported stone dead weight of 245 pounds (111 kg) was applied by suspending bags of lead shot from a basket attached to the clip angle.

Following dead load application, tensile loading was applied to the anchorage configuration normal to the stud using a calibrated hydraulic pump and load cell. Deflections of ½ inch (12.7 mm), greater than the allowable 3/8 inch (9.5 mm), were observed in both the vertical and horizontal directions (designated as D_v and D_h in Figure 1) at a tensile load of approximately 200 pounds (91 kg) at both locations tested.

The second series of in-place load tests was performed at one location on the 12-gauge stud backup structure that incorporated the anchorage system configuration as shown in the schematic provided in Figure 2. The combined dead and tensile (wind) load was applied as before, by suspending bags of lead shot from a basket attached to the clip angle and tensile load applied to the anchorage configuration normal to the stud using a calibrated load cell and hydraulic pump. In an effort to stiffen the backup structure support system, a 4 by 4 by 1/16-inch (10.2 by 10.2 by 0.16 cm) steel plate was centered and mounted behind the clip angle anchor. The anchor was attached to the stud with a self-tapping screw 1/4-inch (6.35 mm) in diameter and 2-inches (5.1 cm) in length.

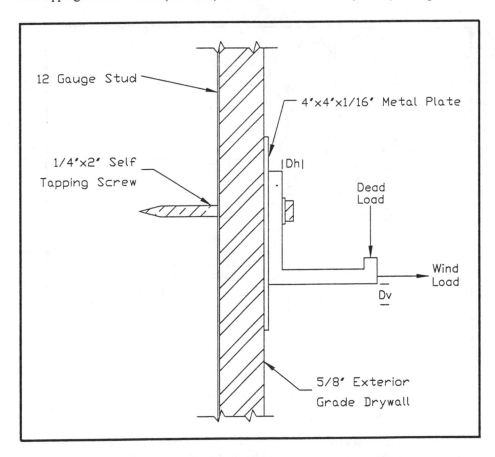

Figure 2 - *Stone Anchor Schematic (12-Gauge Studs)*

Vertical and horizontal deflections of ½ inch (12.7 mm), greater than the allowable 3/8 inch (9.5 mm), were observed at a tensile load of approximately 300 lbf (136 kg). A photograph of the in-place test set-up for the application of the combined dead and tensile (wind) load is shown in Figure 3.

Figure 3 - *In-Place Load Testing Setup*

Stone Anchorage System Evaluation and Redesign

Results of the in-place testing performed on the as-built stone cladding anchorage system configurations indicated that the specified design deflection criteria could not be met. Possible causes for the excessive deflection of the clip angle were most likely attributed to one or a combination of the following:

- deflection of the 1/4-inch (6.35 mm) diameter fasteners within the shims;
- rotation of the fastener thru the light gauge metal;

- crushing of the drywall material under the 1/4-inch (6.35 mm) threaded fastener shank;
- crushing of the drywall under the heel of the clip anchor; and
- defection (bowing) of the metal studs at the point of tensile load application.

Additionally, it was observed that deflection of the stone anchors may have resulted in a load transfer to the stone panel anchors immediately below, causing further deflection and ultimate anchor pull-out.

A modified shelf-anchor design, as shown in Figure 4 was proposed. The proposed anchor spanned across five studs and attachment was made directly to each stud (drywall removed at the point of attachment) using 1/4-inch (6.35 mm) diameter by 2-inch (5.1 cm) long self tapping screws. To provide additional support, the backup structure studs were reinforced with a 1-1/2 by 1-1/2 by 1/8-inch and 12-inch long (3.8 by 3.8 by 0.3 cm and 30.5 cm long) angle centered at each point of anchor attachment. The new anchor configuration with turn-down tabs at each end required the anchor to withstand a tensile wind loading of 1428 pounds (648 kg) and a dead load of 490 pounds (222 kg).

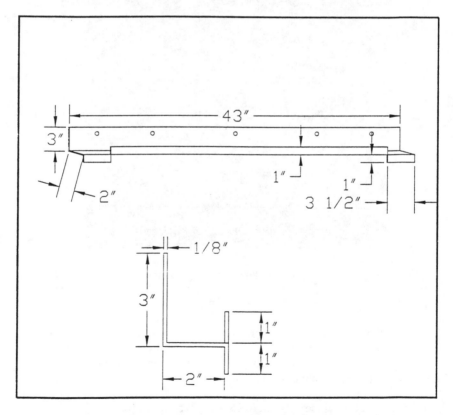

Figure 4 - *Schematic of Proposed Shelf-Anchor*

In-place load testing on the proposed anchorage system design was required. A schematic of the in-place testing configuration is shown on Figure 5 and a photograph of the load test is provided in Figure 6.

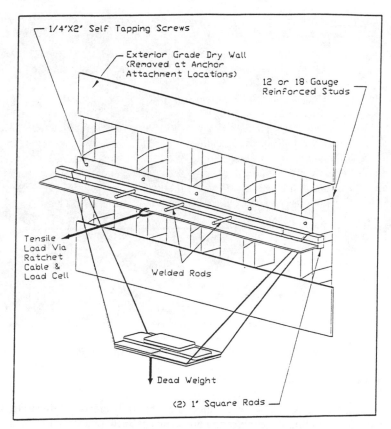

Figure 5 -*In-Place Load Testing Schematic*

Tensile wind load was uniformly transformed across the self anchor by the application of two one-inch (2.54 cm) square rods with one resting across the top of the anchor shelf and the second rod placed directly underneath. Holes were drilled through the stone anchor top and bottom 1-inch (2.54 cm) tabs and the square rods to accept threaded rods secured using nuts attached on the back side of the square rods. Threaded rods were then welded to a metal plate. Three rods were used across the top stone anchor tab and one at each bottom end tab. Welding was performed in the shop and the assembly mounted to the backup structure studs in the field. Stone panel dead weight of 490 pounds (222 kg) was simulated by hanging bags of shot from a basket attached to the ends of the square rods. Required tensile wind loading of 1428 pounds (648 kg) was applied at the midpoint of the plate-rod assembly using a rachet cable and a calibrated load cell.

Testing was performed at three arbitrarily selected locations. A maximum deflection of 1/16 inch (6.25 mm) was observed in both the horizontal and/or vertical axes and these values fall well within the 3/8 inch (9.25 mm) allowable load displacement.

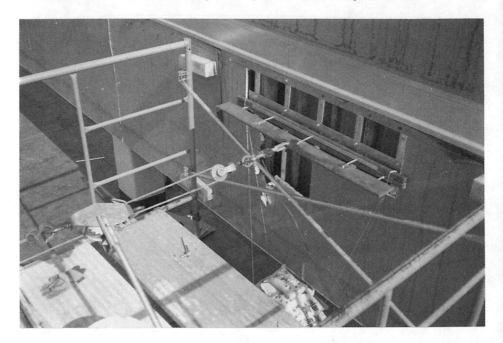

Figure 6 - *Shelf Anchor In-Place Load Test Setup*

Conclusion

As discussed in the ASTM C 1242 Guide, the case study presented illustrates the importance of understanding the engineering properties of anchorage systems, their application to stone cladding and backup structures, and how anchorage system performance integrates with the proposed building designs. Field tests on in-place anchorage of an existing design were used to determine that specified design deflection criteria could not be met. The additional project costs for remediation could have been avoided had in-place testing of the stone anchorage system been performed prior to installation of the stone facade.